Praise for *The Teacher's Ultimate Planning Guide*

"*This is as valuable to the beginning teacher as it is to myself, the 30-year veteran!*"
Shelley Levine, Reading Teacher
New York City Public School

"*This book really seems to focus on the teacher*
and validating."

"*This guide will help educators become successful, excel in their career, and, most of all,*
enable them to create the magic of learning in their classrooms!"
Cathy Ferrara, Teacher
Park School
Ossining, New York

"*Educators who wish to maintain or regain the enthusiasm that initially drew them to*
teaching should read this book and keep it handy."
Diana Agius, Literacy Teacher
Wake County Public School System
Raleigh, North Carolina

"*Management is the key to a successful classroom and* **The Teacher's Ultimate**
Planning Guide *will help ALL teachers be successful!*"
Jill Herbst, Instructional Resource Teacher
Northwoods Elementary
Cary, North Carolina

"*As the director of the NC Teaching Fellows Scholarship Program at UNC Charlotte, our*
preservice teachers are given a copy of this book as a guide to assist them both during and
after student teaching. I highly recommend this book as a 'must-have' for any educator."
Misty Hathcock, Teaching Fellows Director
University of North Carolina, Charlotte

"*This volume should be the companion of every teacher in today's high-stress world.*"
Robert Thabet, Director of Distance Education
Mount Saint Mary College

"*It is a pleasure to use a planbook that addresses the current issues and concerns of edu-*
cation. The author demonstrates a genuine understanding and respect for the teaching
profession and has succeeded in providing teachers with a useful resource."
Christine DiSisto, Kindergarten Teacher
Kent Primary School
Carmel, New York

"**The Teacher's Ultimate Planning Guide** *should be used as a textbook in required col-*
lege courses during a prospective teacher's senior year. It would bring them one step closer
to having a successful teacher career instead of ending one due to teacher burnout."
Anna Chamorro, Teacher
Raleigh, North Carolina

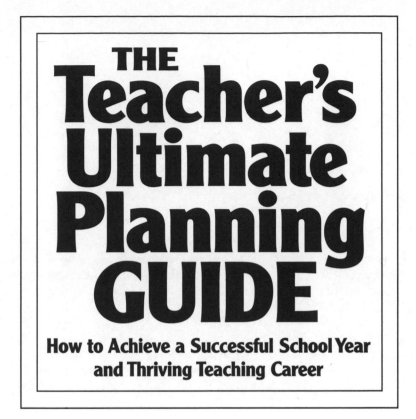

THE
Teacher's
Ultimate
Planning
GUIDE

How to Achieve a Successful School Year and Thriving Teaching Career

Lisa Maria Burke

Skyhorse Publishing

Contents

Preface

WHAT IS THE PURPOSE OF THIS BOOK?

Whether you just started your first teaching assignment or you have years of experience in the classroom, you are working hard to become a successful educator. To help you accomplish this goal, *The Teacher's Ultimate Planning Guide* first presents a summary of the research on successful teaching and then shows you how to achieve it—how to design effective curriculum, prevent and manage student discipline problems, make the most of limited time and resources, handle parent pressures, and much more. This comprehensive guide goes beyond the day-to-day planning and execution of teaching tasks and shows you how to have a thriving teaching career. Creating and maintaining a thriving teaching career demands continual learning, teaching, reflecting, and sharing. These four activities are the roots of both professional and personal growth. This ultimate planning guide shows you how to take control not only of your classroom but also of your career and your life.

WHY DO YOU NEED THIS BOOK?

Studies have found that teachers report some of the highest levels of occupational stress. As a result of this extreme stress, over half of all new teachers leave the profession within their first seven years of teaching, and most of those leave within their first two years. Many teachers leave midcareer due to frustration with their jobs and teacher burnout. Those midcareer teachers who might suffer from teacher burnout but choose to stay in the classroom often lower their teaching performance, sometimes to a bare minimum, to get by. This attrition of new and experienced teachers, coupled with weakening teacher performance, is alarming, especially as we face a growing teacher shortage.

Occupational stress is often caused by not having enough skills to do your job well. In colleges and in emergency teacher preparation programs now in place in many states to help alleviate the growing shortage, prospective teachers are taught how to instruct but receive little training in management. Consequently, they are not prepared to handle the myriad of responsibilities and challenges they will face on a daily basis, including managing large groups of children by themselves. Therefore, many teachers, especially those who enter their classrooms for the first time, are not prepared for all the "other things" that teachers do. No matter how many hours they log in student teaching, many still are not prepared to teach.

Even teachers with several years of experience under their belts may not have mastered the art and science of teaching. Many teachers acquire their teaching experience in what is often described as a "vacuum," receiving little mentoring and coaching from seasoned educators. Most of their learning comes from painful, stressful, frustrating years of trial and error—conditions not conducive to mastering the skills needed to become successful educators. For these beleaguered teachers, this book will reaffirm what they have learned on the job that is effective and supportive of successful teaching, and it will give them what they still need to learn to be the best teachers they can be.

WHO SHOULD READ THIS BOOK?

Teachers of Grades K-12, including all subjects and areas of specialty, such as special education, art, music, and physical education, should read this book, especially teachers who are

- Teaching for the first time, including student teachers
- Experiencing change in their work assignment or work environment
- Reentering the field after several years
- Feeling stressed and burnt out from teaching

This book also provides administrators and school board members with invaluable information for shaping policies and procedures in ways that will ensure teacher success. It also provides a framework for colleges to use for preparing prospective teachers. The epilogue is written specifically for school leaders at every level.

The information in this book is also useful for students who are considering a career in education, thus making it a great resource for college and high school career placement offices.

IN WHAT SETTINGS CAN YOU USE THIS BOOK?

This book is written as a resource for teachers who need more support in becoming successful educators. It is intended for use as

- A comprehensive planning guide for classroom teachers and special subject area teachers already employed in a school setting
- A guide for a staff development seminar
- A textbook for teacher recertification courses

- A prerequisite, supplemental reference guide, or textbook for student teaching
- A supplemental text for classroom management, teaching methods, or curriculum planning courses
- A textbook for teacher induction programs sponsored by state education departments, professional associations, school systems, or schools
- A guide for mentor-teacher and lead-teacher training programs

WHAT ARE THE BENEFITS OF USING THIS BOOK?

This comprehensive planning guide shows teachers how to become successful educators, helping teachers increase their competence and productivity and avoid burnout and early attrition. The desired results of teachers using this book are reduced faculty turnover and increased school stability, which would save schools money and improve student achievement, leading to the ultimate benefit of this book—more successful schools.

WHAT ARE THE BOOK'S SPECIAL FEATURES?

Special features of this book include

- Objectives at the beginning of each chapter
- A summary at the end of each chapter
- Unique questions in every chapter that promote reflection and personalize the text for each reader
- Success Tips, denoted in the text by a hand ringing a bell, to help teachers work more efficiently and effectively
- True Stories, denoted in the text by an apple on a stack of books, to illustrate points made in the text and to offer additional success tips
- Resources for Successful Teaching, denoted in the text by a pair of glasses beside a book, which includes master copies of lesson plan book pages, easy-to-use checklists, lists of professional organizations, and more

HOW CAN YOU GET THE MOST OUT OF THIS BOOK?

To get the most out of this book, it is important to thoroughly answer all the questions posed in each chapter and to record your answers in a notebook. To answer some questions, you may need to consult existing school documents; keep these in a folder near your notebook so that you can easily refer to them as needed. You will also need to have your lesson plan book handy for Section II, Your Action Plans. The Resources for Successful Teaching section at the end of this book has master lesson plan book pages that you can photocopy and place in a three-ring binder for this purpose. Feel free to modify these master pages as you see fit.

WHERE CAN YOU SEND FEEDBACK ABOUT THIS BOOK?

Please e-mail your comments or questions about this book to the author, Lisa Burke, at LMB9@yahoo.com. All feedback is welcome, especially information about what you found most helpful in this edition and what you would like to see improved in future editions.

ACKNOWLEDGMENTS

This book could not have become a reality without all the lessons I have learned from the many fine educators I have had the privilege to meet, speak, and work with over the past several years. Their knowledge and expertise helped inspire this book. I would also like to thank my editor, Faye Zucker, and the rest of the Corwin Press team for their unending support and their invaluable insight and feedback.

Grateful acknowledgment is also made to the following people who have allowed me to use the words of other authors who said it so well that I could not say it better:

- John Wiley & Sons and Jossey-Bass Inc. Publishers for permission to reprint information on p. 58 from *Crisis in Education: Stress and Burnout in the American Teacher* by Barry Farber © 1991 by Jossey-Bass Inc. Publishers.
- Barbara Scaros of the Edith Winthrop Teacher Center of Westchester for permission to reprint information on p. 38 from *Sight on Sites: An Approach to Coping with Teacher Stress—Preventing Burn-out* by Barbara Scaros © 1981 by the New York City Teacher Centers Consortium.
- State University of New York Press for permission to reprint information on pp. 157 and 158 from *Becoming an Effective Classroom Manager: A Resource for Teachers* by Bob F. Steere © 1988 by the State University of New York. All rights reserved.

My deepest gratitude goes out to my family and friends, especially to my husband, James. Without their tremendous support, this book would never have been written. Thank you from the bottom of my heart.

The following reviewers are also gratefully acknowledged:

Raymond Francis
Associate Chair for Student Teaching
College of Education and Human Services
Central Michigan University
Mt. Pleasant, Michigan

David Frankel
Technology Consultant
Wayne County Regional Educational Service Agency
Wayne, Michigan

Sandra Hildreth
Arts Methods Instructor
Education Department
St. Lawrence University
Norwood, New York

Michelle Kocar
Grade 6 Science and Mathematics Teacher
Parkside Intermediate School
Westlake, Ohio

About the Author

Lisa Maria Burke, M. Ed., is a teacher, trainer, and author. She has taught in both regular education and inclusion settings as well as teaching reading resource, college, and continuing education courses. Lisa also has worked as an instructional resource teacher, supporting teachers as a curriculum and instruction specialist. Lisa's workshops and seminars for teachers focus on effective teaching, especially planning and instructional strategies. Her successful publications *7 Steps to Stress Free Teaching: A Stress Prevention Planning Guide for Teachers* and *7 Steps to Stress Free Teaching Plan Book* (Educators' Lighthouse, 1999) were precursors of *The Teacher's Ultimate Planning Guide*. She is a member of the Association for Supervision and Curriculum Development, the International Reading Association, and the Kappa Delta Pi Honor Society. She may be reached via e-mail at LMB9@yahoo.com.

This book is dedicated to all teachers who fill our minds with knowledge about our world, our hearts with compassion for others, and our souls with courage to always do the right thing.

Introduction

The Successful Teacher: What Research Tells Us

INTRODUCTION AND OBJECTIVES

Successful teachers are those who have mastered the art and science of teaching. It is helpful, therefore, to examine the research that identifies the characteristics and behaviors of successful teachers.

The objectives of this introductory chapter are to identify

- What characteristics and behaviors successful teachers demonstrate
- Why some teachers struggle even when they have been exposed to the research on successful teaching
- What stress is and what causes it
- What stressors are and which ones are particularly common for teachers
- How we can apply both the research on preventing teacher stress and the research on successful teachers to enable successful teaching

SUCCESSFUL TEACHERS: WHO ARE THEY?

Most of us think we know successful teachers when we see them—they are enthusiastic, energetic, and appear to be in control of their classrooms. But is there more than meets the eye? Just who are the teachers who succeed?

Successful teachers are effective teachers—ones with the highest student achievement. Because teacher effectiveness is the most powerful predictor of student success, it is imperative that we understand what makes a successful teacher.

Successful teachers exhibit many common characteristics and behaviors. Research shows that it all begins with their expectations of their students and of themselves.

Successful teachers believe that students can and will learn. They set high but attainable goals for academic performance. They review and use research findings to improve their instruction and to examine their own effectiveness. As reflective practitioners, they always strive to improve their teaching performance. They engage in meaningful and ongoing professional development. They also demonstrate a passion for the work they do.

They have a deep knowledge of the subjects they teach. Successful teachers use their knowledge of the subject matter and their students' background information, such as developmental levels and personal interests, to guide their instructional planning. Their instruction matches learners' needs, and they make adjustments as necessary.

They also use a variety of teaching models, including both direct and indirect models, and balance their use to match the developmental levels of their students. They use more direct instruction with lower-achieving and younger students. Successful elementary school teachers use a direct model of teaching more than half the time, especially in reading and math, where teacher-directed approaches yield stronger gains. At the high school level, successful teachers use an indirect mode of instruction, such as questioning and open inquiry, more than half the time. With whatever teaching model they use, successful teachers actively engage their students in learning activities. They effectively group students for instruction, and they use cooperative learning activities.

They design instruction that encourages students to think. They use effective questioning skills and higher-order questions. They cue their students for clarification or elaboration to extend learning, such as "Yes, the answer is 243, and how did you arrive at that answer?" They also provide "wait time" for students to formulate their answers.

Successful teachers emphasize academic goals and activities. They have a goal-oriented instructional program. They plan lessons to daily learning outcomes. They clearly communicate the educational objectives and learning expectations of the lesson, and they use advance organizers to help their students grasp the purpose and scope of the lesson. (*Advance organizers* are organized representations, often in the form of webs or outlines, of what it is to be learned.)

They monitor student progress in a variety of ways and conduct frequent assessments of student learning. They supervise students' work and give timely feedback to both students and their parents.

Researchers have found that giving feedback is the teacher behavior that influences strong student achievement most.

Successful teachers use time masterfully, comfortably pacing instruction and transitioning seamlessly among activities. They spend more time teaching students and assign less busywork. Students are kept on task by offering clear directions and effectively monitoring student activity, making contact with students frequently during seatwork and quickly attending to students' inappropriate behavior to help prevent discipline problems.

Successful teachers' discipline strategies are clear, firm, and consistent. Research has shown that successful teachers punish less, support and reassure more, reprimand softly and only when necessary, and allow offenders to save face. They use positive classroom management strategies, such as positive reinforcement and encouragement, and use praise selectively.

They create a climate of fairness in the classroom and keep morale high. Successful teachers create a relatively relaxed learning environment with a task-oriented focus. They establish a cooperative, family-like atmosphere. They accept feelings and are empathetic toward others. They establish and maintain rapport with students, parents, and colleagues. They encourage parental involvement in student learning and exhibit positive community relations.

> There is a positive and significant relationship between teachers' levels of interpersonal skills—for instance, practicing active listening and showing empathy—and students' attendance, self-esteem, and gains on achievement test scores. Findings show that teachers can develop and improve their interpersonal skills through training, including taking courses and reading available resources on the topic.

WHY DO SOME TEACHERS STRUGGLE TO SUCCEED?

Most teachers graduate from a four-year teacher preparation program that includes three or more years of teaching theory and several months of applying that theory in a working classroom or learning environment. Yet when it comes time to lead their own classrooms, many teachers struggle to succeed during their first few years of teaching. Even teachers with many years of classroom teaching under their belts can feel that they haven't reached a satisfactory performance level—a feeling with which their colleagues or principals may concur. Despite years of experience, these teachers still struggle to succeed.

The root of the problem lies with the nature of the job. Successful teaching is more than just knowing how to use teaching strategies. It is more than just tutoring on a large scale. Successful classroom teaching is rooted in effectively *managing* a large, complex, and diverse learning environment.

In colleges or emergency teacher preparation programs, prospective teachers learn a lot about how to instruct but not how to manage. As a result, they aren't prepared to handle the myriad responsibilities they will face on a daily basis, especially managing large groups of children single-handedly. Many new teachers enter their classrooms for the first time with little idea of all the responsibilities that go along with teaching. No matter how many hours they log in student teaching or spend in teacher preparation courses, many still are not prepared to teach.

The result is stress. Many teachers are overwhelmed with everything they have to do just to survive, let alone thrive. Many tasks are extremely time-consuming and are often emotionally draining. Add a hefty amount of accountability to the mix, and the pressure of everything can be too much. Consequently, many teachers do not succeed, and they will continue to struggle, often until they burn out.

Teachers, Are You Stressed Out?

Ask yourself the following questions to find out if you're stressed out:

- Do you feel excessive pressure from not having enough time to do the things you need to do?
- Are you leaving work frustrated and exhausted?
- Do you suffer from insomnia or other sleeping difficulties?
- Do you find it difficult to let go of work at the end of the day?
- Do you frequently experience gastrointestinal problems such as ulcers, indigestion, or poor appetite?
- Do you have low self-esteem or feelings of hopelessness?
- Do you feel as if you're in a long, dark tunnel without a light in sight?

If you answered yes to one or more of these questions, you might be experiencing stress. But take heart. You're not alone, and you *can* prevent it. You can succeed. This book shows you how.

STRESS: WHAT IS IT?

Stress is a physiological condition that is essential to life. Whether your stress is the result of a major life experience or the cumulative effect of minor everyday worries, your responses to these experiences determine the impact of stress on your life.

Dr. Hans Selye (1974), a physician and prominent researcher on stress, defines stress as the body's physiological response to any demand, pleasant or unpleasant, made on it. This response includes the release of cortisol and adrenaline into the system, which causes increases in blood pressure and heart rate. In addition, muscles tense, senses heighten, and metabolism changes.

The demands made on the body that trigger this physiological response are called stressors. Stressors disrupt a body's natural balance. Your brain detects stressors, interprets the changes in your environment and in your body, and decides when to turn on the stress response.

Stressors are from four basic sources. First, there is your environment, such as noise, traffic, and weather. Second are social situations, such as disagreements, demands on your time by others, and deadlines. The third source is physiology, such as aging, menopause, lack of exercise, and poor nutrition. Finally, your own thoughts can be stressors.

The General Adaptation Syndrome

For all kinds of stressors, the physiological response is the same. Selye named this response the general adaptation syndrome. According to Selye, the general adaptation syndrome has three stages: alarm, resistance, and exhaustion. In the first stage, you become more alert and your body poises for "fight or flight." This occurs whether the situation warrants this type of response or not. The response is left over from our evolutionary past, protecting us from danger in our struggles for survival. The alarm stage is still very useful to us, especially when a stress response is needed for a short time, such as in the face of extreme danger. However, most modern stressors occur over a sustained period. The body stays primed to react, and the alarm response stage spills over into the next stage—resistance.

In the resistance stage, your body uses energy to adapt to the stressor. The length of this stage depends on the intensity of the stressor and your ability to adapt to it. If your body can get used to the stressor, it returns to a state of natural balance. If you never deal with the stressful situation, the long, severe stress eventually depletes your energy and decreases your body's resistance to the stressor. As the stressful situation continues, it leads to the third stage—mental, emotional, and physical exhaustion.

Positive and Negative Stress

The general adaptation syndrome can have a positive or negative trigger, or stressor, so it can create positive or negative stress in your body. Positive stress helps motivate you and enables you to achieve peak performance. For instance, football players experience positive stress during their coach's rousing pep talk moments before a big game.

Negative stress, on the other hand, can make you feel anxious, nervous, depressed, and irritable. It can also decrease your patience and tolerance, affecting your interpersonal relationships. Moreover, it can affect your immune system and lead to health problems such as high blood pressure, migraine headaches, heart attacks, ulcers, and insomnia. If not dealt with, negative stress eventually leads to the state of mental, emotional, and physical exhaustion that defines the third stage of the general adaptation syndrome. In this state, you often experience low self-esteem and feel hopeless, helpless, and weary. This state is often referred to as burnout.

Negative stress, or distress, is the type of stress that plagues most people. Distress is implied every time the word *stress* is used in this book. What we know about stress and its causes has great implications for all people, especially for those who experience it often.

STRESS AND TEACHING: WHAT EVERY TEACHER MUST KNOW

Stress prevents successful teaching. Unfortunately, the American Institute of Stress has found that being a teacher is one of the most stressful occupations. One study concluded that some teachers experience more stress than police officers, miners, air traffic controllers, and even medical interns. Millions of teachers throughout the world are not surprised by this news.

Time and time again, studies have found that teachers report some of the highest levels of occupational stress. High occupational stress is usually caused by physical danger, extreme pressure, or responsibility without control. The teaching profession can have all these characteristics. For most teachers, however, the cause of extreme occupational stress is not an infrequent, intense event, such as those a firefighter might experience, but the cumulative effect of constant, subtle daily stressors involving danger, pressure, and responsibility without control.

Throughout history, teachers have experienced stress. This stress has traditionally been caused by the pressures of accountability, the constant change characterized by the profession, and the loneliness of the job. But the prevailing culture and educational system determine which unique stressors exist at the time. As times change, so do some of the stressors.

When I was growing up, a new child joining the class in the middle of the school year was a rarity. Today I live in a community that is growing and changing rapidly, with multiple real estate transactions occurring daily. Now I have about half a dozen new students join my classes at different points during the school year. Each child becomes a new personality, a new need, and a new stressor for me.

What Causes Teachers' Stress?

For today's teachers, there are three major categories of stressors that cause work-related stress. The first, organizational stressors, includes the social stressors previously described. For teachers, organizational stressors are found in the workplace, including the daily job responsibilities and relationships with colleagues, administrators, and students.

The second category is environmental stressors. These originate outside the workplace and include the students' families, the community, and the teacher's own family and friends.

Individual stressors, which fall under the category of physiological and psychological stressors, as previously described, are the third category of teachers' stressors. These include the teacher's personal characteristics, such as personality type, attitude, and state of physical health.

This book focuses on all three categories of stressors related to the teaching profession.

What Are Your Stressors?

Use the Stress Inventory shown in Figure A.1 to find out which stressors you're struggling with. The inventory helps you identify your stressors, how often they occur, how much control you feel you have over them, how you currently respond to stressors, and how effective your responses are. Copy the table into a notebook that you can also use to complete the questions in the rest of this book (see "How Can You Get the Most Out of This Book?" in the Preface for more information). Provide as many lines in your table as you need.

Figure A.1.   Stress Inventory

Stressor	Frequency	Amount of Control	Your Response	Effectiveness of Response

To help you complete the inventory, answer the following questions:

- *Stressor:* What events cause you stress? Include who or what is involved in the stressor, and begin your statements with verbs. Examples include "completing paperwork on time for weekly department meetings," "interacting with the principal in a one-on-one meeting," "dealing with discipline problems in my last-period class," "helping Sally learn the multiplication facts," and "helping my son with his homework."
- *Frequency:* How often does each one occur? Is it always, frequently, or seldom?
- *Amount of Control:* How much control do you feel you have over each stressor? Is it a high level of control, some control, or no control?
- *Your Response:* How do you currently respond to each stressor? Do you try to overcome it? For example, using the first of the previous examples, you "bring all paperwork home and work all weekend, giving up tons of family time and sleep to complete it." Do you get depressed, frustrated, or angry? Do you just accept it or brush it off? Do you enlist the support of others? Specify exactly what you do for each stressor.
- *Effectiveness of Response:* How effective is your response in removing or managing the stress caused by the stressor? Describe it here

or use a scale: for example, 1 denotes that your response does not effectively deal with the stressor at all, 5 denotes that your response moderately decreases the stress associated with the stressor, and 10 denotes that your response very effectively manages the stress associated with the stressor and thus removes the stress completely.

Look at the stressors you identified. Are any related to your job? Can you group your stressors in any way? Are there any common elements among some or all of your stressors? Which stressors or group of stressors are contributing most to your stress?

Compare your list with what today's teachers find to contribute most to their stress: time management issues; student discipline problems; relationship tensions with administrators, colleagues, parents, and community members; inadequate resources; role conflict; and role ambiguity. Do some or many of your stressors fall within these categories? If so, this book is here to help, offering practical advice and techniques you can use to prevent and effectively manage teachers' work-related stress.

In the Stress Inventory, you also identified the amount of control that you feel you have over the stressors and the way in which you currently manage them. You will use this important information later in this introduction.

Why Must Teachers Learn to Deal With Stress?

Although many teachers are under a great deal of stress, it has been found that over two-thirds of teachers today say they would choose the same career again! This is a sign of dedication, a sign that many teachers feel as I do—that teaching is a calling.

My interest in teaching began in high school when I volunteered to be a reading tutor for younger students. Although my interest in teaching grew, I did not consider it as a career choice. Instead, I decided to join corporate America. When I found work dissatisfying, I began to teach part-time at a community college and volunteered my time to tutor local middle school and high school students. My work with young people was very fulfilling. It made me feel whole. I knew then that I had found my calling.

To make teaching their lifelong profession, teachers must learn and master the skills needed to handle stress. However, teacher preparation programs usually focus on technical skills, not on the stress management and stress prevention skills you need to make your teaching most effective.

Because a lack of stress management and prevention skills has been found to contribute to teacher absenteeism, attrition, and burnout, mastering them is imperative.

Why Focus on Stress Prevention?

Stress management is handling stress after it has occurred. Its purpose is to mitigate the stress, not to prevent it from happening again. It is difficult to cope with stress. Stress management takes a lot of time, energy, and self-discipline.

In contrast, stress prevention takes a proactive, direct approach to stress. A review of research on coping with stress found that a direct approach aimed at improving stress prevention skills was more effective in dealing with stress than approaches aimed at reducing or managing the experience of stress after it occurs. As the saying goes, "An ounce of prevention is worth a pound of cure." Because a teacher does not have a lot of extra time and energy to spend on stress management, prevention is the key.

The focus of the strategies in this book is stress prevention, but maybe you experience stress no matter what you do to prevent it from occurring. If so, there are things you can do to manage the stress, such as breathing techniques, meditation, visualization, self-hypnosis, biofeedback, and thought stopping. You can learn these strategies by taking classes and reading books; consult your local library and community center for more information.

Psychological and Emotional Responses to Stressors

Stress is not external to us. It is an internal response to a stressor. Although the internal physiological response is the same for all stressors, your psychological or emotional response varies depending on the stressors. For example, one stressor scares you while another one frustrates you. In addition, different people can have different psychological and emotional responses to the same stressor. For instance, a stressor that causes you to become depressed might cause your friend to become anxious. Differences in reactions are attributed to different perceptions of the stressor.

How you perceive a stressor determines whether your body responds with stress or stays in a balanced state. Therefore, you need to understand the root of these perceptions before you can successfully prevent stress.

Beliefs: The Root of Stress

Perceptions are determined by beliefs. When you believe that you have no control over a stressor, you generate feelings of uncertainty, frustration, reduced motivation, and eventually burnout. You perceive the stressor as harmful, irritating, or threatening, and your body responds with stress. Research shows that people who feel in control at work feel less stress than those who do not feel influential in their work environment. Therefore, you experience stress when you believe a stressor is out of your control.

Revisit your Stress Inventory. How much control do you feel you have over each of your stressors? The stressors that you feel you have only some control or no control over are probably the ones causing most of your stress.

What Shapes Your Beliefs?

Beliefs are influenced by conditioning factors—internal (such as age or sex) or external (such as parental influences, diet, or medications). As a result, your conditioning factors color your perceptions of different stressors. This explains why you and your colleague might have totally different reactions or different degrees of stress to the *same* stressor. For example, both you and your colleague might identify meeting with the principal as a stressor. But your colleague might feel frustrated by such a meeting because he or she is older than the principal and finds it difficult to take directions from someone younger, while you feel nervous because you've been conditioned to respond that way to people in positions of authority.

Conditioning factors also explain how you can have different stress reactions to similar stressors. For example, in your Stress Inventory, you might have indicated a different psychological or emotional reaction to two different classroom parents, even if you have identified or grouped both parents as *similar* stressors. You might feel nervous when interacting with one parent and irritated when interacting with the other. This happens because each stressor possesses unique characteristics. Because of your conditioning factors, you react differently to each parent's unique characteristics and thus have a slightly different psychological or emotional stress response. For example, you get nervous when interacting with a father who has a volatile temper because he reminds you of the bully who bothered you in high school, and you get irritated when interacting with a mother who is apathetic about her son's lack of achievement because you value education and think it worthy of her utmost interest.

Although each of us is influenced by unique conditioning factors and our stressors have unique characteristics, research has found many common elements among teachers' stress inventories. These elements form the foundation of this book.

Teachers *Can* Prevent Stress

Yes, fellow teacher, you can win the battle with stress! Every day you face countless stressors. If you feel you have only some or no control over a stressor, you'll probably experience stress, but the more control you feel, the less stress you'll experience. The good news is that teachers do have a higher degree of control over most of their stressors than they might believe they have.

Many teaching-related stressors are situations that you, the teacher, can control. Even if the situation seems totally out of your control, there is usually some aspect of it that you can master.

You might be asking, "How do you accomplish this? How do you know what you can control?" The skills needed to identify potential stressors and to implement stress prevention measures can be developed and nurtured by asking the right questions. This book provides those questions.

It was a year from hell. Everything seemed wrong. Most of the time I felt angry, frustrated, and exhausted. I was stressed. When it was finally over, I wanted to find out if my terrible experience was the result of being in the wrong place at the wrong time or of something I did. By talking with other teachers, I found out that most teachers experience a horrible year at some point in their careers, and many experience more than one. Knowing this, "Why me?" turned into "Why us?" and I began to search for answers. From my search, it became evident that teachers can prevent stress. Common threads emerged, and the steps for preventing a stressful year and for achieving a successful school year became apparent. I then contacted teachers from all over the country and found they were interested in my research. With their tremendous encouragement and support, I share my findings in this book.

APPLY THE RESEARCH AND BECOME A SUCCESSFUL TEACHER

The Teacher's Ultimate Planning Guide shows you how to take control of many teaching stressors that can prevent success in the classroom. You've already identified your stressors in the Stress Inventory. The chapters that follow apply the research on successful teachers to show you how to master the elements of successful teaching and prevent your stressors. In each of the following chapters, questions help you develop the skills needed for successful teaching. To internalize these skills, thoroughly answer all the questions. Record your answers in a notebook. For some questions, existing school documents will provide the answers. Keep the documents in a folder near your notebook for easy reference. Also, keep your lesson plan book handy for Section II, Your Action Plans. For your convenience, the Resources for Successful Teaching section at the end of this book has sample lesson plan book pages that you can photocopy and place in a binder. Feel free to modify these pages as you see fit.

The book has different sections to denote the different phases needed for successful teaching. Section I, The First Steps, builds a foundation for proactive teaching. Section II, Your Action Plans, helps you design a comprehensive plan for successful teaching. Section III, Your Momentum, keeps you on track and enables you to measure your teaching effectiveness. The Epilogue, Enabling Successful Teaching: What Educational Leaders at All Levels Must Know, is a discussion of what can be done to foster and support successful teaching. Finally, the Resources for Successful Teaching section at the end of the book is a wealth of easy-to-use resources that support successful teaching.

SUMMARY

In this introduction, you learned the characteristics and behaviors of successful teachers. You also learned that work-related stress can prevent many teachers from becoming successful. After a brief discussion of the main causes of teacher stress, you learned that many of the stressors are usually situations where teachers feel they have low levels of control. Using the Stress Inventory, you identified your personal stressors. The rest of the book will help you prevent the stress caused by your work-related stressors, thus enabling you to become a more effective, successful teacher.

Section I

The First Steps

1

Take Care of Yourself

INTRODUCTION AND OBJECTIVES

Having a successful school year and a thriving teaching career begins with you. The most important element for successful teaching is taking care of yourself, making sure your personal needs are met.

Stress can get in the way of your meeting your personal needs. To prevent the stress that too often overwhelms teachers, you need to attend to three main areas of your life. First is your physical, mental, and emotional health. If you're like most teachers, you place your personal needs after the needs of others. Without providing time and energy to take care of your health, stress continues to build. Eventually, you might experience burnout. Avoid this unfortunate conclusion by setting boundaries to help create the time needed for maintaining good health.

Second, know the administrative details of your employment. For example, understand the terms of your contract and be aware of the criteria used to evaluate your teaching performance. This prevents misunderstandings between you and your employer, as well as the stress associated with them.

Third, take advantage of opportunities for your personal and professional growth and renewal. Such opportunities strengthen self-esteem and improve teaching skills. Taking continuing education classes, working with a mentor, and becoming active in professional associations are some of the opportunities for growth and renewal available to you.

The objectives of this chapter are to help you

- Maintain a healthy physical, mental, and emotional lifestyle
- Understand all the details surrounding your employment contract
- Ensure your personal and professional growth for a successful school year and a thriving teaching career

15

MAINTAIN OPTIMAL HEALTH

Good health is a prerequisite for successful teaching. It helps your body function at its best and prevents stress. When your health is poor, stress can wear out your body and soul, weaken your teaching performance, and degrade your personal effectiveness.

Make Time for Your Health

The first step in attaining good health is building in the time to maintain a healthy and balanced lifestyle. It must be scheduled! To find time, you might have to learn to say no to extra commitments, both work and nonwork related. If you, like many teachers, tend to put others' needs before your own, stop! You must make time to take care of your health in order to operate at peak performance. The first question in this book deals with this issue because it is the most important factor in achieving a successful year and a thriving teaching career.

Open your notebook. Answer the following questions completely. To help you stay organized, the first digit of each question number corresponds with the chapter number.

> 1.1 What can you do to ensure you have enough time for each of the following?
> a. Getting enough rest
> b. Eating balanced meals
> c. Exercising aerobically
> d. Spending time with family and with those you care about
> e. Growing spiritually
> f. Exploring hobbies and non-work-related interests
> g. Exploring personal career growth activities

During lunch, avoid discussing business, eat slowly, and take your full lunch period. To protect your mental and emotional health, try to eat lunch with a staff member who has a positive attitude.

Protect Your Physical Health

Besides making time to maintain a healthy and balanced lifestyle, you need to protect your physical health by integrating safeguards into your daily routine. Children bring many illnesses to school that can spread quickly in the confined space of a classroom. Boost your immunity against colds and other common illnesses by eating well, getting enough rest, drinking lots of water, frequently washing your hands with soap, and using instant hand disinfectant. Maintain your comfort by keeping an extra sweater and a pair of nonrestricting shoes in your classroom.

Most teachers get sick frequently during the first few years of teaching because they have not yet built up immunity against many common illnesses. I was no exception. In my first year of teaching, I caught many colds and had strep throat—for the first time in my life! Although teaching is a very demanding job and it is difficult to be absent, I learned the hard way that it was better to take a sick day when I wasn't feeling well than to go to work. Pushing myself to go to work only prolonged my illness, and it probably made some of my students sick, too. Now I make sure I always have substitute teacher plans ready so I can take a couple of sick days without having to pull together plans at the last minute.

Kidney and bladder infections are another problem for some teachers. This often results from not having enough time to use the restroom during the school day—a common teaching dilemma. Make the time! If you need to, buddy with another teacher and take turns watching each other's class so each of you can get the bathroom breaks you need.

You also need to be aware of procedures related to your health insurance benefits and the procedures for taking sick days and arriving late or leaving early due to an unforeseen illness. Further, if you should be the victim of an accident on the job, you need to know your rights and the procedures that ensure those rights.

1.2 Are there any childhood illnesses or other illnesses that you will probably be exposed to during the school year?
   a. Are there any vaccines available for these illnesses? Where can you get the vaccines? Who pays for them?
   b. What precautions can you take to avoid getting these illnesses?

1.3 Do you get any sick days, "mental health days," personal days, or leave days?
   a. How many do you get?
   b. What is the procedure for taking these days?
   c. Are these paid or unpaid days of absence?

1.4 What are the procedures for arriving late and leaving early? Is there a penalty for doing either of these things?

1.5 What happens if you get hurt on the job or elsewhere?
   a. Are you required to report it? What is the procedure?
   b. What are your rights concerning related absences, sick pay, and keeping your position? What are the procedures for receiving these benefits?

Your Personal Safety

In addition to illnesses, every year more and more teachers have to concern themselves with personal safety. According to the U.S. Department of Education, teachers were the victims of approximately 1,755,000 nonfatal crimes at school, including 1,087,000 thefts and 668,000 violent crimes (such as rape or sexual assault, robbery, aggravated assault, and simple assault) from 1994 through 1998. Among the violent crimes, about 80,000 were classified as serious (such as rape or sexual assault, robbery, or aggravated assault). This translates into roughly 16,000 serious violent crimes each year—an alarming number. Every threat made against you, by a student or parent, must be taken seriously. Report it to your administration immediately. To help prevent potentially life-threatening situations, take the following measures:

- Lock your classroom doors and windows when working alone.
- Make sure you have something in your classroom, such as a telephone or two-way public address system, that allows you to contact the office immediately in case of an emergency. A personal cell phone with programmed emergency numbers is also useful.
- If anyone threatens you in any way, ask to keep your classroom doors locked during the school day until the situation is resolved. However, make sure you are not violating any fire codes and that you and your students still could easily vacate the room in case of a fire or other emergency.
- If your school has a policy requiring all personnel and visitors to wear identification badges, wear yours and question anyone you see who is not wearing one. Refer them to the main office to get one, and if they try to ignore your request, escort them to the office yourself or report them immediately.
- Know the teachers in your neighboring classrooms, and share a signal that you can bang on the walls if you need help.
- Do not stay by yourself in your classroom after most people have gone home, especially after dark and on weekends.
- Close and lock your classroom doors before leaving in the evening.
- If you have to return to school in the evening, park in a well-lit area as close to the door as possible.
- Always walk with another adult to your car in the parking lot, especially after sunset.
- If you have an evening conference, ask another adult to stay with you. Also, meet the parents in a well-lit common area of the building, and walk back to your cars together.

One day I happened to be in the hallway after classes had started, and I noticed two women entering the school through a side door. When I asked them why they were there, they said they came to volunteer in a particular teacher's classroom. I told them they needed to check in at the main office (located at the other end of the building) and get visitors' badges. When they realized that I wasn't going to let them continue down the hallway toward their destination, they became a bit annoyed. Although I hadn't intended to go to the office, I pretended that I did and escorted them myself. I knew that if I left them alone, they would ignore the rules. It was a very uncomfortable situation, but I knew that for everyone's safety, I was doing the right thing.

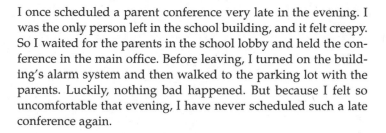

I once scheduled a parent conference very late in the evening. I was the only person left in the school building, and it felt creepy. So I waited for the parents in the school lobby and held the conference in the main office. Before leaving, I turned on the building's alarm system and then walked to the parking lot with the parents. Luckily, nothing bad happened. But because I felt so uncomfortable that evening, I have never scheduled such a late conference again.

- It's always a good idea to be on friendly terms with the custodian. Let your custodian know when you work after school so she or he can stop by to check on you.
- If your life is in danger, do not hesitate to contact the police.

Because of the seriousness of some recent events, most people think that school violence has gotten worse over the past few years. Teachers and administrators agree with this perception, not because of the deadly types of violence that appear to concern the public most, such as drug abuse, weapons possession, and gang activities, but because of the behaviors that indicate incivility, such as verbal intimidation and threats, rumors, pushing and shoving, and sexual harassment. These behaviors—usually seen by others as bullying, acting out, or disruptive behavior—are the *early warning signs* of violence.

Teachers know that children who are at risk for violence usually engage in visible minor behavior problems, such as bullying and poor school attitude, before progressing to using more violent acts. Other early warning signs include (1) strong feelings of rejection, isolation, and loneliness; (2) impulsiveness and chronic bullying, hitting, and intimidation; (3) being socially withdrawn; (4) feelings of being a victim of violence, persecution, or teasing; (5) gang affiliation; (6) low interest in school coupled with poor academic achievement; (7) drawings and writings that express violence; (8) uncontrolled anger; and (9) issuing serious, detailed, and specific threats of violence.

Although students at risk for serious aggression or violence typically exhibit more than one early warning sign, it is important not to overreact to any single incident or behavior. What might be a warning sign at one grade level could be more typical behavior of students at another grade level. In addition, warning signs should not comprise a checklist for labeling, stereotyping, or isolating children. Instead, the behaviors should be seen within the context of the situation and used to establish patterns of behavior.

However, if you see a student who exhibits any of these *imminent warning signs*, you should report it immediately: (1) serious physical fighting with peers and others, (2) severe destruction of personal or others' property, (3) intense rage for minor reasons, (4) detailed and specific threats of lethal violence, (5) possession or use of firearms, or (6) self-inflicting injury or threats of suicide.

Do not touch an enraged student unless the student is a danger to her- or himself, to others, or to property. If you must touch the student, grab her or him to stop the situation, and avoid hitting the student first unless doing so is crucial to protecting yourself from immediate harm.

School or school system policies related to dealing with school violence will vary, but they should have a crisis plan in place and a component dealing with how to report a student who exhibits any of these imminent warning signs. In addition, if a student reports a threat to you, immediately report it to your administrators, your local law enforcement, or whoever else has been designated to receive these reports. It is imperative that all threats of serious violence be taken seriously, for your protection and for the protection of your students. Ways to prevent school violence are further discussed in Chapter 7.

Do everything possible to prevent a violent outburst from happening in the first place. Be proactive with your classroom management plan to prevent and control any classroom disturbance that could escalate into something more serious. Do not react to classroom disturbances, but respond to them. Always keep your cool.

By implementing the personal safety tips described here and by staying alert to both the early and imminent warning signs of violent behavior, you are taking measures to ensure that you and your students are safe, thus preventing unfortunate consequences.

1.6 What precautions can you take to help keep you physically safe from assaults and other types of abuse or personal violations?

1.7 What is the procedure for reporting a threat of school violence?

1.8 What are the different school safety procedures already in place at your school? Are there any others that you feel might be helpful to implement? When will you approach your administrators and colleagues about your concerns and proposals?

Using Substances to Manage Stress

Another health topic that comes up repeatedly in the research is the use of alcohol, tobacco, and other drugs to manage stress. These substances have been found to do more harm than good. Rather than alleviating stress, they temporarily mask it. The stressors are still there. Understand that stress prevention is the place to put your time, energy, and resources— not into a drink or a cigarette.

1.9 If you use alcohol, tobacco, or other drugs to alleviate stress, where can you find help to stop this dependency and find other stress prevention techniques?

Protect Your Mental and Emotional Health

In addition to physical health, good mental and emotional health are important for preventing stress. Mental health involves exercising the mind and keeping it fit. To accomplish this, develop an interest that is not work related, such as gardening or a sport. These activities also help turn your mind's focus away from stressful situations. Schedule the time to pursue these outside interests.

1.10 In which kinds of non-work-related activities are you interested? Which ones will you do? How often? Where? With whom?

Emotional health is crucial for helping you prevent stress. It is very important because your beliefs about yourself and about your relationships with others affect your self-esteem. A healthy self-esteem usually makes you better at relating to others and better at understanding your students' needs. Therefore, if your stress is mostly due to how you feel about yourself or how you feel about your relationships with others, it is imperative that you take care of your emotional health.

Manage Your Negative Thoughts

Controlling your negative thoughts, especially those about yourself, is one way to improve your emotional health. Three ways to manage negative thoughts are replacing them, changing them, and changing your focus.

Whenever a negative thought about yourself or about your teaching enters your mind, interrupt it and replace it with a positive thought. Think instead about past successes in your teaching career, and remember the reasons why you became a teacher in the first place.

Another way to control your negative thoughts is to change them into empowering ones. For example, instead of thinking that you'll never get through grading your stack of papers, say to yourself that you'll do as much as possible in the time you have allocated. If you get them all done, great. If you don't, then you can finish them later. Remind yourself that you are often expected to do a lot more than is humanly possible, so you need to be realistic about what you can accomplish.

I begin every school year with fervor. I have tons of energy and lots of ideas that I add to my to-do list. By the third week of school, I'm swamped. My list is filled with things I have to do in addition to all the things I want to do. However, the differences among the items on my list get blurred, and I put a lot of pressure on myself to accomplish all of them. As a result, negative thoughts about myself run rampant. Then I know I have lost sight of what I can do. When this happens, I step back and look at my list again. I prioritize the items and try to be realistic about what I can accomplish within the time I have.

Changing your focus also helps remove negative thoughts. An easy way to accomplish this is by changing your activity. For example, when you are having a negative thought, change your focus by reading a good professional resource or by rearranging your bulletin boards. Keep a list of these activities taped to the inside back cover of your plan book so that the ideas are handy when you need them.

Sometimes you might find yourself in the presence of a negative colleague. If this person's negative attitude begins to influence your thoughts, politely remove yourself from the situation. Getting away might help change your focus and thus your negative thoughts.

Good emotional health has a lot to do with your thoughts about yourself. You need to stop beating yourself up! Every time a negative thought crosses your mind, you must interrupt it. Remember, you have complete control over what you are thinking. To prevent stress, it is imperative that you change how you think and what you focus on.

1.11 Do you have any pervasive negative thoughts about yourself or about your teaching?
   a. What teaching successes have you had that you can use to replace your negative thoughts?
   b. In what ways can you change the negative thoughts into empowering ones?
   c. What kinds of activities can you do to change your focus, especially when you are teaching?

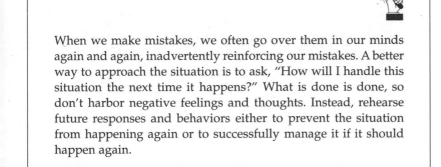

When we make mistakes, we often go over them in our minds again and again, inadvertently reinforcing our mistakes. A better way to approach the situation is to ask, "How will I handle this situation the next time it happens?" What is done is done, so don't harbor negative feelings and thoughts. Instead, rehearse future responses and behaviors either to prevent the situation from happening again or to successfully manage it if it should happen again.

Positive Affirmations Can Empower You

You can also use affirmations to achieve emotional health. You can create positive affirmations about yourself, both personal and professional. For an affirmation to be effective, you must truly believe it and repeat it to yourself with all the positive emotion you can generate. A sample empowering affirmation might be, "I am a competent and caring professional who does not react but responds to stressors in my environment." Use this one, or create one of your own.

1.12 What affirmations can you create that would empower you when you think of them? When and how often will you say them?

Communicate Effectively by Being Assertive

It has been found that teachers handle stress better when they are in a supportive environment. You might be thinking, "How do you get this support?" At first glance, you might feel that gaining support from administrators, colleagues, parents, and others is impossible. However, by becoming assertive, your chances of enlisting the support of others increase.

Being assertive can reduce your stress because it teaches you how to enlist the support of others by communicating your thoughts and needs efficiently and effectively using "I statements." An example is, "I feel . . . when you . . . because. . . ." You might also want to add "and I want . . ." or "and I need. . . ." Often, you need to use these statements when someone requests that you do something for them. Being assertive helps you say no to things you know you should not or cannot do. It enables you to stand up for yourself without bullying others or letting others bully you.

If being assertive is not easy for you, don't answer the request immediately. Ask for some time, and tell the other person when you will respond. Next, weigh the request against the things you have on your plate, as well as against your values. Then decide on your response and be willing to explain how you arrived at your decision.

Being assertive is one way to control the one thing you have complete control over—yourself. Take full advantage of this fact for helping you prevent stress. Several books are available to teach you how to become more assertive. If you would like more help, check out continuing education programs offered by your community or a local college.

1.13 Where can you learn more about becoming assertive? How can you ensure that you set aside enough time to learn and practice this skill?

One way to take care of yourself is to know your limitations. During the first few weeks of school, you will be asked to serve on many different committees and to take on extra duties. Because you know yourself best, only you can determine when you need to decline these invitations. Don't be afraid to say no! Learn to be assertive or else suffer the stressful consequences of biting off more than you can chew.

Organize a Support System

It is also important to identify to whom and where you can turn for help and support in times of emotional strife. Make sure that those you identify are people you can trust. Sometimes the person you thought you could trust stabs you in the back. Be careful! If you don't have a colleague or administrator you can trust, confide in a spouse, a friend, or even a pet. Be wary of including your students or their parents in your personal support system, because they can easily use the information you shared with them against you. If you are friends with any retired teachers, you should consider them a great source of support. Because they have walked in your shoes, they can offer some good ideas, materials, and advice.

As part of their benefits package, employers sometimes contract with outside agencies to provide free counseling for employees on an as-needed basis. Check with your school's human resources or guidance departments to find out if this benefit is available to you.

If you feel like you are going to explode and have no one you can turn to, write in a journal. Get it all out on paper. Although verbal feedback from a journal is impossible, most people get a sense of relief from putting their stresses in writing because it provides an outlet for venting emotions and sorting out events. It offers a nonthreatening environment in which to be very honest about a situation and about the role you played in making it a stressor. Many times, just by being able to sort out events, you find the clues for overcoming and preventing similar situations from occurring in the future.

I began writing in a journal the first evening of my first day of student teaching. I got hooked and have kept a journal ever since. I find that it helps me vent my frustrations. It also helps me sort out the events of my life—both inside and outside school. For me, journal writing is therapeutic. As a bonus, I can look back at old entries to see how much I have changed, how much I have grown. That always gives my self-esteem a boost.

1.14 Who can you trust when you need emotional support? If they are not available, what options do you have for getting the support you need?

UNDERSTAND THE DETAILS OF YOUR EMPLOYMENT CONTRACT

The details of your employment include all the paperwork required by your employer for your personnel file. There are many potential stressors in this area. Luckily, teachers have a lot of control over most of them. This part of taking care of yourself involves analyzing the terms of your employment to help you determine exactly how much control you have over each one.

What to Do Before You Are Hired

First, briefly examine what an employer might require you to have before you are even hired.

1.15 What do you need to be employed by this particular school?
   a. A background check? If yes, what kind, who pays for it, and what forms need to be completed?
   b. A formal application with the employer?
   c. Proof of past work experience? What kind of proof?
   d. A teaching certification? If so, what type?

1.16 Who do you contact to find out the following?
   a. Has your employer received all the required documents and information?
   b. Is any additional information required?

Understand Your Contract

Once you have secured a job, read your contract—including the fine print. Read all paperwork, booklets, and forms associated with your employment that are mailed to you from your school system's central office. This is where many teachers unconsciously abdicate their control. By ignoring these important documents, they set themselves up for turning simple, easy-to-handle situations into stressful experiences. Do not let this happen to you! You'll probably get the answers to many of the following questions during your interview, but don't take anything for granted. Verify the answers with your school system's central office and with the paperwork you receive.

1.17 What are the terms of your contract?
   a. What is the difference between a continuing, terminating, or other type of contract? What type of contract did you receive?
   b. Is tenure an option? How can you earn it? How can you lose it?
   c. What is expected of you in your new position? What responsibilities and duties are stated in your contract and in your job description? Which ones are not stated but implied?
   d. Are inservice classes or other types of courses required to keep your job and your certification?
   e. Are you required to sign up for extra duties, committees, chaperoning, detention, coaching, and other activities? If yes, which ones and how many? What are the commitments and responsibilities of each? Do you receive a stipend for them?
   f. What is the schedule for standing meetings that you are required to attend for your grade level or department, school, and school system?

g. Are you required to attend meetings (such as faculty and PTA meetings, workshops, and seminars) outside school hours and during your personal time? Are you compensated for your time with money or with extra time off?

If a written job description is not available, check the performance evaluation forms used by your school. It usually contains a list of the criteria used to evaluate your work. These criteria will outline the responsibilities and duties that are expected of you.

Is Your Class Roster Fair?

An issue that tends to cause teachers undue stress that might or might not be included in your contract is the assignment of a greater than average number of students with major behavioral problems. If you are a special education teacher assigned to teach this type of population, this might not be an issue for you, but for "regular education" teachers at all grade levels, it can be a significant stressor.

To ensure that your class roster is fair, first determine the school's average number of "difficult students" per class by asking your colleagues, administration, and office staff. Second, check your students' cumulative records as soon as you have your class roster. If you feel that you have received an unfair load, discuss it with your principal as soon as possible.

1.18 In your school, what is an average number of students per class who have significant behavior problems?

1.19 After checking your students' cumulative records, do you find you have several of these kinds of students in your class? When can you speak with the principal regarding your concern?

Know the Details of Your Health Insurance Benefits

Most teaching positions also have a health insurance benefits package. Especially with the advent of health maintenance organizations (HMOs), completing the proper forms and following the correct timelines and procedures are imperative for preventing stress. The time, energy, and money lost by not following proper filing procedures can be enormous. Make sure you understand your benefits and how to get access to them.

1.20 What are your health insurance benefits?

a. Who do you need to contact to find out if you have received all the proper filing documents for obtaining or maintaining any health insurance benefits you might be entitled to?

    b. Have you correctly completed and handed in all the proper documents to obtain or maintain any health insurance benefits you would like to receive?

    c. Does the benefits enrollment office have your information recorded correctly?

    d. When you visit a doctor, what are the proper filing procedures for receiving your health insurance benefits?

    e. When do your health insurance benefits become active, such as the first day you begin working or the first day of the next complete calendar month you are employed?

Keep Tabs on Your Financial Benefits

In addition to health insurance benefits, you also have financial benefits. You need to complete additional forms to receive the proper salary and to have the correct amount of taxes withheld from your paycheck. If you do not take care of this paperwork, you will most likely experience a lot of stress.

1.21 What are your financial benefits?

    a. Who do you need to contact to find out if you have received all the proper tax withholding, retirement, beneficiary, investment (such as 401K or 403B), direct deposit, and other financially related documents you are required or have the option to complete? Where do you send them after you complete them?

    b. To obtain the salary you are entitled to, what kinds of proof of past work experience, degrees, and certifications are required?

    c. Which department or person has to see these proofs?

    d. Is the information on your first pay stub correct?

When I began teaching, I was so excited to have a job that I completely ignored all the information on my pay stub. After a few months, as I began to settle into my new job, I finally took the time to look at my pay stub—to *really* look at it. I did the math and realized there was a discrepancy between what I thought I was supposed to be paid and what I was actually being paid. I called the payroll department and inquired about the discrepancy. It turned out that my certification level was recorded incorrectly because the state had not yet notified them of my graduate degree certification status. It took a few more months to get my back pay, but I always wondered if I would have received the money if I had not brought it to my employer's attention.

How to Augment Your Salary

Due to the use of a fixed salary scale, most teachers' salaries are based solely on years of experience. Usually, salary scales are based on the total number of years you have completed working as a teacher in a full-time capacity. In addition, years spent teaching part-time or partial years of full-time employment are often not included in the total. Therefore, it is difficult for some teachers to climb the pay scale. In most school systems, staying employed full-time is the best way to obtain salary increases. Nevertheless, find out from your employer the exact rules and procedures for pay-scale advancement.

Another way to increase your salary is to volunteer for duties or extra responsibilities that pay a stipend—for example, serving as department chairperson, club leader, or testing coordinator. If you are interested in augmenting your salary, find out whether your school has any of these opportunities and whether you qualify.

1.22 What extra duties and responsibilities pay a stipend? What are the qualifications for these positions? Are you interested in pursuing any of them? Do you have the time and energy to commit to any of them?

Because the first year or two of teaching can be overwhelming in terms of the volume of work, it is wise not to volunteer for additional, nonrequired duties during that time. The extra responsibilities will only add to the enormous amount of stress you will experience as a new teacher, and you will probably find that the stipend is not worth the extra pressure. Wait until you have a solid command of your day-to-day responsibilities before volunteering for extra duties.

Ensure Favorable Performance Evaluations

Maintaining acceptable performance evaluations is a condition of employment in most contracts. Evaluations can cause teachers a tremendous amount of stress. Minimize the stress by finding out the exact evaluation procedures and the criteria used for evaluation. Trends in performance evaluations show an increase in the use of different types of assessments, such as professional portfolios, in addition to the traditional observation conducted by a principal or assistant principal. Therefore, it is important to find out what your performance evaluations will entail.

You should also get to know who will be evaluating your job performance. Schedule a preevaluation meeting to glean what your evaluator's priorities are. Ask the evaluator or your colleagues about which teaching styles and teacher attributes the evaluator approves of and endorses. If you feel you can improve your chances of a positive evaluation without compromising your own teaching philosophy, try to develop these styles and attributes.

When meeting with your evaluator, have all the information you will need in a folder. Keep your notes in order, and prepare a list of questions for the meeting. If you feel uneasy about the impending meeting, get a friend or colleague to role-play your meeting with you.

You should also understand the postevaluation process and your rights as an employee if you should receive a poor evaluation. Ascertaining the process beforehand helps prevent intensifying the stress you might already be experiencing from such a negative situation.

1.23 How will your performance be evaluated?
    a. What are the components—such as observations, videos, and portfolios—of your evaluation?
    b. What are the evaluation criteria?
    c. How many evaluations are required, and when are they done?
    d. Are there any informal interim evaluations that can give you an idea about how you are doing, including your strengths and areas that you need to improve?
    e. How is the evaluation conducted?
    f. Who formally evaluates you? When can you schedule a pre-evaluation conference with the evaluator? What aspects of the teaching process are most important to the evaluator? Which teacher does the evaluator consider excellent? What attributes or teaching style does that teacher have? Should you focus on developing and emulating any of those attributes or that style to help you obtain a positive evaluation?
    g. What happens if you receive a good evaluation?
    h. What happens if you receive a poor evaluation? What are your rights as an employee?
    i. When can you schedule a time to audiotape and videotape one of your lessons for critiquing your own teaching? Whose audio and video equipment can you use?

Audiotape and videotape your lessons. Audiotaping is a very effective self-assessment tool because it helps you isolate your tone of voice and inflections better than using a video camera. In addition to being easier to borrow and set up than a video camera, a cassette recorder is more inconspicuous than a video camera, thus discouraging your students from "putting on a show" for the camera. On the other hand, videotaping your lessons can also be very helpful, especially if you want to see the whole picture, including how your students are behaving and how you are attending to different stimuli in the classroom, both verbally and nonverbally.

Most evaluations will be the result of observations conducted by your principal or assistant principal. When your observation is scheduled, prepare the lesson plan for the class to be observed. Ask an experienced colleague or mentor to review your plan to make sure that it is an appropriate activity for a formal observation. Since you are the expert in your classroom, also prepare a data sheet for the class that you will be teaching for your observation. The data sheet should include a seating chart or class roll with diagnostic information about each child, including any special problems, disabilities, or health problems. Be sure to include an explanation of anything that might happen during your class period that the evaluator might question or misinterpret, such as a child quietly leaving the classroom to go to a regularly scheduled resource class. If a significant interruption is scheduled to occur during your observation, such as a fire drill, find out how it will be handled, whether the observation will be stopped and rescheduled or will continue after the interruption even if you do not have enough time left in the period to complete your lesson plan. In addition, an evaluator who is new to your school may not be familiar with your subject or grade. In this case, be prepared to share your curriculum guides and show how your lesson plan supports the curriculum goals outlined in the guides. Share as much information as possible about your lesson plan and your class during your preevaluation conference to prevent any misunderstandings from surfacing during the observation.

As soon as possible after the observation, make notes about what you felt you did well and what you could have done better. List suggestions of things you could do to overcome the weaknesses you identified. Also, note any event that could have been interpreted in a negative manner by your evaluator. Bring your notes to your postevaluation conference.

During the follow-up conference, request the observation data and ask specific questions about areas of strength and weakness the evaluator observed. For example, if you received high marks for classroom discipline, ask the evaluator what you did to deserve those marks. To avoid self-incrimination, allow the evaluator to identify the deficiencies. If she mentions a weakness that you had also identified, let her know that you are aware of it and discuss the suggestions for improvement you had brainstormed. Ask for her help and involvement as you work to improve your areas of weakness. Have the evaluator put in writing any additional recommendations for improvement, with timelines for completion of activities. Finally, request copies of all data collected during the observation or evaluation and a copy of your final evaluation.

If you have a positive feeling about your observation and your pre- and postevaluation conferences went well, send a note thanking the evaluator for making the experience a pleasure rather than a hardship. The evaluator will feel appreciated and happy to have been helpful.

During your evaluation feedback sessions with your evaluator, make sure you learn the following:

1.24 How are you doing? What are your areas of strength and weakness?

1.25 Where is your school and school system heading in terms of curriculum program goals, and how do you fit into the short- and long-term plans?

1.26 What additional skills or education do you need to progress?

1.27 If you continue with your current level of performance, what can you expect for the future, including teaching assignments and performance evaluations?

1.28 If a problem develops, what kinds and amount of support can you expect from your evaluator?

Remember to make copies of all your evaluations and keep them in a safe place for future reference. You might need them to help update your résumé, or you might need them as supportive evidence if your teaching practices are ever questioned.

Maintain a Professional Portfolio

A professional portfolio can be a valuable tool. Many professionals—architects, engineers, artists, and writers, for instance—have portfolios that highlight their accomplishments. For years, teachers have known the power of portfolios in presenting student achievement. Likewise, you can use a professional portfolio for demonstrating your achievements to students, parents, administrators, and potential employers. You can be creative in compiling a portfolio, but it should contain some standard pieces:

- An updated résumé
- Teaching certificates
- College transcripts
- A statement of your teaching philosophy
- Sample unit and lesson plans
- Professional development plans and evidence that supports progress and completion of these plans (which are discussed later in this chapter)
- Records of any work-related seminars, courses, or workshops you have attended
- Performance evaluations
- Documentation of awards, commendations, honors, or letters of praise you have received
- Photographs of your students at work
- Photographs of your classroom and bulletin boards

Every year I take pictures of all my students doing different activities. I keep them in a photo album with all the previous years' photos. Near the end of the year, I bring the photo album to school to share with my students. Many of them are interested in seeing what I have done in the past (especially if they recognize older students in the photos), and they love seeing pictures of themselves!

Whether or not you create a professional portfolio, reference letters and a reference list are good things to have in case someone requests them. Remember, discuss with your references ahead of time what they would say about you if they were ever asked. Many times your references just ask you to tell them what you would like them to say. Make sure you know what they will say before you use them as references!

1.29 Do you want or need to build a professional portfolio?
   a. What should it contain?
   b. Which pieces do you want to obtain this school year?

1.30 Do you need references?
   a. Who can you ask to write a reference letter on your behalf to keep in your personal professional portfolio?
   b. Who can you ask to be on your list of references?

Display your degrees and your teaching certificates in your classroom. Other professionals have these documents displayed, and teachers should, too. The display usually has a positive effect on parents, students, and administrators.

GROW PERSONALLY AND PROFESSIONALLY

Finding opportunities for personal and professional growth is a common concern among teachers. Teachers understand that learning does not end when you receive a diploma. Learning more skills, both work and non-work related, must continue for professional and personal growth—the foundation for a thriving teaching career. Teachers also understand that learning occurs in many different ways and in many different places, not just in classrooms. This section helps you find different opportunities for continuing your education, both inside and outside the classroom.

Professional Development Plans: Guiding Personal Growth

Some school systems require every teacher to have some sort of professional development plan that outlines areas for the teacher's further investigation and learning. The plan should be created collaboratively with your principal and be based on your needs as well as those of the school and the school system. If you are undecided about your goals, select ones that address your job's performance standards, as outlined by your performance evaluation criteria. The plan should be directed at changing teacher behavior rather than student behavior. In addition, it should include formative and summative evaluations and be reviewed periodically and revised as needed. If your school system does not require a plan, you might consider creating one for yourself anyway. You can use it as a guide for continuing your growth as a teacher and as a person. See Resource 1.1 in the Resources for Successful Teaching section for an outline of a professional development plan.

Resource 1.1

When completing a professional and educational development plan, make sure the items are specific, reasonable, measurable, and time bound. Limit the plan to no more than three goals with two or three strategies each. It should include at least one long-range goal. Consider including an item or two related to strengthening your understanding of the content or population you will be teaching. Finally, make sure you collect written documentation to provide evidence of progress, completion, and achievement of your plan's goals.

1.31 Does your school system require you to have a professional development plan?
   a. What information must you include in the plan?
   b. Do you write it collaboratively? Are goals determined collaboratively?
   c. Do you have to complete a form?
   d. Who has to sign it?
   e. To whom do you submit the plan?
   f. How often is it reviewed?
   g. What is the procedure to update the plan?

A professional development plan usually includes any additional education courses required by your employer. Besides the required courses, there may be other things you would like to learn about, career or non-career related. Whether or not they are part of an official professional development plan, make time to pursue your interests.

1.32 Are any additional courses or education required by your employer, such as inservice classes, certification renewal credits, or classes toward a graduate (master's or doctorate) degree?

1.33 If additional education is not required, do you still want to take some career-related courses or to do your own investigative learning about something related to your work, such as improving your classroom management skills?

1.34 Is tuition assistance available? How do you apply for it?

1.35 Do you want to learn about something that is not work related?

1.36 How can you arrange your schedule to allow time for attending classes and completing assignments?

1.37 How will you evaluate, both formatively and summatively, whether this education has helped you?

1.38 What kinds of rewards and incentives can you include to motivate yourself to follow through on your plan?

1.39 How often will you update your educational plan?

Networking: Nurturing Your Professional Relationships

Becoming actively involved in your profession provides for both personal and professional growth. By joining teacher organizations, you have the opportunity to network with other teachers and to fill your calendar with social activities that support your career goals.

1.40 What local, state, and national unions and associations exist for the following?
   a. Teachers in general
   b. Teachers in your particular field (subject, grade level, and so forth)

1.41 How do you become a member?

Networking provides the opportunity to learn from other teachers by watching them, listening to them, and sharing with them. You can find these teachers in professional organizations, but don't overlook the teacher next door! Your colleagues in your school and school system are treasures, so do not isolate yourself. They are invaluable in helping you grow, both personally and professionally.

One kind of special teacher that can have a tremendous role in helping you become an effective teacher is a mentor-teacher. Since a mentor usually works closely with you, he or she can help you identify and deal with many of the potential stressors you might face in your teaching assignment. Make the time to get to know your mentor.

Master (excellent) teachers in your school are like angels sent from heaven. You can learn so much from these wonderful teachers! Most of these people have their potential stressors under control. Watch and learn from them. Do not underestimate the value of this kind of learning. It is imperative that you find master teachers and develop and nurture relationships with them. To learn additional teaching strategies, observe them during your planning periods. You might want to schedule a time to observe a master teacher teaching a lesson that you will also be doing or, for the sake of comparison, a lesson that you have already done.

Your relationships do not need to be one-sided—give as well as receive. For example, for those who have helped you, offer to watch their classes during your free periods or write a sincere note of appreciation and courtesy copy your principal.

1.42 Will you be assigned a mentor?
   a. Who is your mentor?
   b. What is the relationship between you and your mentor?
   c. In what ways can a mentor help you?
   d. What are your responsibilities to your mentor?

1.43 Who are the master teachers in your school and in your school system?
   a. What kinds of things can you learn from them?
   b. How can you learn from them? Can you schedule a time to meet or to observe master teachers?
   c. May you ask one of them to be your mentor?

1.44 What kinds of things can you do to show your appreciation for these special people?

The Truth About Giving and Receiving

When you give your time and resources to other teachers, you receive much more in return. By helping your colleagues solve their stress-related problems, you gain insight into your own stress and actually decrease the amount of stress you are feeling. Through mutual support, you reduce feelings of isolation and helplessness and become more emotionally and socially healthy individuals. If an entire group of teachers supports one another, the teaching team becomes more effective. Therefore, you need to examine ways in which you can work together with other teachers to prevent and deal with stress.

Peer Coaching: An Effective Way to Give and Receive Professional Support

Peer coaching is one way to give and receive professional support. In peer coaching, two or more teachers with mutual trust and rapport agree to observe and coach one another. When teachers observe each other, the one teaching is often the coach, demonstrating effective teaching practices. The teachers focus on helping one another sharpen specific teaching strategies and skills they feel they need to improve.

Peer coaching is a collegial process. It begins with two or more teachers discussing their staff development needs and teaching practices. The teachers decide which teacher behaviors (teaching strategies and skills) they wish to improve. Then they make plans to watch each other teach and decide on what instruments the observer will use to objectively record data that will identify strengths and weaknesses in the observed teaching behaviors. Afterward, they discuss their experiences and review the data collected during the observations. Using constructive feedback, they then discuss what improvements can be made, study new skills needed to implement the improvements, and plan for additional observations. Because teachers are not evaluating one another, peer coaching is a nonthreatening way to give and receive support.

Another way to implement peer coaching is to create a team of teachers that agree to present model lessons for one another. In this way, no one is critiquing anyone else and everyone is learning from each other.

If you are interested in trying peer coaching, approach your colleagues and principal about it. A school that does not already have a peer coaching program might offer to allow you and your interested colleagues to get formal training in this very successful, effective method for professional development.

1.45 Is peer coaching something that you are interested in pursuing? If yes, which teachers do you feel you can help and who will give you the most honest feedback in a supportive manner?

Peer Support Groups: Building a Support Team

Another way of working together to prevent stress is establishing peer support groups. The purpose of these support groups is to help one another clarify stress-related problems and come up with possible solutions. Effective support groups have a deep level of trust and rapport. They also start and stop on time. They have a set agenda and stick to it. According to Scaros (1981), the procedure for conducting a peer support group meeting is as follows:

1. Form a support group with four to six colleagues with whom you feel comfortable and who exhibit mutual respect, trust, and support.

2. Select a mutually convenient meeting time and place.

3. Select one person to go first and to discuss a work-related problem or challenge that she or he is having. This teacher is considered the "focus person" for that particular meeting.

4. The group asks questions to clarify the problem, and the problem is documented.

5. The group then discusses the problem and documents possible solutions.

6. The focus person then takes the opportunity to clarify any or all the suggestions.

7. The remainder of the time is used for helping the focus person decide what is the best action to take based on the suggestions. The action is documented in contract form—for example, "I, . . . , will . . . by . . ."—and it is signed by the focus person and the other members of the support group.

8. Another meeting time for additional support and follow-up is scheduled.

9. A new person becomes the focus person, and the steps are repeated.

Like a journal, peer support groups give a teacher a nonthreatening environment in which to be honest and objective about a stressor. An additional benefit of establishing a peer support group is having several people you can trust when you need help.

1.46 Have peer support groups already been established in your school or school system? If yes, how does a teacher join one? If no, can you start one? What will you need to establish a group?

Sharing Information With Colleagues

As a teacher, you are bombarded with information. You may not find a lot of this information useful, but someone else might. Pass the information along. It could help another teacher solve a problem and prevent stress. In addition, when we help others deal with their stress, our own stress level decreases. Therefore, it is very important that we never lose sight of the fact that in giving, we receive.

1.47 In what ways can you help other teachers?
  a. What kinds of things can you share with them?
  b. If you attend a workshop or seminar, how can you share with your colleagues what you have learned?
  c. What vehicles can you use to share information with other teachers in your grade level or department, school, school system, state, country, and world?

We are sometimes forced to work with colleagues who appear to be very territorial with their materials and ideas. Perhaps they feel threatened by other teachers or do not respect their peers' teaching styles and expertise. Some colleagues might believe that beginning and less experienced teachers need to go through their rites of passage alone (just as veteran teachers did when they began teaching many years ago). Perhaps they feel that they will be viewed as interfering, or they might think that assisting teachers is the principal's responsibility, not theirs. Maybe they get so caught up in their own classes that they can't see what else is going on around them. Nevertheless, colleagues who do not share their expertise perpetuate the "sink or swim" situation in which many teachers often find themselves. As mentioned earlier, teaching can be a very lonely job, especially if you are surrounded by colleagues who keep their ideas and materials to themselves. Unfortunately, I've experienced this more than once. All teachers, experienced and new, have something to offer. If we take the time and effort to share with one another, we will help one another and strengthen our profession.

SUMMARY

Taking care of yourself includes taking care of both your personal and your professional needs. In addition to taking control of your life, it is important to help others gain control of their lives. Helping others solve their stress-related problems also helps you relieve your own stress. Your teaching team becomes more effective and thus more successful. Therefore, identify where and when you can help other teachers and actively do so. Taking care of yourself is the most important step because it shows you how to take control of the only thing you can completely control—yourself.

Identify and Understand Expectations

INTRODUCTION AND OBJECTIVES

Significant factors in your becoming a successful teacher are identifying and understanding the expectations placed on you as a teacher—by others as well as by yourself. If you do not understand these expectations, you will experience stress. For example, when your expectations about your role as a teacher are different from your employer's, you can be sure that there will be tension. This tension is a stressor for you and for everyone else involved. If you identify and understand your employer's expectations before the possibility of a confrontation, you have more control over the situation. You have the choice either to meet the expectations or to take an assertive approach to try to resolve your differences amicably.

Two kinds of stressors relate to expectations: role conflict and role ambiguity. When you are pulled in different directions by parents, students, administrators, and colleagues, you experience role conflict. You get conflicting demands on your time and conflicting ideas about what you are supposed to do. For example, you might be encouraged by your school system administration to use cooperative learning centers, yet school administrators expect you to operate a teacher-centered classroom where your students work quietly by themselves. The conflicting messages about which teaching style you should use can cause stress.

On the other hand, you experience role ambiguity when you don't know the exact expectations and goals of your job. For example, if you don't have a curriculum guide, course of study, or some other kind of outline for the subject or grade level you are teaching, you might not be sure what you are supposed to teach. Also, if you aren't informed of the criteria your school uses for teacher evaluations, you won't know how you'll be judged. As a result, you'll experience role ambiguity and the stress that comes with it.

To prevent role conflict and role ambiguity, identify and understand your own expectations first. Second, identify and understand the expectations of all the people you interface with. Learn as much as you can about others' expectations before you start your teaching assignment. But after you start the assignment, inevitably you'll experience daily challenges to your expectations of your job and of your role as a teacher. Be prepared! Try to understand as much as you can before your first day. Be assertive! Try to resolve any mismatches in expectations before they become issues for either you or the other person.

The objectives of this chapter are to help you

- Identify and understand your expectations about teaching and learning
- Identify and understand your state's and country's expectations for your work
- Identify and understand your local community's expectations for you and your school
- Identify and understand your students' expectations about how you will conduct your work
- Establish an effective way to share your expectations with others that improves communication among you, your students, and your students' parents

WHAT ARE YOUR EXPECTATIONS?

The first step in preventing role conflict and role ambiguity is to determine exactly what you expect of yourself and your career. But before you write your expectations in concrete, realize and accept the fact that they will change over time. They change because you change. Faced with new challenges day after day, year after year, you grow. If you understand this up front, it might help you be more flexible and less frustrated when your new knowledge and experience challenge your current expectations.

It's important to keep in mind the research about effective teaching that was discussed in the introduction to the book as you formulate your current expectations. The research can help shape your expectations about your role as a teacher and your philosophy of education in general. In addition, don't forget to do your own research. Look around you and identify the most effective teachers in your school. They are usually

As a new teacher, I was very idealistic. My expectations about my students, my job, and myself were unrealistic. And I know many new teachers, regardless of their age or their assignment, who have had similar experiences. Does this idealism stem from romantic notions of what teaching should be? Perhaps it's the excitement of a new job, a fresh start, a clean slate. Or maybe it's the conviction that teachers can make a difference in students' lives no matter what is happening outside school. I don't know. What I do know, however, is that over time, I changed. I grew because of my experiences, both positive and negative, and my expectations changed accordingly. To be realistic, I also expect my expectations to keep changing as I continue to grow.

the ones who are highly respected by administrators, students, and parents. Figure out why. If the attributes and attitudes that make them successful are congruent with your beliefs and values, emulate them. Also, use the same teaching strategies, set up your classroom in a similar way, and follow a similar routine. Copy the things they do that you feel would be most beneficial in helping you, too, become an effective teacher.

Finally, research shows that effective teaching is based on the philosophy that all students can and will learn. Rather than accepting the common belief that basic student performance derives from family background, effective teachers believe that their and their school's responses to students' family backgrounds are what promote student success. Many teachers and schools across the country are working with students with significant societal disadvantages and helping them succeed by effectively responding to students' needs, whether those needs stem from inside or outside school. If you want to become a successful teacher, it is imperative that you not only understand this foundation for effective teaching but also adopt this belief and make it your own.

2.1 Which teachers in your school are effective? Why? What are their expectations about teaching, administrators, students, and parents? Which attributes and attitudes would be helpful to emulate? Which things that they do would be helpful to copy?

2.2 In light of the research findings mentioned here, what are your beliefs about what is necessary for effective teaching? In addition, what is your philosophy about the following?

a. The goals of schooling
b. Your role as a teacher
c. How children learn and which instructional strategies are most effective with the population you teach
d. Assessing and evaluating learning
e. Homework and parents' role in homework
f. Parents' role in their child's education
g. Discipline and the roles you, parents, and administrators play as disciplinarians
h. Reward systems for behavior and for academic achievement

2.3 Using your philosophy about effective teaching as a base, what do you expect from your teaching job?

a. What teaching assignments and classes are you expecting to get? How many students?
b. What kinds of student needs do you expect to be faced with? How do you expect your students to be in terms of behavior, motivation, values, and beliefs?
c. What do you think your job will be like?

2.4 What are your expectations of others?

a. How much support do you expect to receive from administrators? colleagues? students? parents?
b. How do you expect to be addressed by students? parents? colleagues and administrators?

Now that you have identified your expectations, it is important for you to identify what others expect of you.

I began my elementary school teaching career in a newly built school. Because the school had no history, every procedure and rule had to be created. Every detail of opening a new school had to be attended to. This left very little time and energy to support the handful of first-year teachers like me. This experience taught me that first-year teachers should look very closely at the school they'll be working in. Investigate how much collegial support you can expect to receive, because you'll need lots of it that first year. Don't underestimate this need.

WHAT ARE THE GOVERNMENT'S EXPECTATIONS?

Although expectations coming from the federal and state governments are not directed to you personally, you are involved in a profession that must comply with certain laws and government regulations, such as the Individuals with Disabilities Education Act, or IDEA (for more information about IDEA and other federal mandates, go to the IDEA Web site at http://www.ideapractices.org/finalregs.htm.). This means that you must do your part to help your school comply with these laws and regulations, which also include Occupational Safety and Health Administration (OSHA) regulations, laws related to reporting child abuse or neglect, corporal punishment laws, state-mandated assessment and remediation requirements, and state curriculum requirements such as teaching patriotism, citizenship, civics, drug abuse prevention, health education, fire drill instruction and fire arson prevention, humane treatment of animals and birds, and the conservation of natural resources.

You must be especially aware of laws that, if violated, open the door for lawsuits against your school system, your school, and you. To prevent possible legal fallout, learn about the laws that affect you and your students from your school system's special education department. Federal and state departments of education are also good sources of information. Know the law and understand how it is interpreted.

2.5 What federal and state education laws affect your school?

2.6 What other laws or regulations must your school comply with?

Many teachers reviewed this book before it was printed. It is interesting to note that although none of the newer teachers made any notes in this section, most of the teachers with 20 or more years of experience wrote comments emphasizing the importance of this topic.

WHAT ARE THE COMMUNITY'S EXPECTATIONS?

The community is the predominant force in defining the expectations of your school. Therefore, it is important that you get to know the community that your school and school system serve. Subscribe to the local paper. Walk around the area and patronize local establishments. Call or visit the chamber of commerce and visitor's center. Getting to know the social and emotional climate of the community tells you a lot about what you can expect as a teacher in that community's schools.

What the community expects from your school is reflected in your school system's mission statement. The community's expectations of its schools and the laws with which the school system must comply are funneled together to create a mission statement for the school system. Sometimes additional statements are created for each individual school. Understanding these mission statements and how they are achieved gives you a general understanding of your role as an educator in this particular school system.

2.7 What are the mission statements of your school system? of your school?

2.8 How are these missions achieved by the school system? by the school?

School System Policies

Mission statements might tell you what a school system believes it is supposed to do, but school system policies show you how the system intends to act on what it believes. School system policies, which are sometimes further embellished at the school, grade, or department level, are highly reflective of the expectations of the community that the system serves. Staff, parent, and student handbooks are good sources for this information. If they exist, read them.

2.9 Does your school provide staff, student, and parent handbooks? Where can you obtain copies?

2.10 What are the policies, written and unwritten, of your school system, school, grade, and department for students and staff (when applicable) regarding the following?
   a. Discipline (including assault, fighting, stealing, sexual harassment, weapons, gangs, drugs, alcohol, profanity, and so forth). Are there any specific procedures or forms to be completed when involving administrators in discipline-related matters, such as sending a student to the office or to detention?
   b. Appearance (including dress code)
   c. Instruction, including acceptable teaching styles and teaching strategies
   d. Homework, including amount of homework and parents' role in homework completion

Rights and Freedoms

In addition to federal and state education laws and local policies, you must also be aware of the U.S. Bill of Rights and how your community supports it. Although these rights are protected by the federal government, you need to find out what boundaries your school system places on them. The boundaries reflect the values and expectations of the community, and understanding them helps you understand your role in meeting the expectations of your community.

2.11 What boundaries, if any, are placed on the freedoms of speech, the press, assembling peaceably, and petitioning? How do these boundaries affect you and your role as a teacher?

2.12 Does your school or school system limit the use of certain materials or discourage certain topics from being explored and discussed?
   a. Does your school or school system discourage or even prohibit the use of any books or resources?
   b. Does your school or school system discourage or even prohibit the discussion of any topics or themes?

Curriculum Expectations

In continuing to find out what you are not supposed to discuss, it is also very important to find out what you must discuss. This is usually documented in a curriculum guide or standard course of study. In addition to the subject matter to be taught, the curriculum guide or course of study specifies what materials, instructional strategies, and classroom climate you are expected to use to meet the curriculum goals.

2.13 What is the curriculum or standard course of study for the class you teach?

2.14 What materials and instructional strategies are you expected to use?

2.15 What kind of classroom climate is expected?

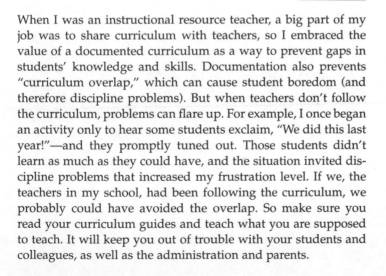

When I was an instructional resource teacher, a big part of my job was to share curriculum with teachers, so I embraced the value of a documented curriculum as a way to prevent gaps in students' knowledge and skills. Documentation also prevents "curriculum overlap," which can cause student boredom (and therefore discipline problems). But when teachers don't follow the curriculum, problems can flare up. For example, I once began an activity only to hear some students exclaim, "We did this last year!"—and they promptly tuned out. Those students didn't learn as much as they could have, and the situation invited discipline problems that increased my frustration level. If we, the teachers in my school, had been following the curriculum, we probably could have avoided the overlap. So make sure you read your curriculum guides and teach what you are supposed to teach. It will keep you out of trouble with your students and colleagues, as well as the administration and parents.

Programs for Exceptional Students

Because children function at very different developmental stages regardless of their grade level or placement, curriculum goals and objectives might need modification to meet students' needs. Although there are laws protecting exceptional students—especially those who are low achieving or have been found to have physical, psychological, or emotional disabilities—the local community might demand more from its school system for meeting the needs of these students.

How much the curriculum is modified or enhanced beyond what the law would normally provide for these children is very reflective of the values and beliefs of vocal people in the community. These people might push for a more individualized and more challenging curriculum for high-achieving students, who are sometimes labeled "academically gifted." Some community members might push for special services on an Individual Education Plan (IEP) for a child with physical and psychological needs. Therefore, you need to know if there are any extra programs and services that the school system or school has set up to meet the demands of the community.

2.16 How does your school system and school meet the needs of its exceptional children? What programs, such as academically gifted programs, and strategies, such as inclusion, are in place for the following students?
   a. Above-average academic achievers
   b. Musically, artistically, and athletically gifted
   c. Below-average academic achievers
   d. Children with physical, psychological, or emotional disabilities

2.17 What is your role in identifying and placing exceptional students into these programs? What is your role in implementing any of these programs, whether you are a program specialist or a "regular education" classroom teacher?

School Rules and Procedures

In addition to programs for exceptional students, there are also school rules and procedures that affect all students. These rules and procedures also affect staff and parents. They have been put in place to help the school system and school run smoothly, and they must be followed. The following questions outline some of the issues you need to be aware of:

2.18 What are the rules and procedures for students and staff regarding the following?
   a. Arrival at school (inside and outside the school building)
   b. Early-morning programs (for those who arrive for morning on-site day care or other programs)
   c. Dismissal (inside and outside the school building)
   d. After-school programs (after-school day care or other programs)

2.19 How does your school handle student attendance?
   a. Where are the records kept?
   b. Who does the recording?
   c. Is it recorded in pen or pencil?
   d. What are the symbols used for recording an absence?
   e. What are considered excused and unexcused absences?
   f. Is any documentation from home required when a student returns to school after being absent?
   g. How is tardiness recorded?
   h. Who gets the daily attendance record after it is completed and by what time?
   i. What is the follow-up procedure if a student is absent? Who does it?
   j. What is the procedure for signing in and out during the instructional day?
   k. Is the absentee list posted daily, especially for use by resource teachers and other specialists that work with students in a pull-out program (a program where the students go to another classroom for instruction) or push-in program (a program where a special teacher comes into the classroom to work with a student or group of students)?

2.20 What are the school discipline rules that your class must follow and the discipline programs that your class must use?
   a. Are teachers allowed to send students to the office? Under what circumstances?
   b. What can students expect when they meet with a disciplinarian in the office?

2.21 What are the rules and the procedures for the use of the following?
   a. Hallways
      i. Are you required to escort your students in the hallways?
      ii. Are hallway passes required? How do you write one? Do you need to use preprinted forms?
   b. Hallway lavatories
   c. Cafeteria
      i. How do students and teachers obtain lunch tickets or accounts?
      ii. Where can you obtain copies of free and reduced lunch application forms?
      iii. Do you need to take lunch count and collect lunch money in the mornings?
      iv. Are there assigned seats?
      v. Do you need to use a specific traffic pattern?
      vi. Where are trays, plates, and utensils returned, and where is trash thrown out?
      vii. Do students and/or teachers have cleaning duties?

To prevent stressful situations in the cafeteria, review with younger students how to get and pay for food, how to eat neatly, and how to avoid spills. To prevent garbage from falling off their trays, show your students how to insert their napkins and utensils into their milk carton before walking to the trash can.

    d. Media center/library
       i. Are library passes required?
      ii. How long can a student and a teacher keep a book on loan?

When you want the media center for research projects, let the media specialist know of your plans ahead of time. Often he or she can prepare some materials for your class in advance. Also, review with your students the goal of their visit, the media center's rules and procedures, and the research skills they need to complete their assignment.

    e. Gymnasium
    f. Computer room
    g. Auditorium
    h. Playground areas
    i. Playground equipment
    j. Parking lots. Do students and staff get assigned parking spaces?
    k. School bus
    l. Common areas (inside and outside)
    m. Photocopying machines and other machines or tools in the teacher workroom

2.22 What are your responsibilities regarding emergencies that occur at your school?
    a. What emergency procedures must your class follow for the following?
       i. Fire
      ii. Severe weather
     iii. Injury
     iv. Illness

b. Are you required to post any of the procedures?

c. After an accident, are you required to fill out an accident report? How much time do you have to complete it?

Share emergency procedures with your students. Post fire and severe-weather escape routes by your classroom door. Review all emergency procedures often to help your students internalize them before a major catastrophe or crisis strikes your school.

2.23 How is your school's health office managed?

a. How do the health office's personnel support you and your class?

b. What are the health office's rules and procedures?

c. Which student illnesses (for example, head lice, chicken pox, and so forth) are you required to report to the health office?

d. What emergency contact information is collected from your students? Are you required to collect it? When? How?

e. What is the procedure for calling parents when a student is sick and needs to go home? How do you find out who is allowed to pick up the student from school?

f. Are first-aid kits available?

g. What are the rules and procedures for administering medications to students?

   i. What associated forms must be completed by the student's parents? physician? teachers?

   ii. Who contacts the parent or physician when prescriptions need refilling?

   iii. Are students allowed to self-medicate?

2.24 What is the procedure for lost and found items?

2.25 What are the procedures and rules regarding the use of the school's petty cash account? Do you get reimbursed for any out-of-pocket expenses? If yes, what is the procedure for getting your reimbursement?

2.26 What are the procedures and rules regarding handing in money collected from students for field trips, fund-raisers, or other purposes?

a. Who is the money given to? By what time each day must this person collect the money?

b. Is there a form that you must complete to accompany your deposit?

I'll never forget the first time I collected field trip money. Each day I collected the money and kept it locked in my file cabinet. One day the school secretary asked me when I was going to start collecting the field trip money. I told her I already had, and she exclaimed that I was supposed to give my collections to her by noon every day. I was also required to complete and sign a special form stating how much I had given to her and when. Until that day, I never knew that teachers had to deposit on a daily basis any money they had collected from students. Luckily, my school secretary was very understanding.

2.27   What is the procedure for reserving a classroom or a conference room for meetings or other gatherings?

2.28   Which school telephones can you use for personal use and for work-related use?

2.29   Are school supplies such as paper, pencils, and pens provided for your students, or are they expected to supply their own?
   a. If they are to supply their own and cannot afford them, who provides the school supplies for them?
   b. Can you request a list of school supplies, monetary contributions, or other donations from students and their families?
   c. Who orders the school's supplies? Does each teacher, grade level, or department do their own ordering, or does your school make one large order? Can supplies be ordered throughout the school year, or are they ordered only once per year?

2.30   What is the procedure to follow when a student loses a textbook or a library book?

2.31   What are the end-of-year procedures for storing materials, collecting books, taking inventory, collecting fines, completing students' permanent records and portfolios, and so forth?

Prevent stress by doing as many end-of-year procedures as you can several weeks before the hectic last days of school.

Many of the rules and procedures mentioned here are needed in the first few days and weeks of school. Have this information prepared for students and parents as soon as possible. You might want to add it to a classroom handbook (which will be discussed later in this chapter) and distribute it to your students and their parents on the first day of school.

Rules and Procedures for Special Activities

Special activities that occur throughout the year might also have rules and procedures associated with them. It's never too early to begin planning classroom holiday activities, especially those that involve parent participation. Use the following questions to find out what they are:

2.32 Which special events or holidays are you allowed to celebrate in your classes? Which ones do you want to celebrate?

   a. What can and cannot be done to celebrate holidays? See Resource 2.1 in the Resources for Successful Teaching section for tips on planning celebrations.

Resource 2.1

   b. Does anyone have to be notified of these activities? Does anyone have to sign off on these activities?

   c. What is the policy for the following?

     i. Having religious holiday paraphernalia displayed (such as a Christmas tree, a menorah, and so forth)

     ii. Discussing religious holidays in your class

     iii. Purchasing gifts for your students for gift-giving holidays, such as Christmas

If it is the tradition at your school to exchange Valentine's Day cards, encourage your students to give them to all their classmates. If you have ever been a teacher or a parent of a student who was "left out," you know how heart-wrenching it is to see children overlooked by their peers on this special day of love and respect. Explaining this important real-life lesson to your students will help prevent hurt feelings in your classroom.

2.33 What can and cannot be done to celebrate a student's or a colleague's birthday during school hours and on school campus?

2.34 Are there programs or events in which your grade level or department traditionally host or participate? When are they held? What is your role in organizing and participating in the events?

2.35 What is the tradition at your school regarding end-of-year picnics and celebrations? Is each class responsible to set up their own, or are they schoolwide events?

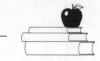

I worked at a school where some teachers held their own end-of-year class picnics in addition to the traditional schoolwide celebrations. Since I was unaware of this tradition, I was one of the few teachers that didn't plan for it. My students and their parents asked me repeatedly about having a picnic, but when they began asking, it was already too late in the year. I felt bad for my students and vowed never to let a "fun" tradition pass by me again!

2.36 What fund-raisers occur, if any? What is your role in these activities?

Resource 2.2

2.37 Are you expected and allowed to take class trips? If yes, see Resource 2.2 for tips on planning class trips.

2.38 Are any book fairs scheduled at your school?
   a. If your students need assistance in choosing books, who helps them?
   b. Do any of your students qualify for any free books due to prizes or financial assistance?
   c. Are you allowed to create a "wish list" for parents to use as a guide when purchasing books to donate to your classroom?

2.39 Are you required to have a classroom student recognition program (such as Student of the Week, Show and Tell, and so forth)?

Send home a list of good books for gift-giving ideas the month before each student's birthday or in mid-November for holiday gifts. List mostly books your students would find interesting and entertaining and ones that have some relationship to your subject area and units you plan to cover during the school year.

Unstated School Rules and Procedures

Every school has a unique culture. For example, certain schools expect you to be involved in every faculty social activity, while other schools do not. Consequently, every school has unstated rules and procedures that reflect their unique culture. Get to know these rules by observing and speaking with your colleagues.

2.40 What is the professional etiquette in your school? What do your colleagues expect from you professionally?

2.41 What are the unstated rules of the teachers' lounge? Who pays for the coffee and who makes it? Who gets to eat the "free food" people sometimes place in the lounge?

2.42 What are the rules (stated and unstated) for borrowing materials from your school's professional library? How many items can you have on loan at one time? How long can you keep them?

Copy Figure 2.1 onto a sheet of paper, adding as many lines as you need. Put it into the three-ring binder you are using as your lesson plan book or tape it onto the inside cover of your spiral-bound lesson plan book. The "yes" responses in the first column will help you see at a glance which resources you have lent out, making it easier to keep track of your personal resources.

Figure 2.1.   Resource Log

Is the Resource Yours?	Resource Title	Person Loaned To or Borrowed From	Date Loaned or Borrowed	Date Returned

For several months, I kept checking my school's professional library for a resource I needed. Some of the other teachers repeatedly assured me that it was there, but I just couldn't find it. At the end of the school year, I discovered that one of my colleagues had used it and kept it in her classroom practically the entire year. Through my frustration, I learned a valuable lesson in stress prevention. Now I ask all my colleagues about missing resources, not just a few.

2.43 Are you expected to welcome unannounced classroom visits and observations by administrators? parents?

2.44 Are you expected to join the PTA?

2.45 Are you expected to attend student activities, such as sporting events, choral performances, and school plays?

2.46 If you witness an argument or other problem outside your classroom, are you expected to discipline students who you do not teach? How much are you expected to do before calling other school personnel for help?

2.47 What is expected of you if your students are involved in intramural sports, band, music lessons, cheerleading, color guard, and other extracurricular activities?
   a. Are there any special activities that occur during the school year for such students? What is your role in these special activities?
   b. Are you expected to allow students to leave early from class or come late to class to participate in any of these activities?
   c. Are you expected to make any changes in assignments, such as due dates, for students involved in particular extracurricular activities?

2.48 Are you expected to help students complete college application forms? Are you expected to write letters of reference for your students?

Your Responsibilities and Accountability for Student Progress

Besides knowing and following rules and procedures, there are many things that you have to do as a teacher. They are your responsibilities. Most of them are documented in a staff handbook if one exists. If your school doesn't have a staff handbook, the following questions help point out key responsibilities that most teachers have:

2.49 What paperwork, if any, is required for your position? (See Figure 2.2.)
   a. To whom do you deliver it?
   b. When is it due?
   c. Are there any preprinted forms you are required to use for some of your paperwork?
   d. What is the frequency of completing this paperwork?
   e. What format is required?
   f. Are you collecting enough data, such as grades and anecdotal notes, to be able to complete your paperwork?

Figure 2.2. Possible Types of Paperwork

Check to see if forms already exist for some of these or if particular formats are expected.

- Attendance, tardy, and absentee notices
- Milk money and lunch forms
- Lesson plans
- Students' assignments (grading and filing)

- Student progress reports for school administrators

- Tests (creating and grading)

- Grade book

- Plan book
- Report cards and other student evaluation reports, such as progress reports
- Daily or weekly homework folders

- Academic and behavior contracts
- Student referral forms for special services and IEPs

- Grade-level/course retention paperwork
- Weekly newsletters
- Parent notes
- Parent-teacher conference records (both telephone and in-person conferences)
- Daily or weekly academic and behavior reports and detention slips
- Parent questionnaires and surveys
- Students' cumulative/permanent records
- Meeting minutes
- Substitute teacher folders (creating and maintaining)

- Student "self-discipline" (including effort and behavior) reports
- Emergency contact cards

- End-of-year card summarizing student's achievement and placement for following year

2.50 What is your responsibility to update and maintain students' cumulative and permanent folders?
   a. What information goes in them?
   b. Where are the folders kept?
   c. In what order are the documents placed in the folders?
   d. Is there anything you believe you should save for each child, such as tests, graded papers, reports, projects, parent notes, and your anecdotal notes, even though it is not required to be saved? How many years is it prudent to save these documents? Where can you store them?

I know a veteran teacher who saves every piece of graded work for every student for at least three years. She allows her students to bring graded work home to show their parents, but they must return their papers the next day with their parents' signatures. When I asked her about this unusual practice that appeared to take up a lot of precious storage space in her classroom, she told me it began when one of her student's parents contested the grade that their child received. As the teacher, she had to defend the grade she had given the child, but because the child's work had been sent home and subsequently lost, she had no way to prove to the parents that their child's grade was earned. The situation escalated to a point where many administrators had to become involved. She now saves every piece of graded work, including graded homework, and has parents sign each piece to show that they had seen it and accepted the grade given as a fair evaluation of the work.

2.51 What are your responsibilities regarding lesson plans?
   a. Is there a lesson plan format that you must use?
   b. Are your lesson plans or plan book reviewed? How often and by whom?
   c. Are you required to leave your plan book at school?

2.52 What are your responsibilities regarding extra duties?
   a. Are you assigned any extra duties, or are you expected to volunteer for them?
   b. What are the responsibilities of the different extra duties available?
   c. Are you assigned to chaperone student events?

2.53 Are you required to attend certain meetings, such as grade-level or committee meetings? When and where are they held?

2.54 Do you have to complete purchase orders for teaching and student materials you use for any reason—for example, your classes, your grade level, your department, special classes (such as art, music, media, P.E., foreign language, and so forth), or resource classes? What is the procedure for completing a purchase order and getting it preapproved by the person in charge of your school's funds?

2.55 Are you required to stay with your students during their special classes, such as art, music, P.E., foreign language, and so forth, or during their lunch period?

Accounting for student progress is one of your responsibilities. The community at large expects a lot from its schools, and thus a lot from you.

Barry Farber (1991) describes these expectations well: "Society expects [teachers] to educate, socialize, and graduate virtually every student who comes to school, regardless of the social, economic, familial, or psychological difficulties some of these students bring with them" (p. 61). He adds that parents, psychologists, social workers, and agencies can fail, but teachers cannot, and if they do, they will be held accountable. Farber believes that the push for accountability is just a way of expecting schools to cure the ills of society. Farber poses an interesting point of view. Many teachers who have experienced disgruntled parents and community members know that there is some truth to what he is saying.

The community, especially parents of school-age children, are crying for accountability. They want to know if their schools are doing their job. They want to know if children are learning. To determine these things, the community and the government rely very heavily on standardized test results. The recent surge in high-stakes testing, with teacher and administrator bonuses tied to test results, is further proof of the push for accountability and the carrot-and-stick approach to education reform. Whether this approach is working to improve our schools is debatable and beyond the scope of this book. However, it is important to note that although standardized testing is not new in education, the pressure is new for many teachers. Thus, for today's teachers, high-stakes standardized testing is a significant stressor, and it needs to be addressed.

There are different things that teachers can do to help prevent much of the stress associated with high-stakes standardized testing. First, you must prepare your students for the tests. This includes teaching students effective strategies for answering multiple-choice questions and any other types of questions that their standardized tests will contain. It also includes showing students how to fill in their answer sheets correctly. And because we all know children who never finish tests as well as children who rush through tests, making several careless errors along the way, all students must be taught effective self-pacing strategies.

For a standardized exam that allows only enough time to compose a draft version of an essay response, teach students how to quickly sketch an outline of their responses. An outline takes only a few moments to create, and if it is checked against the question, it serves as a guide to ensure that they are answering all parts of the question. An outline helps organize their responses, and it helps keep their writing from drifting away from the topic.

Second, if the high-stakes test is written to test your students' achievement against your state's curriculum, it is imperative that you teach to your state's curriculum guides. Make sure that your unit plans and lesson plans directly address the goals outlined in your state's curriculum.

Third, set up standardized testing practice sessions. Although it is usually impractical to administer a complete mock exam, you can administer "mini-mock" standardized exams, perhaps comprising only five to ten questions each and allowing approximately 20 minutes for students to complete. These timed mini-mock tests should be written in the same style and format as the high-stakes standardized test. Your state, school system, or school may have created or purchased mini-mock tests for you to use; find out if they're available. If they aren't, consider creating some using practice booklets often distributed for the exams.

Finally, acknowledge your students' anxiety about the tests and comfort them. Allow for many practice sessions. Familiarity with the test's format and with testing conditions will help increase their self-confidence and reduce their stress about the test.

> One year, when I was a reading resource teacher, I had the responsibility to work with about 45 third-, fourth-, and fifth-grade students who had not passed or had barely passed the state's standardized test in reading the previous year. My job was to improve my students' reading levels and prepare them for the standardized test in reading to be given at the end of the year. I'll never forget one little boy who quickly completed our first mini-mock exam with plenty of time to spare. After he completed it, he sat there daydreaming for the remaining time while his classmates continued to work. When the time for the test was up, we went over the questions, and this child had several incorrect answers. Because he demonstrated a higher level of skill and understanding during our class discussions, I immediately felt that the test wasn't an accurate indication of his level of achievement. As a group, we discussed different test-taking strategies that the students used during our mock test. During our discussion of how to refer back to the reading passage when you can't remember a specific detail, this particular boy exclaimed in a completely surprised voice, "I didn't know you could go back!" It was a revelation for him and for me. I knew at that point that it was imperative that I teach my students effective test-taking strategies. I am happy to report that at the end of the school year, the boy passed the test with flying colors.

The system used to show accountability is usually representative of the community's expectations. But be forewarned! Some community members, especially parents, are not satisfied with the reporting mechanisms currently in place. They want more information. Ask your colleagues and principal about whether parents are looking for additional assessment information or for the information to be presented in a different format. Furthermore, many parents find some reporting mechanisms unfamiliar and confusing. Sometimes using nontechnical terms to explain what the grades and test results mean and to compare them to an *average* student's achievement level helps clear up confusion and alleviate parent frustrations and fears. Effective communication about student achievement goes a long way in helping you and them prevent stress.

2.56 What standardized tests are used in your school?
   a. Which ones will your students be taking?
   b. When and how do the test results get shared with students and parents?
   c. What do you need to do to help prepare your students for these tests?
   d. What do you need to do to prepare yourself for administering these tests?

2.57 What are the procedures for reporting student progress?
   a. What is reported on report cards or their equivalent?
   b. Are portfolios required? What is the minimum required content?
   c. How are grades determined? Do effort, participation, and homework completion get factored into the grades?
   d. Are report cards, or their equivalent, reviewed by your principal or anyone else on the staff before being shared with the students and their parents?
   e. Are parent-teacher conferences required? When and where?
   f. Do parents expect daily or weekly reports on student "self-discipline" (including effort and behavior)?
   g. Are daily or weekly homework or class work folders expected to be sent home with students?

I worked in a school that allowed each teacher to choose the day that was best for them to send home weekly class work folders. As a result, there was a lot of inconsistency, even among teachers at the same grade level. At the middle of the year, a new assistant principal was hired, and she felt it was necessary to be consistent across all classes in the school. As a result, all the teachers chose the same day to send home weekly folders. This common routine brought a sense of unity to our school and made a positive impression on parents.

Have Substitute Teacher Plans Available at All Times

You're held accountable for your students' learning even when you are absent. Because of this, put together excellent emergency substitute teacher plans. Emergency substitute teacher plans are lesson plans that can be used at any time during the day or school year because they are not tied to any particular topic or theme, yet they are supportive of your required curriculum goals. Developing at least five days of emergency plans is prudent in case of an unexpected, prolonged absence. Although creating substitute teacher plans is sometimes put at the bottom of teachers' to-do lists, make it a priority. Lesson plans are the last thing you want to do from your sickbed! Your mind and body will be stressed enough from your illness or accident. Having enough quality substitute teacher plans in place helps you prevent stress when you need to prevent it the most.

Resource 2.3

2.58 What are your responsibilities regarding substitute teacher plans?

    a. What must they include? If your school has no guidelines, what kinds of information does the substitute teacher need to have a successful, productive day? See Resource 2.3 for a sample list.

    b. Can the directions left be easily understood by a substitute teacher and by your students?

    c. To prevent student discipline problems, are the lessons stimulating, with a high student interest level? Do the plans keep students actively involved and on task? Do the activities ensure a high success rate?

    d. How many days of substitute plans are you required to have prepared?

    e. Where are you supposed to keep them (in the classroom, in the main office, or some other place)? If there is no set rule, where can you keep them so a substitute can access them easily in an emergency?

    f. How often are you required to update your emergency substitute teacher plans? If there is no requirement, how often do you feel is necessary?

WHAT ARE PARENTS' EXPECTATIONS?

Communication is the key to building strong relationships with parents—relationships based on the fact that you are all adults concerned about children's progress in school. You are not best buddies, nor are you enemies. When teachers work together with parents toward a common goal of helping their children, the atmosphere and climate for learning improve.

You need to know parents' expectations of you to help build successful relationships. Find out what they expect from you by asking them. Send home a simple survey at the beginning of the year addressing many of the points mentioned in the questions that follow. Also, you might want to ask your colleagues what they believe parents want, especially the colleagues that taught your students the previous year. However, just like everyone else, people do change, and some parents might have different expectations this year. Some might even want to wipe the slate clean with the new school year. If this is the impression that you get when you meet them, respect their wishes.

2.59 What kinds of information do parents want?

2.60 What types of communication vehicles do parents expect you to use (such as letters, newsletters, telephone calls, or conferences) when communicating with them?

A newsletter feature that promotes positive communication between home and school and between parent and child is a "Questions to Ask Your Learner This Week" section. Include at least six questions, each one reflective of a different level of Bloom's Taxonomy (knowledge, comprehension, application, analysis, synthesis, evaluation), that will prompt students to describe to their parents what they learned about that week. You can have all the questions focus on one unit of study for the week, or you can include questions about different units. For example, if your class was studying a unit on American history, specifically the history of the Thanksgiving holiday, questions might include "Where did the Pilgrims' first Thanksgiving in America take place?" (knowledge level), "Why did they have this feast?" (comprehension level), and "What are you thankful for today? Why?" (evaluation level).

2.61 Does your school prescribe the frequency of your communication with parents? Do you get to decide on the frequency, or do you communicate only on an as-needed basis?

When calling a parent on the telephone, remember that it is courteous to first ask if it is a good time to talk. If not, reschedule for a time that's convenient for both of you.

Successful Parent-Teacher Conferences

Before any parent-teacher conference, parent or teacher initiated, send a questionnaire to the parents asking them what they think are their child's strengths and weaknesses. You might also want to find out if they have any concerns about their child's progress, what their beliefs are about what they can do at home to support their child's progress, and if they have any questions. The following are possible questions to include in your questionnaire:

- What are your child's strengths?
- In which subjects do you feel your child is doing well?
- What are your child's needs?
- In which subjects do you feel your child needs to improve?
- What does your child enjoy doing at school?
- What does your child like least about school?
- What are your concerns?
- What are your goals for your child?
- What are some things that you can do to help your child succeed?
- Which questions would you like to ask me? Which topics would you like to discuss?

Resource 2.4

This questionnaire should be returned to you well in advance of the conference so you can prepare yourself and your supporting materials. See Resource 2.4 for tips on conducting successful parent-teacher conferences.

Keep a log of all parent-teacher conferences in each student's cumulative folder, whether you conducted them in person or over the telephone. The log should contain (1) the date and location of the conference, such as classroom, home, or telephone; (2) the nature of the conference, such as routine report, problem, or emergency; (3) who initiated the conference; (4) the participants; and (5) a brief summary of what was discussed and the action plan put in place as a result of the conference. Record the dates and times you tried to initiate a conference but failed, and note the reasons why, such as the parent did not return your call or invitation.

Keeping the Tone Positive

Parents expect that their school system will make them feel proud of their children and of the school system and community to which they belong. Find out how your school system and school meet this expectation and your role in accomplishing it.

2.62 What does your school system and school do to encourage parents to feel proud of their children?
   a. Of their school and school system?
   b. Of their community?

2.63 What specific programs do your school system and school have in place for student recognition?

2.64 What is your role in accomplishing the efforts of your school and school system in raising parents' pride?

2.65 What more can you do to further this effort? ·

Involving Parents in Their Child's Education

Another way to get parents (and community members) to feel proud of their school is to get them involved in positive activities. However, not everyone will, or even wants to, get involved. There appears to be more parent volunteering when students are younger, possibly because the likelihood of there being a stay-at-home parent with a relatively flexible schedule is greater during the child's formative years than it is later.

Nevertheless, you might have three types of parents represented in your class: those who are occasionally involved, those who are too involved, and those who are rarely or never involved. Overinvolved parents can actually become a burden to you unless you channel their energies into classroom-enhancing activities. On the other end of the spectrum, the parents who are rarely or never involved can also be a burden to you because you might have to spend a great deal of time and effort just to contact them. Regardless of the types of parents you have, you need to find out what their expectations are for involvement, and you need to get them involved.

Both parents and students are normally enthusiastic at the beginning of a school year, so parents are more apt to commit to volunteer opportunities at that time. Seize the moment by sending a volunteer request letter to parents on the first day of school, asking for specific help during the school year. To do this most effectively, have your curriculum mapped out ahead of time, and the more months you have planned, the better (more on how to accomplish this in Chapter 6). Examples of requests include, "I need five parents to chaperone our field trip to the zoo on September 25th," "I need three parents for two hours in the morning on December 15th to set up booths for our international festival activity," and "I need two parents to volunteer on Tuesday and Thursday afternoons during the month of October for tutoring students in math." Also include an option for parents to indicate they are unable to commit to anything specific at this time but would like to be called if their assistance is needed for a special need or event.

If you are not able to map out your volunteer opportunities before the first day of school, send a more generic letter that asks parents if they are willing to volunteer inside or outside your classroom, which days and times are better for them, and what activities they would like to participate in, such as tutoring, correcting papers, reading with students, or making photocopies. Include information about your classroom parents committee, if you have one, and how a parent can become involved with that group (more on classroom parents committees in Chapter 7). Finally, attach a form to your letter that outlines your requests and allows parents to easily check the volunteer opportunities in which they would like to participate. Ask that the form be signed and returned by the end of the first week of school. Because the requests are specific and manageable, most teachers who try this find that they will get more volunteers than they requested.

2.66 How do parents (working and nonworking) expect to be involved in their child's school life and in their school?

2.67 What do your school system and school expect you to do to involve parents (working and nonworking)? other community members?

2.68 What can you ask parents and community members to do or not to do?

I know of a school that has a committee to set up guidelines for parent involvement. These guidelines are included in a parent handbook to help parents, especially those who volunteer often, understand the school's expectations of their involvement. In this way, the guidelines offer documented limits for both parents and teachers.

When Parents Are Not Satisfied

One final note with respect to working with parents: When parents have concerns about their child's education, they sometimes make demands for some particular change that they feel will help correct the situation. For example, they might demand a change in the placement of their child in a particular class or course. They might also make demands about your class's curriculum and instruction.

You need to know how your principal and school system administrator respond to these types of demands and how they expect you to respond. Furthermore, you need to understand how parents expect you to react. Do they expect you to meet their demands? Do they expect you to compromise? Do they expect you to refer them to someone else? If a parent has been used to having teachers and administrators cave in to her or his demands and you do not back down, you can be sure that you will have a sticky situation on your hands. You might be able to diffuse the situation simply by remaining calm.

This type of situation can cause significant role conflict for a teacher. Beware of this major stressor, and take precautions by knowing others' expectations and being prepared with your responses ahead of time.

2.69 How does each parent expect you to respond when they make demands about a change in their child's curriculum, instruction, or placement?

2.70 How does your employer respond to parent demands?

2.71 How does your employer expect you to respond to parent demands?

How Others Can Report Grievances Against You and Your School

No matter what the school system and your school do to meet the expectations of the community they serve, there still might be someone who is not satisfied. When this occurs, there usually is a policy or procedure for parents and other community members to communicate grievances and obtain responses. Find out what the policy or procedure is and recommend it to people with grievances regarding issues outside your control. It helps them direct their energies into the proper channels and helps you decrease, or even remove, a stressor in your life.

2.72 What is the procedure that parents and other community members can use to communicate grievances against you, your school, or your school system?

WHAT DO YOUR STUDENTS EXPECT OF YOU?

In addition to all the expectations generated by the adults in your school's community, you need to remember that your students also have expectations. They range from how they expect you to behave to what their educational experience should be. Before you meet your students, you can take an educated guess about what they are expecting. If and when the subject is appropriate, you might even want to ask your students directly.

Besides using a shoe box to collect suggestions and input from students, try having students write a response to one of the following questions and then use it as a ticket to leave the classroom for their next period or when leaving for the day: "What do you like most and like least about this class?" "How can I help you succeed in class?" or "What could I do to make the class more interesting for you?" You could also use sentence starters instead, such as "I would like to learn more about . . ." or "I feel . . ." or "I wish . . . ."

2.73 How do your students expect you to dress and behave?

2.74 What things do your students expect you to do or say in the following instances?
   a. When they need support, both academic and emotional
   b. When they need help feeling proud of themselves, of their school, and of their academic and affective progress
   c. When they need feedback

2.75 What do they think are your expectations of them?

2.76 What are their expectations regarding how their progress is assessed and graded?

2.77 Do your students expect rewards for good behavior, good work, and so forth?

> Others often expect teachers to have beautiful, legible penmanship, both print and cursive. Unfortunately, I did not. My penmanship was often illegible, especially when I was writing quickly on a chalkboard. A colleague of mine told me that she once had the same problem but solved it by buying penmanship templates from her local teaching supply store and practicing both print and cursive every time she sat down to watch television or talk on the telephone. I tried the same thing, and now my penmanship is extremely legible, and I form the letters properly and according to the penmanship style taught in my school system. I often used the following sentence to practice because it contains every letter of the alphabet: "The quick brown fox jumped over the lazy dog." A good tip for writing legibly on the blackboard is to stand farther away from the board than you think you need to stand. This seems to help keep your printing level and your letters uniform in size.

Students are bound to have some expectations about how you determine their grades. They might also have a belief that you give them grades—that you're the king or queen handing down rewards and punishments. For reasons relating to conditioning and associations of past experiences with grades, many students have not learned that their grades are earned. As their teacher, you must help them understand that concept and that, for the most part, their grades are determined by the amount of effort they put into their learning. Research shows that effort and persistence are greater in those students who believe that their achievement is the result of factors over which they have control. Therefore, if you can show them that they have control over their grades, the ownership of learning is transferred to your students (and rightfully so), and you prevent a potential stressor.

When students submit unacceptable work, tell them you believe that you know they can do better. Point out ways that the work can be improved, and then ask them to make those improvements. By telling students how to improve their work and asking them to do so, you encourage both student responsibility and academic success.

SHARING YOUR EXPECTATIONS: THE CLASSROOM HANDBOOK

Understand that expectations flow in both directions. Just as you want to learn about what others expect of you, others, especially your students and their parents, want to know what you expect of them. Although there are many ways to share your expectations, a classroom handbook is a great vehicle, especially for students and their parents.

Resource 2.5 shows a sample table of contents for a classroom handbook. A good idea is to share this information with your students on the first day of school and with parents at an Open House or Back to School Night. Your principal might be interested in this information, too.

Resource 2.5

2.78 How can you make your expectations known to the following?
   a. Employer
   b. Colleagues
   c. Students
   d. Students' parents

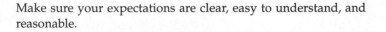

Make sure your expectations are clear, easy to understand, and reasonable.

A FINAL NOTE
ABOUT EXPECTATIONS

Expectations are dynamic. They can and do change. Circumstances, sometimes totally beyond your control, warrant changes to expectations, even after the first day of school.

If a change in expectations forces you to alter what you're doing or what you've planned, discuss possible solutions with your colleagues and phase in the change. Be realistic. Don't try to be superhuman. You can only implement changes at a rate that is comfortable for you.

Be careful not to think that once you've answered all the questions posed in this chapter that you are set for the school year. Accept the fact that your expectations change and others' expectations change, too. Keep your eyes and ears open at all times for any changes. And until you are aware of any changes that need to be made, use what you now know as a frame of reference while completing the remaining chapters in this book.

SUMMARY

Understanding what you expect from your teaching experience and what others expect of you as a teacher helps prevent role conflict and role ambiguity, two major stressors for teachers. Becoming aware of the expectations before you begin your teaching assignment is the key to effective stress prevention, a prerequisite for a successful school year. Finally, if you disagree with an expectation that is made of you, remember to be assertive and to try to resolve your differences in a proactive, amicable way.

3

Know Your Resources

INTRODUCTION AND OBJECTIVES

Knowing the resources that are available to you is an important part of becoming a successful teacher. Being familiar with your resources helps you know who and what you can rely on and when. Teachers cite inadequate resources as one of their major stressors. If you are aware of any inadequacies ahead of time, you can take measures to deal with them in an assertive, proactive way. This avoids the stress you might get when you go to use a resource and find it is not available.

Resources come in all shapes and sizes. They include time, people, and materials. The key is to know what resources exist and how to gain access to them.

The objectives of this chapter are to help you

- Analyze the amount of time you have to do your work
- Identify and tap into people who can be invaluable resources to you
- Identify and effectively use all the teaching tools available to you and your students

TIME: IS THERE EVER ENOUGH?

Most teachers feel they never have enough time to do all the things they need and want to do. Lack of time is many teachers' number-one stressor, making them feel overwhelmed, helpless, and out of control. Often, the time teachers have for noninstructional duties is very fragmented and filled with extra responsibilities. With the loss of the large block of time needed for efficient planning comes stress.

71

During my first year of teaching, I had 35 minutes of planning time four days a week. Needless to say, that wasn't enough, especially for a new teacher. This lack of time was a major stressor for me, and boy, was I stressed! Since then, I've learned to carve out more planning time within the schedule I'm given. (More on how to accomplish this in Section II, Your Action Plans.)

To get a handle on this precious resource, you need to examine how you manage time. Figure out how much time you have to spend and how you need to spend it. To get an idea of how you currently spend your time, every 15 minutes write down in a log what you have been doing. Evaluate your log on a daily or weekly basis to see where you spend your time, and analyze whether you are spending too much time on low-priority items. To use your time more efficiently, first identify any deadlines or events that direct your daily activities. Second, realize that you cannot control the passage of time, but you can control how you use the time you are given.

First, find out how much time you really have.

3.1 What is the school calendar (including holidays, half days, early release days, teacher workdays, Open House, parent-teacher conference days, and so forth)?

3.2 What is the calendar of school and school system events that involve you and your students (including marking period dates, standardized testing dates, assemblies, picnics, field days, vision/hearing/lice screenings, and so forth)?

3.3 When is your first meeting with your grade level, department, or team? When and how often are these meetings held?

3.4 What is your students' schedule for the following activities?
   a. Art
   b. Music
   c. P.E.
   d. Media
   e. Other electives
   f. Academically gifted programs
   g. Resource programs
   h. Recess and the use of the playground areas

3.5 Can you help decide the schedule for special classes and programs?

3.6 What is your commitment schedule for the following?
   a. Extra duties
   b. Extracurricular activities that you have already committed to do both inside and outside school

    c. Nonschool responsibilities (for example, your own children's day care drop-off and pickup times, soccer game schedules, and so forth)?

3.7 How much planning time do you have?

    a. During the days before the first day of school, are any school system, school, grade-level, or department meetings scheduled? How much time do you have to spend in your classroom during these particular days?

    b. Do you have planning time built into the school day? before and after school?

    c. Do you have time for lesson planning when you're at home?

YOUR SUPPORT NETWORK

People—your colleagues, administrators, parents, students, and most important, yourself—are invaluable resources to you. Like most people, you probably underestimate your own creativity and ability to solve problems, and you may not realize that what you might lack in skills and ideas, someone else might have. The strengths and weaknesses of others can complement yours. Working together, you all can make astounding contributions.

You Are Your Greatest Resource

You are a source of energy, filled with creative ideas. Look beyond the obvious. You are capable of much more than you realize.

3.8 What are your strengths? What things can you do to capitalize on your strengths?

3.9 What are your weaknesses? What are some things you can do to improve your weaknesses?

3.10 Where can you get help in learning how to unleash your creativity?

School Employees

School employees include your teaching colleagues, administration, office staff, and many others. These people can become true pillars of support for you and your students. Take a moment to find out who they are.

3.11 Using the following list as a starting point, determine who your colleagues are. Consider the other teachers at your school and those from other schools. What are their job descriptions and responsibilities? How can they help you and your students?

    a. Regular education teachers (note their grade levels or departments)

    b. Music teachers

    c. Art teachers

    d. Media specialists (or librarians)

    e. P.E. teachers

    f. Computer teachers

    g. Foreign language teachers

    h. Bilingual resource teachers

    i. Reading specialists

    j. Special educators

    k. Speech therapists

    l. Occupational therapists

    m. School psychologists

    n. School social workers

    o. School guidance counselors

    p. Curriculum specialists or instructional resource teachers

3.12 Is peer coaching available? How can you get involved?

3.13 Is team teaching available? How can you get involved?

3.14 Are mentor-teachers available? How can you get involved?
    a. If you are assigned a mentor, what can he or she help you with?
    b. If you are not assigned a mentor, with whom can you establish a mentor/mentee type of relationship?

3.15 Do you have an assistant teacher (paid or unpaid)?
    a. How many hours or days per week is an assistant assigned to your class?
    b. What are the assistant's job description and responsibilities?
    c. Are there any legal constraints with respect to the assistant's responsibilities in the classroom?
    d. What are your assistant's teaching and discipline philosophies?
    e. Have you discussed with your assistant your teaching program and his or her role in it?
    f. Have you trained your assistant in the tasks he or she is responsible for?
    g. In what ways can you show appreciation for your assistant's help?

I once had a full-time assistant teacher. She was a certified teacher with many years of experience. I learned a lot about teaching from watching her work with my students. To me, she became more than an assistant; she became a good friend and a trusted mentor.

3.16 How can your administrators and district office personnel support you and help you grow as a professional teacher?

3.17 Who is on the following staffs at your school? What are their responsibilities? How do they help your students? Are they available for you and your students only during certain hours or on certain days? Do they sponsor any programs, including contests, for you and your students? How can you help them do their jobs?
   a. Office (including the school secretary and receptionist)
   b. Cafeteria
   c. Custodial
   d. After-hours janitorial service
   e. Nursing
   f. Security

Your Students and Their Families

Now take a look at your students, their siblings, and their parents. They are resources that go virtually untapped in many classrooms. To keep the information about these resources handy, you might want to set up a folder or card file for each of your students, noting the following pertinent information about them and their parents:

3.18 Who does your class roster include? Include names, addresses, telephone numbers, and parents' work telephone numbers.

3.19 Where are your students' confidential, permanent records kept? How and when can you get access to them? From these records (and additional information you gather after meeting them), what can you determine about who your students are?
   a. What are their strengths and weaknesses?
   b. What are their lives like outside school?
   c. What are their wants and needs as individuals? as a group?
   d. What are their interests as individuals? as a group?
   e. What hobbies or expertise can they contribute and share with their classmates?

Parents are one of your greatest resources, and they are often underutilized. Parent volunteers are common in the lower grades, especially in kindergarten. But it's normal for parent involvement to wane as students get older. It's important to maintain parent participation throughout children's school career because it has been found that higher parental involvement produces higher student achievement. Further, if you don't make the time and effort to get parents involved, you're losing an invaluable resource.

3.20 Who are your students' parents?
   a. What hobbies or expertise can they contribute and share with your classes? See Resource 3.1 in the Resources for Successful Teaching section for a sample parent survey you can use to collect this information.

Resource 3.1

b. Which parents are more supportive of your students and of your class as a whole?

3.21 What ways do your school and school system provide for parents (working and nonworking) and community members (such as the elderly, older siblings, or business owners) to become involved in your school and in your class?
   a. Is there an organized PTA or PTO already in place? How does it work?
   b. How can they receive information about the school system, school, or classroom happenings?
   c. How can they contribute or donate supplies, items, or money?
   d. How can you recognize and thank them for their contributions to enriching your classes' learning experiences? Are gifts purchased for them? By whom and with which funds?

3.22 What else can you do to support efforts to involve parents and community members?

3.23 In what ways can older and younger students in your school assist you and your students (for example, as cross-age tutors, as helpers for younger students during dismissal, or as buddy classes)?

Support Programs and Services

People are the foundation of support programs and services, which exist both inside and outside school.

Look at What Your School Offers

Your school system undoubtedly has programs and services (such as help lines and buddy programs) for you and your students. Find out which ones are available.

3.24 What support programs or services are in place for teachers? How does a teacher get access to them?

3.25 What programs and services (such as tutoring or mentor programs) are available for students who need extra help or extra enrichment? How does a student get access to them?

3.26 Is there a school-based or school-system-based team (such as a student support team, a pupil review team, or a student assistance team) that can assist you in determining better educational strategies to support the students who you might have a difficult time reaching?
   a. What is the name of this team?
   b. In what ways can this team help you and your student?
   c. Who is on the team?
   d. What is the procedure for referring a student to this team?

e. Do you need to document the teaching strategies you have been using with this student? Are you required to document these strategies for a certain period, such as six weeks, before referring a student?

f. What forms, if any, do you need to complete before the meeting?

g. Are parents invited to attend the meeting? Who sends the invitation?

The procedures for referring students to school-based assistance teams can be confusing. Over the years, I've been a member of two different assistance teams and have referred students to two additional teams. Although each team's mission was similar, each had slightly different rules and procedures. I realized that it was a good idea to find out ahead of time how my school's assistance team operated before I ever needed its help. This proactive approach helped save a lot of time (and stress) when the need for their assistance arose.

3.27 What kinds of support does the school or school system provide for your classroom?

a. Does someone clean your classrooms? How often? What is cleaned?

b. If something is broken, what is the procedure for getting it repaired?

c. If you need to, can you get access to your classroom over the weekend? How?

Look to Your Community for Support

There are also support programs for you and your students organized and supported by groups outside the school system. For you, there are teacher associations, organizations, and agencies available. See Resource 3.2 for names and addresses of many such teacher associations. For your students, a school counselor or social worker might be very helpful in pointing out which educational, social, recreational, and cultural programs and services exist for them. In addition, support programs and services exist for linking your classroom with others.

Resource 3.2

3.28 What teaching associations, organizations, and agencies are available?

3.29 What programs and services organized and supported by the community are available for your students?

3.30 Are any awards or contests in your county, state, or country available for your students? your school? you?

3.31 Are there opportunities to connect with other schools to work together on projects?

3.32 Are intraschool, interschool, and U.S. Postal Service mail and courier services available for you and your students to use? What are the procedures for using each type of service?

TEACHING TOOLS AND MATERIALS

It's hard to think about a teacher without conjuring up the images of a piece of chalk, a chalkboard, a ruler, or a globe. These tools and materials are the hallmarks of teaching, but there are many more.

When your classroom is not equipped with the tools and materials needed for teaching and learning, it becomes a major stressor because you cannot function as effectively or efficiently as you want and need to function. To prevent this from happening, you must know what tools and materials are available to you and your students. Because money is a crucial factor in determining the availability of tools and materials, you might never have all you feel are necessary to do your job. This is where you need to tap into your creativity and that of those around you for ideas to buy or make teaching tools and materials for your students.

First look at the obvious. As soon as you receive your classroom key, take an inventory of what's there. Use Figures 3.1 and 3.2 to record this information, and keep them with your plan book so they are always at your fingertips when you plan. Then search beyond the obvious. Seek out those people you have identified as able to help you find what's available at your school.

Figure 3.1. Equipment Inventory

Equipment (including A/V, lab, machine, and computer)	Serial Numbers

Figure 3.2. Curriculum Materials Inventory

Curriculum Materials (including curriculum guides, teacher's guides, professional resources, teacher's magazines, software, manipulatives, posters, and student texts)	

What Your School Provides

When you start investigating what items your school supplies for you and for your students, first get the most important items—your curriculum guides or standard courses of study.

3.33 Where can you get copies of the curriculum guides or standard courses of study for the classes you are teaching?

3.34 What diagnostic tests and tools are available for assessing your students' needs, achievement, interests, and attitudes?

If you will be using a new textbook series this year, borrow and review the teacher's manual before the school year begins. This will help ensure that you are familiar with the format of the series and with the resources that come with it.

3.35 Which textbooks, basal reading series, and so forth, does the school or school system use?
   a. Are you required to use them?
   b. How do you get them?
   c. Are you responsible for issuing and accounting for your students' textbooks?
   d. Are you responsible for collecting your students' textbooks at the end of the school year?
   e. Where do you get the teacher's guides and other supplementary materials provided by the publisher for these books, if they exist?
   f. Are any books shared among teachers or students? Which ones?
   g. Can you order additional or different books? From where are you authorized to purchase them? Who pays for them? What is the procedure for ordering them?
   h. Are all these books free of any gender, racial, ethnic, cultural, or age stereotypes? Are they free of any bias?

3.36 What school supplies—consumable and nonconsumable, including cleaning supplies, paid for with school funds—are available for you and your students? See Resource 3.3 for a list of possible supplies.
   a. Where do you get them?
      i. The grade level's or the department's supplies closet?
      ii. The school's supplies closet?

Resource 3.3

    iii. The school's or school system's warehouse?

    iv. Trade catalogs?

  b. What is the procedure for obtaining these supplies?

  c. How long is the stock expected to last?

  d. What are the procedures for reordering when stock is running low?

  e. Are any of these supplies shared among teachers or students?

3.37 Are photocopiers, laminating machines, and overhead transparency makers available at your school or somewhere in your school system? What are the procedures, rules, and restrictions regarding their use?

Every laminating machine I've ever used needed to be preheated to a high temperature before it would work properly. I've gotten burned (no pun intended!) many times because either I was too impatient to wait for it to get hot enough or someone accidentally turned it off before I got to use it. When the laminator isn't hot enough, the plastic film doesn't adhere properly to the paper, and you're left with something that comes apart over time. I've found that the worst situation is when the film partly adheres and you have to try to remove it with a straight pin without tearing your paper—a totally frustrating experience!

3.38 Is your classroom or school equipped with a place where you can store your personal belongings, such as your coat, purse, and professional books?

3.39 What is the layout of your school building? Where are the bathrooms, water fountains, emergency exits, and so forth?

3.40 How do you sign up for the use of the cafeteria, multipurpose room, and other large gathering places outside your scheduled time?

3.41 Does your classroom or school have extra children's clothing on hand for students in case of any accidents?

One day, one of my eight-year-old students was not feeling well and accidentally had a bowel movement in her pants. To compound her embarrassment, we didn't have a change of clothes for her. Luckily, a teacher across the hall had a bag full of extra clothing. My student was able to borrow some clothes—and save face with her peers. A similar embarrassing incident happened to a middle school student who began menses and was not prepared. The moral of the story: Keep some extra clothes on hand, regardless of the age of your students.

Take Advantage of the Latest Technology

Most schools provide computers and other technology for their teachers and students. Computers are more common today in schools and homes than ever before, yet their effective use as a teaching and learning tool has been slow to progress. The main hindrance has been the lack of teacher training in both how to use the technology and even more in how to effectively integrate the technology into daily instructional plans. Nevertheless, when computers are used effectively, they increase student motivation, promote student ownership of learning, and improve student achievement. The beauty of computers is that the wide array of technology and programs enables teachers to easily differentiate instruction to match a variety of learning styles and needs.

Sign up for computer training that not only teaches you how to use a particular software application, such as a word processor, but also shows you how to effectively use the Internet and educational software to improve student learning. Brainstorm with colleagues on how to use technology in your classrooms and lesson plans, and continue to support one another as you develop this very important skill.

Computers can be used in many different ways to enhance teaching and learning. In classrooms, computers can be used for drill and practice, using software programs that teach a concept and provide questions and drills to see how well the concept was learned. They can also be used for simulations, where software enables students, usually working in teams, to role-play and solve complex, realistic problems. Teachers can easily create crossword puzzles, word searches, worksheets, and so forth, using utility applications. Tools such as word processors, spreadsheets, and databases are also helpful to both teachers and students. Gathering research with the computer, using packaged software or the Internet, is another way computers enhance teaching and learning. Finally, computers can be used for communication with things such as e-mail, listservs, and online bulletin boards and discussion groups.

For helping teachers manage many routine tasks such as keeping a grade book and communicating with parents, a school can set up an intranet (a network of all computers in the school or school system) and classroom Web sites. Many Internet companies also offer these types of services for teachers free of charge or for a nominal fee. These types of tools help teachers work more efficiently and thus more effectively.

There are numerous educational software titles on the market today. Remember that the quality of the packaged software—not the mere fact that it is computerized—is what makes computer-based instruction an effective tool. Therefore, it is imperative that you read software reviews (which you can find in teacher's magazines or through an Internet search), use the software, and evaluate it before integrating the application into your lesson plans.

The Internet is another powerful resource for you and your students. With Internet access, you have virtually an infinite number of resources at your fingertips. It offers you and your students access to the latest information on any topic. It also gives you access to educational products and services (some of which are free) as well as hundreds of ongoing discussion groups that enable teachers and students from around the world to interact and collaborate. In addition to online discussion groups, Internet e-mail offers you and your students the opportunity to communicate quickly, easily, and inexpensively with other teachers and students from anywhere in the world. The possibilities are endless.

By making the Internet part of your lesson plans, you can enhance learning in a variety of ways. Students can use the Internet for research purposes or as a springboard for response activities that call for students to create graphic organizers of their reactions to what they have seen and read on Web sites. Finally, students can use the Internet as a starting point for a processing activity, applying the information on a Web site to a process or product.

Because the Internet offers you and your students thousands of resources, using a search engine such as Yahoo!® with your Internet browser is one of the best ways to find what you're looking for. When you find a Web site that appears to be very useful or that you're visiting often,

Make sure you check the validity and ease of use of Web sites you plan to use in your lesson before allowing your students to use them. To save time during your lesson, bookmark the sites you want your students to use and then teach your students how to access the bookmarks.

add a bookmark for it in your browser. This saves you a lot of work the next time you want to access that particular Web site.

The Internet is dynamic. Thousands of Web sites are added every day. At the same time, hundreds of other Web sites have address changes or are removed. So it's futile to list all the sites that could be helpful to you and your students, but a few are worth mentioning. For the latest educational research and news, good places to start are the Web sites of the U.S. Department of Education (http://www.ed.gov), any state's department of education, and the Educational Resources Information Center (ERIC) database (http://www.eric.ed.gov). Two other federally supported Web sites worth noting are the Federal Resources for Educational Excellence (FREE) database (http://www.ed.gov/free) and the Gateway to Educational Materials (GEM) database (http://www.thegateway.org). The FREE database lists free federally supported teaching and learning resources; it has been created and is continually updated by more than 30 federal agencies. The GEM database includes collections of educational materials found on various federal, state, university, nonprofit, and commercial Internet sites. Both Web sites offer materials in a variety of subjects, including language arts, mathematics, science, social studies, foreign languages, health, arts, physical education, educational technology, vocational education, and more.

All these Web sites have a wealth of information for teachers trying to find the best teaching resources on the Internet. A search engine can also help you find helpful sites. But user beware! In addition to all the good material on the Internet, there's a huge amount of misinformation and unreliable data. Therefore, if you use the Internet to gather facts, proceed with caution and use common sense.

Learn about the Internet by taking classes and reading books and articles about it. And don't forget to ask your school's technology teachers about how this resource can become a tremendous asset to you and your students. The time spent learning about the Internet is time well spent, because the

Internet brings an infinite amount of resources to you quickly and easily. Just as important, it links you to other teachers who have similar interests and problems. These teachers can become part of your support system (as discussed in Chapter 1) helping you solve problems, deal with stressors, and prevent stress.

At this point, you might be asking, "Where do I begin? How do I incorporate technology into my daily lesson plans so that my students' achievement will improve?" To use educational software and the Internet as an effective teaching and learning tool, begin with your curriculum. The learning goals drive how the technology could and should be implemented. Don't gravitate toward a computer-based lesson plan just because you found a visually appealing Web site or an entertaining piece of educational software. Focus on your learning goals and topic, and then make decisions about your resources (computers or other) and activities from that perspective. For example, if the instructional goal is reinforcement of a particular skill, it would be appropriate to incorporate a drill and practice software program that helps students practice that particular skill.

The next step is to collect computer software programs, Web sites, e-mail addresses, Internet links to online experts, videoconference opportunities, and so forth, that support your learning objectives. Then you can use your collection to create activities. Self-contained packaged software often comes with preset activities and learning goals, but the Internet can be more versatile.

Once you've designed your activities, take a step back and look at your entire unit. Do your computer-based activities support your learning goals? Make sure that all the activities connect to your unit's topic. Then implement your activities and evaluate whether your students have mastered the learning objectives.

Use the following questions to help you identify the computer and other technology resources available to you and your students:

3.42 What computer hardware and peripherals (printers, modems, CD-ROM drives, CD-RW drives, and so forth) can you access for teaching and for personal use? What computer technology do your students have access to for learning and for their personal use?

a. Is there a computer lab for your class's use or for your students' personal use?

b. When can you and your students use the above technology? Is there a schedule?

c. What is your school's or school system's technology plan?

3.43 Do you or your students have Internet access? What is the procedure for obtaining an Internet account? Where can you go for

If you have a limited number of computers at your disposal and your students have to take turns, use a simple timer to make students' turns equal in length (if that is what you want) and to signal when a turn is over. Teach your students how to set the timer themselves, and post a list of your students' names by the computer. When the timer rings, ask the student at the computer to get the next student on the list. By making the computer usage procedure an independent one, you remain free to continue working with the rest of your class.

help in learning about the Internet and what it has to offer?

3.44 What are some useful Internet Web sites and discussion groups?

3.45 Where can you go to learn more about the Internet and how to use it to help improve your students' achievement?

3.46 What kinds of computer software programs, CDs, DVDs, videos, laser discs, films, and audiocassette tapes are available to you and your students through your school and school system?
   a. What is the procedure for borrowing them?
   b. Can you get them from retail stores? Who pays for them?
   c. Do they come with teaching manuals that you can borrow?
   d. Are all these materials free of any gender, racial, ethnic, cultural, or age stereotypes? Are they free of any bias?

3.47 What audio/visual equipment (such as televisions, VCRs, camcorders, digital cameras, overhead projectors, film projectors, filmstrip projectors, slide projectors, boom boxes, CD players, and headphones) do you have access to?
   a. What is the procedure for getting this equipment?
   b. Is this equipment shared among teachers and staff? Is there a schedule?
   c. If you are assigned equipment, is it in proper working order equipped with emergency parts such as extra light bulbs and batteries?
   d. Are you familiar with how to use this equipment efficiently and effectively?

A rule of thumb for creating transparencies is to print the visual on an 8.5-by-11-inch sheet of paper, set it on the floor, and stand on a sturdy chair above it. Make sure you can read it easily. If you can't, increase the size of the text or graphic. In addition, to prevent discipline problems, always ask your students if they can easily see and read transparencies and other visuals that you use in class.

What Your School System Provides

After you have done an exhaustive search for resources in your school, look outward. Your school system might have a teacher's resource center or office stocked with extra teaching tools and materials. If not, perhaps there is one in your local area that is affiliated with a state or county teacher support system, such as the public university system.

3.48 Is there a teacher resource center available? Where is it located? When is it open?

Keep a list of supplies that are running low. Purchase more or let the person in charge of ordering supplies know about the situation before you completely run out of them. Refer to this list the following year to help you estimate how much you need to order at the beginning of the school year.

Visit Your Local Libraries

Use the public libraries. They are carrying more teaching-related books and materials all the time. Also, visit libraries at local universities, especially those that confer degrees in education. Their curriculum libraries have an abundance of materials.

3.49 What libraries are available for you to use and to borrow from?
a. Town or public libraries
b. University or college libraries

Every few weeks, I go to my local public library and bring large canvas tote bags. I usually fill them with two to three dozen books I plan to read with my students over the following few weeks. Each time I go, I notice others checking out a similar number of books. Some even bring milk crates strapped onto hand trucks to make carrying the books easier. When I ask, I find out that these people are teachers, too—no surprise!

Tap Into Your Colleagues' Expertise

Borrowing from colleagues is another way to find the resources you might need. Your colleagues, especially those who have taught the same grade level or subject as you, usually have a wealth of resources already collected and organized. All it usually takes to get access to their resources is to simply ask. Many of your colleagues are probably extremely supportive and are more than willing to share what they have.

3.50 Which teachers in your school have taught your grade level or subject before?

Teacher Organizations and Associations

Besides support, teaching associations and education agencies offer a lot of education-related information. See Resource 3.2 for their names and addresses. They offer newsletters, periodicals, books, and other materials regarding effective teaching. Most of this information is packaged well and presented clearly.

Resource 3.2

There are also agencies and organizations not related to teaching that want to promote their missions or causes. They might also be sources of free or inexpensive materials that you can use in your lessons.

3.51 What teaching associations, organizations, and agencies can help you obtain teaching tools and materials?

3.52 What other agencies and organizations might have free or inexpensive materials that you can integrate into your lessons?

Sources of Additional Funds

Unfortunately, most schools grapple with the money issues—the lack of it, that is—forcing teachers to find other means of obtaining needed and wanted resources. Grants, donations, earned bonus points from various book clubs, and free donations are just some of the ways you can get the resources you want and need.

Many resources list places where you can obtain free or very inexpensive teaching materials. Educators Progress Service publishes books whose titles begin with the words *Educators Guide to Free* (for example, *Educators Guide to Free Science Materials*). These books are updated annually and sell out quickly. Several other books are also available from your local teaching supply store or bookstore. Professional teaching magazines, such as Scholastic's *Instructor* and The Education Center's *The Mailbox*, are also very good sources of free and inexpensive materials. Check the media center to see if your school subscribes to these magazines.

Use the following questions to help you examine these options:

3.53 How do you find out about which grants are available? What are the school's rules and procedures for applying for them?

3.54 Which book clubs can you join that also have bonus point systems, such as children's book clubs (Troll or Scholastic, for instance) and adult book clubs (Doubleday Select is one example)?

3.55 Are there any computer user groups that you can join for mutual support?

3.56 Are there any places or organizations that give away free materials?

3.57 Are donations (monetary or other), free presentations, and free tours available from parents? local businesses?

When asking for donations, be specific about what you want and why; otherwise, you might end up with material that you can't use and are then responsible for storing or disposing of properly. Try to time the request appropriately and emphasize its educational purpose. Also emphasize the possibility that it could be a tax-deductible donation. Finally, remember to send thank-you notes after receiving any donations.

Recycled Materials

Comb the yellow pages for businesses that discard items you might find useful. This is a great way for businesses to recycle what they can no longer use. For example, contact a local supermarket for paper and plastic bags, styrofoam trays, and clean cardboard cartons. Ask the local newspaper for unsold newspapers. Contact a carpet store for remnants and the paint and wallpaper store for old wallpaper books; you can use the carpets to create a wonderful sitting area in your classroom, and the wallpaper is great for book covers. Again, be specific about the items you would like and be willing to explain what you will be doing with them.

Your last resort might be to simply look through the garbage. Yes, there's truth in the saying, "One man's trash is another man's treasure," so consider sifting through unwanted items.

First, check out your own throw-aways. Go through your closets to find anything that you think you could recycle into something useful for your class. For example, take old dress shirts and use them as painting smocks. And don't throw away those fabric scraps! Use them for making book covers for student-authored books.

Next, check your school's garbage. There might be old teacher's manuals, old workbooks, and the like, especially if your school has recently adopted a new textbook series. Clean boxes and other storage items in your school's garbage might also be good things to save. Be creative.

3.58 What are some treasures that you might be able to create from discarded, unwanted items?

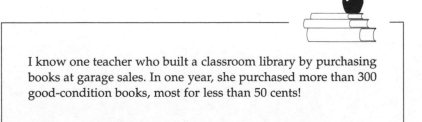

An inexpensive way to help students be more efficient is to offer them Post-it brand tape flags to help them quickly and easily reach different sections in their textbooks, such as the glossary, index, and the chapter they are currently studying. Because the flags do not damage the paper, they can easily be moved to different parts of the book as the year progresses.

The Last Resort: Your Personal Funds

If you must use your own money or are lucky enough to get an allowance from the school, try to invest in items that are nonconsumable, sturdy, and adaptable for meeting the needs of different students. Large discount stores, thrift stores, and garage sales are often good sources for such items, and the prices are usually very affordable.

3.59 How can you keep your personal spending to a minimum when obtaining tools and materials that you can't get in any other way?

I know one teacher who built a classroom library by purchasing books at garage sales. In one year, she purchased more than 300 good-condition books, most for less than 50 cents!

SUMMARY

Resources are all around you. Find out as much as you can about them so that inadequate resources do not become a major stressor for you and you can be the most effective teacher as possible. To continually find new and better resources for you and your students, always keep your eyes and ears open. And above all, keep an open mind.

Section II

Your Action Plans

4

Determine Your Goals

INTRODUCTION AND OBJECTIVES

Before you can develop action plans, you need to know where you're heading. Determining your personal, professional, instructional, and classroom climate goals gives you the direction you need.

The objectives of this chapter are to help you

- Clarify your personal and professional goals
- Identify your instructional goals
- Determine your classroom climate goals

YOUR PERSONAL AND PROFESSIONAL GOALS: TAKE CONTROL

In Chapters 1 and 2, you examined your wants and needs. Now you can focus on clarifying your personal goals. You should consider them first because of their importance in helping you take control of your life, a key ingredient for a thriving teaching career.

What do you want to accomplish in your life? What do you want to accomplish this year in your teaching assignment? Look at where you are and where you want to go, and then answer the following questions:

4.1 What are your personal goals for the following areas of your life?
  a. Physical health
  b. Family and friends
  c. Spirituality
  d. Hobbies and interests

4.2 What are your professional goals?
   a. What grade and subject do you want to teach?
   b. What image do you want your students, parents, colleagues, and administrators to have of you?
   c. How do you want to be remembered by your former students?

In addition to the broad professional goals you have just recorded, you might also have more specific professional goals. For example, this year you might want to learn more about using technology as a teaching tool, or you might want to become more involved in a professional teaching organization or association. Answer the following questions:

4.3 What do you want to learn this year?

4.4 Are there any professional teaching organizations or associations in which you would like to become more involved?

Your professional goals also include the things you would like to do with your class this year. All your teaching experiences so far have helped shape your opinions about what does and does not work for you and your students. As a result, you might have ideas about activities that you want to do this year.

4.5 Are there any activities you have done in the past that you would like to do again this year? would like to change this year? would not like to do at all this year?

4.6 Is there something new that you want to try this year with your students?

Every year I make new distinctions about what works in the classroom. And I know that what works with one group of students doesn't always work with another group. Yet I am always eager to try new things. One example is using learning centers in the classroom. I had used centers effectively as a primary grade teacher. But in every school where I taught upper elementary grade levels, I found that centers were rarely used. So I decided to make centers an integral part of my third- through fifth-grade classes one year. I read many professional resources and spoke with other teachers about how they managed centers in their classrooms. Drawing on my experience teaching primary grades and some of the new ideas I had learned, I successfully integrated learning centers into my classes. The centers enhanced my teaching and improved my students' achievement.

YOUR INSTRUCTIONAL GOALS: FULFILL CURRICULUM EXPECTATIONS

"My students will become lifelong learners." "My students will get accepted into college." "My students will learn the multiplication tables." These are all excellent goals to strive for, but you have to ask yourself if these are goals you are expected to pursue. Perhaps they are. Perhaps they are only reflections of your personal goals for your students. Having student goals that are not supported by your employer can be a cause for role ambiguity and role conflict. So be careful.

Remove any role ambiguity and role conflict by making sure you help your students reach the goals you were hired to help them achieve. If you choose to work toward different goals, you might place unnecessary pressure on yourself and on your students. Unnecessary pressure can lead to unwanted stress.

The simplest way to find the required goals is to consult your curriculum guides, standard course of study, grade-level proficiency lists, or scope and sequence charts. They should consist of cognitive, affective, and psychomotor goals for your students. If they do not exist or are incomplete, ask your colleagues, your principal, or your school system curriculum administrators. If there are no curriculum goals for your teaching assignment, find out the state and national guidelines, including standards and guidelines from national councils such as the National Council of Teachers of Mathematics (NCTM), the National Council of Teachers of English (NCTE), and others.

4.7 Using all the curriculum guides or other curriculum documents for your assigned teaching positions, determine the following:
   a. Which parts of the curriculum are you responsible to teach?
   b. What are your curriculum goals?

If there are any parts of the curriculum documents that appear vague, ask your principal and colleagues for clarification. For example, if they state students must learn to write legibly but do not specify the exact style of handwriting, find out from your principal or colleagues which style the school or district recommends that you teach.

Often there is miscommunication among teachers, students, and parents when it comes to using the word *writing*. When speaking with students and parents, make sure you explain that *writing* is the process of creating a story, essay, letter, and so forth, whereas *handwriting* or *penmanship* are the proper words used to signify the actual skill of forming letters, either in print or in cursive.

Unfortunately, it is not enough to identify curriculum goals based solely on the curriculum documents. You also need to look at your students. You might be assigned students who either have not achieved the prerequisite skills needed to be successful in your class or have already achieved the goals you have outlined here. In either case, you might need to modify some of the goals on your list for certain students. The goals you establish must be appropriate for each student you teach.

Examine your students' permanent records and identify any students who might need modified goals. Any student who has an Individualized Education Plan (IEP) or equivalent probably needs modified or additional goals.

4.8 Are there any curriculum goals that need to be modified for your students?
   a. Which students?
   b. Which goals need modification?
   c. Do these students need any additional goals?

If you use small-group instruction, use different-colored markers to highlight in your lesson plan book how often you meet with each group during the week. Check to make sure you are spending an equitable, not necessarily equal, amount of time with each group.

YOUR CLASSROOM CLIMATE GOALS: NURTURE HEALTHY RELATIONSHIPS

To have a successful school year, you also need to establish a classroom climate that supports an effective learning environment. Climate is all about relationships—the emotional health of the relationships among a group of people. Climate, therefore, is the atmosphere or tone created by the emotional health of the relationships that exist among the members of your classroom and those that exist between your classroom and everyone else. As the teacher, you have tremendous control over your classroom climate.

Discipline problems, cited as a major stressor for most teachers, play a significant role in classroom climate. Discipline problems result when students use inappropriate behaviors to deal with demands or expectations placed on them. Students feel pressured into a corner and try to get out any way they know how—from fighting to daydreaming. Discipline problems erode the emotional health of those involved and of bystanders.

These problems become a strain on the classroom climate. When they occur, you need to have the skills to deal with the inappropriate behavior. Many of these skills are discussed in Chapter 7. There is a wealth of resources you can use to learn these skills; check your school's professional library and stores that sell teacher resources.

As the classroom leader, you have the power to create a climate that can help you prevent stress. Use the following questions to help you identify your climate goals and to determine if you are committed to this very important stress prevention strategy:

4.9   What is your current classroom climate like? What has your past classroom climate been like?

4.10 What are your climate goals for this school year?

4.11 What are your school's climate goals? How do your climate goals support the school's climate goals?

Are you calling on girls and boys at equal rates? Find out if you are by nonchalantly placing a paper clip in your right pocket every time you call on a girl and a paper clip in your left pocket every time you call on a boy. Most students won't notice what you are doing, and you'll have your answer at the end of the day.

SUMMARY

Identifying your personal, professional, instructional, and classroom climate goals is the first step in creating action plans for a successful school year and a thriving teaching career. These goals drive the actions you take to become an effective, successful teacher.

5

Your Schedule: The Framework for Your Action Plans

INTRODUCTION AND OBJECTIVES

How much time you have to create and execute your action plans is determined by your daily schedule. As the framework of your action plans, a carefully recorded daily schedule is the key to examining how to maximize your planning time so you can achieve your instructional and climate plans.

The objectives of this chapter are to help you

- Prioritize your activities so you can achieve your personal and professional development goals
- Examine and record school and student schedules as well as your teaching schedule
- Analyze your planning time
- Maximize your planning time through effective time management strategies

CAN YOU MAKE TIME TO ACHIEVE YOUR GOALS?

Perhaps the real question is, can you afford *not* to make the time to achieve your goals? A successful school year and thriving teaching career depend on your ability to work toward your goals. Making the time to work toward all your goals—personal, professional, instructional, and climate—allows you to lead a balanced life, a requisite for stress-free teaching. Therefore, consider the following guidelines when creating your schedule:

- Keep a steady, comfortable pace; don't try to do everything in one day.
- Use time wisely, especially the hours you are at school.
- Build buffers into your schedule to accommodate unforeseen delays and help ensure that you meet deadlines.
- Coordinate personal and school events so that you are not involved in too many highly stressful situations at once.
- Stay as organized as you can to help you feel less overwhelmed and more in control of your time.
- Be flexible and understand that you might need to rearrange your schedule as the days and weeks go by.

Control your time by carefully planning your daily activities. To help you allocate enough time for the important things you need and want to do, photocopy Resources 5.1, 5.2, and 5.3 in the Resources for Successful Teaching section. As you read the rest of this chapter, use these resources to record your scheduled activities and those of your school and students. Armed with this information, you will be able to maximize your time.

WHAT DO YOU DO FOR YOURSELF AND YOUR PROFESSION?

Resource 5.1

Using Resource 5.1, block out the time you are required to be at work, including the time you need to travel to and from school. Then schedule the activities you need to pursue to fulfill your personal goals. Schedule your personal life as carefully as you schedule your lesson plans. Although you might have to adjust this schedule as the year progresses, jot it down now so your personal plans get the priority they need.

Include as many personal activities as you know of at this time. Some of the activities to consider scheduling now are the time needed for sleeping, eating properly, and exercising. Also mark in the time you want to set aside for family and friends, spiritual growth, hobbies, health maintenance activities (annual physicals, dental, and eye care appointments for you and your family), extracurricular activities (yours and your family's, including the travel time to and from these activities), and professional development activities. After you have set aside time for these activities, make sure you schedule some time to just relax—"me time." This is time to do whatever you please, however you please.

Teaching is not just a job, it's a profession. And it's the kind of work that's hard to "turn off." Like it or not, you usually take work home with you, whether it's papers to grade or just thoughts of what's happened during the day. When I began teaching, it was very hard to separate my work from my personal life. As a result, my family time and my "me time" were virtually all taken up by my work. This was not good. I was very stressed, and within a few months, I felt completely burnt out. In the years that followed, I made time for my family and me. I scheduled it. Although I couldn't always follow my exact schedule every day, I was able to follow it most of the time. My stress decreased sharply, and I became not only a much happier person but also a much more effective teacher.

WHAT'S HAPPENING AT YOUR SCHOOL?

Obtain a copy of your school calendar. Using Resource 5.2 and the weekly lesson plan pages in your plan book, mark which days are vacation days, holidays, half days, teacher workdays, Open House, parent-teacher conferences, marking period end dates, and any other kinds of special days that are identified on the school calendar. Don't forget to include other special school or school system events that involve you and your students, even if they are not listed on the school calendar. Figure 5.1 has additional special days that you might want to include. When you finish transferring the dates, tape your school calendar to the inside back cover of your plan book to use as a handy reference during the school year.

Resource 5.2

Figure 5.1. Special Dailys to Remember

July
4 – Independence Day
 	
August
Friendship Day (1st Sunday)
 	
September
National Grandparent's Day
   (1st Sunday)
Labor Day (1st Monday)
First day of autumn (3rd week)
 	
October
31 – Halloween
Columbus Day (2nd Monday)
 	
November
11 – Veteran's Day
Election Day (1st Tuesday)
Thanksgiving (4th Thursday)
National Book Week (3rd week)
 	
December
25 – Christmas
First day of winter (3rd week)
Hanukkah (date varies)
 	
January
1 – New Year's Day
15 – Martin Luther King Jr.'s
   Birthday
Chinese New Year (date varies)
	February
	2 – Ground Hog Day
	12 – Abraham Lincoln's Birthday
	22 – George Washington's Birthday
	President's Day (3rd Monday)
	
	March
	17 – St. Patrick's Day
	First day of spring (3rd week)
	Health Week (last week)
	Easter (date varies, may occur in
	   April)
	Passover (date varies, may occur in
	   April)
	
	April
	1 – April Fool's Day
	22 – Earth Day Anniversary
	National Arbor Day (last Friday)
	Easter (date varies, may occur in
	   March)
	Passover (date varies, may occur in
	   March)
	
	May
	1 – May Day
	5 – Cinco de Mayo
	18 – Peace Day
	Mother's Day (2nd Sunday)
	Memorial Day (last Monday)
	
	June
	14 – Flag Day
	Father's Day (usually 3rd Sunday)
	First day of summer (3rd week)

WHAT ARE YOUR STUDENTS DOING?

If you teach in a self-contained class, obtain a schedule of your class's special activities, such as lunch, art, music, and so forth (for a complete list, see Chapter 3). Also obtain a schedule of your students' pull-out times for resource and enrichment classes and record these student schedules on a copy of Figure 5.2 and include it in your lesson plan book.

Figure 5.2. Special Daily Schedules for Students

Students: Schedule:	Students: Schedule:
Students: Schedule:	Students: Schedule:

At the beginning of the school year, you'll want to record these schedules only in the first two weeks of your plan book pages. Save yourself a lot of work by not copying this information on the rest of your plan book pages until the schedules are solid. These schedules can change often in the first few of weeks of school, especially in high-growth communities where higher-than-expected student registration creates many last-minute changes in classes and schedules. If you do not have a lesson plan book, make several copies of Resource 5.3 and place them in a three-ring binder.

Resource 5.3

Rather than writing in the same activities over and over each week, devise a shorthand or set of symbols for standing activities, such as L for lunch. Remember to include a key with your substitute teacher kit so that your substitute teacher can easily understand your plan book.

WHAT'S YOUR TEACHING SCHEDULE?

Obtain the schedule for your duties and meetings. If you teach several classes during the day, find out when you are required to teach and when you have extra duties. You also need to obtain the schedule of any weekly meetings you're involved in. As you did with your students' schedules, indicate these times only on the first two weeks of your plan book to save yourself work if the schedules should change soon after school starts. With these times marked, you have an idea of how much time you have for planning.

Using a three-ring binder for your lesson plan book makes it easy to add important papers, tables, charts, and so forth, or make other changes as the school year progresses. It also allows you to customize your plan book pages to meet your unique needs. Once you have created a plan book page style that meets your needs, record any standing weekly activities such as lunch and duties and make enough photocopies to cover the rest of your semester or school year.

DO YOU HAVE ENOUGH PLANNING TIME?

Compare Your Personal Schedule (Resource 5.1) with your teaching schedule in your plan book. Identify all your planning time. Your planning time is made up of all blocks of free time—before, during, and after the school day. It's important to be aware of all the planning time you have available, because you will need it to develop your instructional and climate plans. Don't panic if you believe you don't have enough planning time; this chapter offers help for maximizing the time you have available.

5.1 How much time do you have for planning? When is it?

5.2 What time of day are you most alert and energetic? Is there a way to make your planning time coincide with your "best time"?

If possible, adjust your schedules to accommodate your best time. This is the first step in helping you maximize the use of your time and thus prevent stress.

You can grade papers while waiting in the doctor's office, read professional journals while waiting for the bus, and so forth. So take work with you in a folder or briefcase and try to take advantage of any free time you might have.

TIME MANAGEMENT: THE KEY TO EFFECTIVE PLANNING

Managing your planning time effectively and efficiently is critical to preventing stress. A general time management strategy consists of five steps:

1. *Analyze:* Record how you spend your time. Figure out what you spend too much time on.

2. *Set goals:* Identify the things that you want to accomplish and by what time.

3. *Prioritize:* Decide which goals you must achieve first. Group similar tasks together to save even more time.

4. *Delegate:* Farm out some of the work that someone else can do. Delegate tasks to your students, students' parents, assistant teachers, volunteers, and your own family members, if they don't mind.

5. *Plan:* Create an action plan that describes how you can achieve your goals identified in step 2.

Your action plan that describes how you can achieve your goals can include several of the following tips to help maximize your efficiency. There have been several books written about time management over the past couple of decades. Check them out for timesaving ideas.

- Prioritize activities.
- Avoid extra work by learning how to say no.
- Structure time by allotting a reasonable amount of time for a task and moving on to something else when the time is over.
- Take short breaks.
- Pace yourself.
- Do the toughest tasks early in the day.
- Handle each piece of paper once (either act on it immediately, file it for future action, refer it to someone else, or throw it out).
- Expect that you might not be done at the end of the day; there's always more to do.
- Do one thing at a time.
- Don't let others waste your time.
- Delegate paperwork or other chores that someone else, such as a student, aide, or volunteer, could do with less than four hours of training.
- Avoid perfectionism.
- Organize your desk and materials.
- Minimize procrastination by deciding what to do first and starting on small tasks.
- Break the job down into smaller tasks.
- Give yourself a reward after completing a task.

- Set a deadline that is earlier than the real deadline.
- Group telephone calls.
- Make the most of downtime. Bring books to read, papers to grade, and lesson plans to write while waiting for appointments and other personal "wait times."
- Take breaks to restore energy.

Your colleagues have undoubtedly learned lots of unique ways to save time, so tap into their creativity, and use your own to think of some other ways. The following are some time management tips specifically for teachers that perhaps you can also use:

- Create forms for recording information from meetings, observations of students, grades, and anecdotal notes.
- Create a conference form that includes a place for you to record questions you need to ask and a place to record outcomes of the conversation.
- Prioritize students' assignments and which parts of them you will check (for example, the first and last problems on homework assignments).
- Check students' in-class or homework assignments only on certain days of the week, and allow students to check their own or each other's work often.
- Make classroom learning centers cover work previously covered in class, and make them self-checking.
- Keep folders or index cards with each child's emergency information handy.
- Use a spreadsheet program or other software to record and average grades.
- Ask a parent to help you run off materials, grade objective-type papers, set up and take down bulletin boards, and make games.
- Use the computer to document, update, and save lesson plans.
- When you're unable to answer the phone, use voice mail or an answering machine or ask the school secretary to give callers a specific time to call back. If a caller is not available at that time, ask for a time that they will be available to take your call.
- Keep a notepad by your bed to record those late-night inspirations that are too often lost by morning.
- When you record a meeting in your plan book, include details regarding what, when, why, and details about any personal responsibilities or materials you might need. By including this information right in your plan book, you avoid having to search for it as the meeting nears. Also, create a folder where you keep all the materials you will need for future meetings so you don't waste time gathering your materials at the last minute.
- Write down everything you have to do, in the order of importance, and scratch off items as you complete them.
- Store items of similar use together.

Ask yourself the following questions to help you identify your biggest time wasters and to put some plans in place to address them:

5.3 How do you spend your planning time? Do you spend too much time on certain tasks?

5.4 How can you structure your planning time and organize yourself so that you can accomplish as much as possible?

5.5 Which time management tips can you use to maximize your efficiency?

SUMMARY

In this chapter, you examined your entire schedule. You set aside the time to achieve your personal and professional development goals by scheduling these activities first. You then recorded schedules for school and student activities as well as your classroom teaching schedule. With these schedules identified and recorded, you were able to identify and analyze your planning time. In addition, you considered some time management strategies to help you make the most of your planning time. Congratulations! You've laid out your entire schedule. It now becomes the framework for the instructional and climate action plans you will develop in the next two chapters.

6

Develop an Instructional Plan

INTRODUCTION AND OBJECTIVES

Once you've mapped out your schedule, you can focus on developing your instructional plan. You probably had extensive training in developing instructional plans when you were studying to become a teacher. Since instructing is the focus of a teacher's job, resources in every aspect of developing an effective instructional plan are abundant. Therefore, this chapter only highlights the process. However, if you feel you need more help, don't hesitate to revisit your college textbooks and notes, ask your colleagues for assistance, get help from your local teacher association(s), find support and information at Web sites for teachers, or obtain some of the many quality curriculum resources now available on the market.

The objectives of this chapter are to help you

- Design quality unit plans
- Use strategies that enhance your lesson plans for maximum learning

DESIGN QUALITY UNIT PLANS

Quality unit plans are thorough and effective in helping your students achieve instructional goals. By keeping your students interested and on task, quality unit plans prevent student discipline problems and thus help you avoid a major stressor. Your students enjoy the success they achieve through high-quality unit plans, as do their parents and your administrators. Therefore, it is important to learn how to create excellent unit plans within the planning time you have identified.

If you're a new teacher, creating unit plans is probably the skill in which you've had the most training and the least experience. If you're a veteran teacher, you probably have a lot of experience creating unit plans, but perhaps your creativity needs a jump start or the process isn't as efficient as you'd like it to be. Whether you're just starting your teaching career or you've been teaching for years, the brief review offered here can help you create great unit plans.

What Are Unit Plans?

Unit plans are not lesson plans, although any good unit plan includes lesson plans. Unit plans are developed topics or themes that teach several related goals over the course of a few days, a few weeks, or even a few months. The related goals might be from one subject, such as mathematics, or they might be from two or more subjects, such as social studies and language arts. A table of contents for a unit plan consists of an introduction (a brief summary justifying the use of the topic or theme), goals and behavioral objectives, subject matter, possible methods of starting the unit, possible lesson activities, possible culminating projects, suggested methods of evaluation (formative and summative), resources, and lesson plans. Most veteran teachers agree that the more time and effort you put into creating these units up front, the more use you get out of them later.

How to Create a Unit Plan

To help you prevent stress, fully develop only one or two units at a time, but develop an outline or framework of all the units you'll need for the entire year. To create a framework for the school year, map your curriculum goals by using the process described in the sections that follow. Then all you have left to do during the school year is to develop your behavioral objectives and lesson plans. Keep in mind, however, that many teachers recommend preparing a lesson, with associated materials and handouts, at least one week before the day you present it. Many teachers say they need at least two weeks' preparation to prevent stress most effectively.

Right now, just concentrate on completing steps 1 through 6. In Chapter 8, you'll map out the use of your future planning time to complete the remaining steps (which include lesson planning).

Step 1: Identify Your Instructional Goals

Start with all the instructional goals you identified in Chapter 4. Write each one on a separate strip of paper. To save some time, you can photocopy the goals from your curriculum guide, standard course of study, or learning results outline (whichever your school system uses), using a different-colored sheet of paper for each subject area, such as language arts, math, science, and so forth. Then cut out each goal. Having them separate will be helpful later when you try to combine the goals into logical combinations.

Step 2: Classify Your Instructional Goals

Using a large sheet of paper (bulletin board paper or butcher paper is helpful), create a chart with the different curriculum areas you are responsible to teach labeled across the top (this could be different subjects, such as math, science, and social studies, or it could be areas within a subject, such as counting, classification, and patterning for the subject of mathematics). Down the left side, place three labels: content, skills, and attitudes. Figure 6.1 is a sample chart.

Figure 6.1. Sample Curriculum Chart

	Reading	Writing	Social Studies	Math	Science
Content					
Skills					
Attitudes					

Complete the chart by placing your goals in the correct areas and color-coding each goal using different-colored markers to identify which curriculum area and which kind of goal it is. For example, place a yellow dot on all content goals, a blue dot on all skill goals, and a pink dot on all attitude goals. Color-coding your goals will help save time later.

Step 3: Make Logical Connections Among Your Goals

After color-coding your goals, begin to make logical connections among them. Examine all your goals and identify which ones you can logically teach within the same unit.

Many goals can be taught and learned together very effectively because they are the content, skills, and attitudes needed to answer a particular real-life question. For example, several mathematics and science goals can be taught together. Some of the topics that cross both these subjects are collecting, organizing, and displaying data. Therefore, a real-life question that ties a particular science and mathematics unit together might be, "What are different ways to collect, organize, and display data?" A theme that might be used to answer this question is air and atmosphere. Another theme that could be used is rocks and minerals. The theme chosen is usually driven by the content goals that you identified in Step 2.

Make your instruction relevant. Be sure your students see how the content relates to them and the world of work.

Notice that the theme is not the focus of your unit. The focus of your unit is the real-life question, also known as the essential question. Most units will have two to five logical, sequential essential questions for a three-week to three-month unit. The questions are the unifying elements of all the goals in the unit and they reflect your conceptual priorities. They drive your unit because they help determine which activities you should do in your unit. Essential questions, when shared with and understood by your students, provide a meaningful reason to learn the content, skills, and attitudes outlined in your curriculum. The majority of students who drop out of school have no idea why they were in school in the first place.

Essential questions help your students see a purpose to what they are learning and a reason to come to school. For the duration of each unit you teach, post essential questions in your classroom to remind your students of the main goals of your unit. To develop essential questions, consider the following:

6.1 What are the most important concepts that your students should investigate about the unit?

6.2 What are the most important concepts that they should remember a year from now and reflect on?

I didn't always create units around questions. I used to choose my themes first and then try to group a bunch of my goals into them, whether they fit together logically or not. I also used to think that I was integrating curriculum when I used plastic bear counters in a math lesson during my "bear unit." I learned that what I was doing was just inserting a cute idea, not integrating curriculum. Most important, I learned that once you've made logical, real-life connections among the goals and developed unifying essential questions, you need to share those questions with your students. Essential questions become the driving force behind the unit because they stimulate thinking and motivate learning. As the name implies, these questions are the essential element of effective instruction.

As you combine your goals into logical groups, try to balance the groups with content, skills, and attitude goals so that one group does not have all content goals and another has all attitude goals. This helps keep your units balanced. Note that it doesn't matter if one unit has several more goals than another. The real measure of merit is whether the combination of goals makes sense.

After trying to see which goals logically fit together, you might end up with a handful of goals that really don't fit logically with any other goals. Illogical, meaningless connections only weaken your unit, so don't force goals to fit. Some goals—learning the multiplication tables, for instance—can be taught in isolation. If you find you have a handful of goals left over, just remember to make time to teach them.

6.3 Which goals just don't fit with any others and should be taught separate from any unit?

Make essential questions very powerful by creating ones that present problems that are relevant to students and that they believe are important to solve. An example is, "How does recycling affect the future?"

Step 4: Choose Themes for Your Units

Themes are the content labels for your units. For example, two themes might be the Civil War and plants. Find out from your grade-level or department colleagues if there's a list of reserved themes for your grade level or subject. If it does exist, you have a head start. If it does not exist, identify some possible themes by examining your units. The content goals within each unit will help you identify the best theme for each unit. If you teach a self-contained class and are responsible for teaching all subjects, the content goals within each unit (especially for social studies and science) are a good place to start. If you are a high school teacher responsible for teaching one discipline and have chosen not to do integrated units with other departments, the content goals for your discipline will also be the best place to start to find the best themes.

You can get ideas for the grade level or subject you teach by reviewing your collection of resources. These include teacher's manuals, textbooks, computer programs, and any other professional resources you can find for your grade level or subject. Peruse these resources for reoccurring content themes or topics.

Also, keep in mind your students' interests and developmental levels. Simply ask your students to tell you what interests them. Another way to figure out your students' interests is to put books about different content-appropriate themes all around your classroom and ask your students to look at them. Notice which ones they naturally gravitate toward. Keep in mind your interests and expertise, too. If you are already interested in and familiar with a theme, it's easier for you to develop it into a unit plan.

Finally, keep in mind the philosophies and policies of the school, parents, and community. Are there any themes that are encouraged or discouraged? In addition, don't forget to find out if any themes are reserved for other grade levels or departments. You don't want to step on anyone's toes!

Choose a sufficient number of themes for the entire school year. This number depends on the grade level you teach. Ask your colleagues for some sort of number. If you still have no idea, begin with six to eight themes. Develop one or two before you start the school year. You can change the others if your students' interests are different. If you teach all subjects, make sure you balance social studies and science-dominant themes.

6.4 What is the rationale for the themes chosen?
    a. Are they consistent with the curriculum and with the expectations?
    b. Are the themes meaningful, interesting, and developmentally appropriate for your students?

Research tells us that people learn concepts more easily and remember them longer when they explain them to others. Therefore, provide students with many opportunities to explain what they have learned to one another. One strategy is a pair review, where two students take 30-second turns for a total of a couple of minutes to explain to each other their understanding of a certain concept or topic. The goal is to share as much of their knowledge about a concept or topic and make as many connections as possible. The students speaking can use notes and resources as they share and must avoid repeating themselves or their partners. While a student is speaking, the listener is not allowed to ask any clarifying questions. To begin the activity, you might want to provide different starter questions to each team member to help them begin their oral review.

Step 5: Sequence Your Units

Put the units you have created and any goals that were left over into a rough timeline. Sequence the units as logically as possible, and estimate the amount of time you believe each unit will take to complete. Use Resource 6.1 in the Resources for Successful Teaching section or the pacing chart in your lesson plan book for this step.

Step 6: Gather Materials to Develop Your Units

Once you have determined your themes, learn as much as you can about them. Check your libraries, the Internet—anything and anywhere. Visit the children's literature section in your school and public libraries. They have a wealth of information that has already been prepared for students, often making the themes or topics easier to understand than adult nonfiction books on the same subject. Determine if there is enough unbiased information available on the topic. If not, you might want to see if there is a different theme that would be easier for you to develop into a unit plan. Also, if possible, find out what your students already know about the topic to help save time. You can conduct an informal survey or create a KWL chart (what we know, want to know, and have learned).

Finally, learn as much as you can about the theme. Use the resources you have gathered and do any additional research if necessary to increase your knowledge about the topic. You are the instructional leader of the unit, so you need to be the class "expert" on the theme.

6.5 Are there enough quality resources available to create a unit plan for each of the themes? If not, what are other possible themes?

Step 7: Brainstorm Possible Unit Activities

Using everything you have learned about your themes, think about and list what activities you could do with each of them. Sample activities include reading a novel, role-playing, taking a field trip, participating in a lab experiment, doing a demonstration, and so forth. The possibilities are endless. One way to generate these lists is to write down what you think of when you think of the particular theme. You can also write down what you would like to learn about with respect to the theme. At the same time, identify which curriculum goals can be achieved with each of these activities.

To help alleviate late-winter doldrums, look back through your lesson plan book and find lessons that ignited your students' love for learning. Update their content to match your current curriculum goals and objectives, and reuse these dynamite lesson plans to brighten up the gray days of winter.

Step 8: Write Behavioral Objectives

Use the goals and activities to write behavioral objectives. A behavioral objective is a statement that has three parts: a student's observable behavior (written as an action verb with a direct object), a condition that exists for the behavior to occur (such as the materials or learning strategies that are used), and the criteria used to determine minimally acceptable performance or achievement. An example of a behavioral objective is, "Using a graphic organizer, the student will categorize the different modes of transportation into at least three different categories." "Using a graphic organizer" is the condition, "categorize the different modes of transportation" is the observable behavior, and "at least three different categories" is the minimum criterion for acceptable performance. Keep in mind your students' IEP goals and objectives as you do this. Use the following question to assess the quality of your objectives:

6.6 Is the group of objectives for each unit representative of all the levels in Bloom's Taxonomy (knowledge, comprehension, application, analysis, synthesis, evaluation)?

Step 9: Design Effective Lesson Plans

Behavioral objectives, which include the activities, goals, and evaluation criteria, are the framework for your lesson plans. If the objectives are clear, meaningful, and realistic, it is easy to write effective lesson plans. And if the lesson plans are effective, your students are more likely to succeed, achieving higher test scores, better retention, and more positive attitudes toward school.

The greater the structure of a lesson and the more precise the directions are for activities and tasks, the higher the achievement rate of students.

You might not always design an effective lesson. If you find that something is not working well during a lesson, be flexible and change it. Have a backup plan available, and make a note on the lesson plan of what went wrong so that you can improve the lesson for next time.

An effective lesson plan includes

- The time allotted for the lesson
- The instructional goals
- The behavioral objectives

- The materials needed
- A "focus and review" activity to get students' attention and to relate the current lesson to previous learning
- A motivational introduction to get students involved early
- Teacher input for the lesson, including the teaching strategies and activities that will be used and what the teacher will model to help students meet the objectives
- A guided (supervised) practice activity to help students practice the newly learned content, skill, or attitude and allow the teacher to prevent students from practicing errors
- Formative assessment activities that show how the teacher will check for understanding during the teacher input part of the lesson and the guided practice
- An independent practice activity (done in class or for homework) to allow students to internalize the new learning
- Ways to give constructive feedback to students (this is a must because research shows that feedback is the teacher behavior that matters most for strong student achievement)
- Closure that reviews and summarizes the main ideas of the lesson and what students learned
- A homework assignment for further practice of mastered skills
- Summative assessment activities to measure the achievement of the instructional goals of the lesson

While creating your lesson plans, be aware of how much time you have to do the lesson with your students. Also, make a note of how you plan to group your students (one large group or several small groups). Remember to add a note in your lesson plan to explain to students how they are assessed and any due dates for their independent and homework assignments.

Begin the lesson with a rich activity, leaving reading assignments for later. Students thus get the background and motivation needed to understand the reading material.

Assess the quality of your lesson plans by answering these questions:

6.7 Have you provided diversification in the following?
   a. Types of activities
   b. Instructional strategies (including small- and large-group instruction)
   c. Teaching styles

     d. Matching different learning styles
     e. Accommodating different learning modalities
     f. Supporting and strengthening the multiple intelligences

6.8   Do the activities keep students actively involved?

6.9   Is there enough individualization to ensure success for all of your students?

6.10 Are the lessons interesting and worthwhile?

6.11 Do you create small groups of students for instruction or for certain activities?
     a. How are the groups determined (for example, by language or by ability)?
     b. How often are these groups used?
     c. How do the lists of members change and how often?
     d. Are these groups empowering or inhibiting for your students?

6.12 Have you included information about what students should do if they finish the guided and independent assignments before their peers?

6.13 Do you have or want to have extra-credit activities?

6.14 Do any of the lessons have potential points of failure? Is there anything in the lesson you can change to avoid failure? If the lesson should not go as planned, do you have a "plan B" available?

Step 10: Plan for Assessments and Evaluations

Plan for different types of assessments and evaluations, both formative and summative. How to do this is discussed in more depth later in this chapter. Don't forget to analyze your lesson plans to make sure they include assessment activities.

6.15 What kinds of assessment do your lessons include?
     a. Do your lessons have built-in mechanisms that provide for manageable ways of collecting the information needed for ongoing assessment or grades?
     b. Do the lessons give students the experience of different types of assessments, such as paper-and-pencil tests, presentations, rubrics, and others? Is each type of assessment appropriate for the task or project it is assessing?
     c. Do you have a portfolio set up for each student? What items from this unit will go into students' portfolios?
     d. How many grades or evaluations do you need to get a true picture of a student's achievement?
     e. Is the grading and evaluation practice you have chosen consistent with school policy?

Also, design pre- and posttests for your unit goals. Pretests help determine whether your students have the prerequisite knowledge they need to succeed with the unit. Combined with posttests, they help you quantify your students' growth and progress as a result of the unit. The test results also help you evaluate the effectiveness of your unit as a whole. See Figure 6.2 for some test administration tips to help you and your students prevent the stress usually associated with test administration and test taking.

Figure 6.2. Test Administration Tips

Tests are just one way to assess achievement. Use these test administration tips to help you and your students successfully handle the stress associated with test taking.

Before giving the test:
- Prepare students for the test by giving them the test date and any review material they might need several days in advance.
- Schedule the test well in advance of any grade-reporting deadlines so you have enough time to correct the tests.

During the test:
- Make sure students are comfortable and have enough elbow room.
- Seat students away from others that might pressure them to rush through their test.
- Schedule enough time to give the test so you and your students do not feel pressured by time constraints.
- Tell them how much time they have to complete the test.
- Review what you expect them to do in case of a fire drill or other type of interruption.
- Reiterate that they should do their own work, and explain the consequences if they are caught cheating.
- Review how to ask for help during the test if they should need it.
- Review what they should do if they finish the test early.
- Wait until there are no more questions before handing out the test.

Note that at the beginning of the year, you need to perform a special assessment of your students to determine their achievement and retention of curriculum goals from the previous school year. You can use ready-made diagnostic or achievement tests, or you can make your own using review items from textbooks and materials your students used the previous year. Analyzing your students' work samples from the previous year and from the first few days of school also gives you clues of their achievement to date. Making observations, conducting interviews, and administering interest and attitude surveys are additional ways to assess your students.

To help in designing assessments, ask, "What are the learning outcomes?" "Why are you assessing and how will the results be used?" and "For whom are the results intended?" Check the validity of your assessments by asking, "Is it possible for a student to have mastered the learning outcomes and not be able to do well on this task?" and "Is it possible for a student to do this task well and not have mastered the learning outcome?" If you can answer yes to either of the last two questions, alter the assessment until you can answer no to both.

Step 11: Evaluate the Unit

Both you and your students should do a summative evaluation of each unit. Your students should write (if developmentally appropriate) about the parts of the unit they feel were the best and the worst and why they feel this way. This gives you some insight into what to alter for next time. They can also offer ideas about activities that can be added to the unit. You too need to reflect on the unit. Make notes of these things before you put the unit back on the shelf. Ask yourself the following questions:

6.16 What do you think went well and was effective? Which lessons are worth repeating? Which need some work? Which need to be scrapped?

6.17 Was the unit fun for you and your students?

6.18 Was the unit focused and teachable?

6.19 Did the unit have a wide variety of activities?

STRATEGIES THAT ENHANCE LESSON PLANS FOR MAXIMUM LEARNING

This section examines some of the latest research in education that you can use to improve the effectiveness of your lesson plans. The information highlighted in this section includes

- The latest brain research and what it means for teachers
- How people process and acquire information
- The different kinds of intelligences all people possess
- Effective questioning techniques
- How to use different types of assessments effectively

Apply the Latest Brain Research

The past decade has witnessed tremendous progress in the area of brain research, particularly in how the brain learns. By applying this new research, you can make teaching and learning more effective.

Brain research clearly supports the link between a person's emotions and the ability to learn. For example, when a person is stressed, chemicals are released in the body that impair memory and learning. As a result, teachers must create a supportive classroom climate that reduces student stress so effective learning can take place. The process of creating a supportive classroom climate will be discussed in the next chapter.

Brain research also shows that learning occurs when neural connections grow. This happens when an electrical current passes along the nerve cells and chemicals are discharged into neighboring cells. The more often these pathways are exercised, the greater the retention of the activity or material. Therefore, the more students repeat a learning task, the more automatic or learned the task becomes.

Further, because different parts of the brain store different parts of a memory, learning requires both the acquisition of information as well as the ability to reconstruct the information from different parts of the brain. It has been found that differences in learning styles affect how the student retrieves and reconstructs stored information. Therefore, it is important to accommodate different learning styles in your lesson plans. Repeating the learning in a variety of modes or learning styles is best.

Take advantage of the fact that words set to music are easier to recall than words without music. Borrow a popular tune that your students have already memorized and have your students change the words to match the concepts, skills, and attitudes you want them to learn and remember. Add movement to the mix and further enhance learning with this additional modality.

Research has also found that the brain uses less energy when a person performs familiar or similar functions than when learning a completely new skill. Therefore, design lessons that allow students to use prior knowledge to learn a skill, attitude, or information. In addition to explicitly demonstrating the links to prior knowledge, teach students how to identify similarities and patterns that underlie concepts so that when you are removed from the learning process, they will still have the skill to find the connections themselves.

Finally, experiential learning, or hands-on learning, has been found to exercise the parts of the brain responsible for higher-order thinking. It also has shown that the brain exerts less effort in learning when hands-on tasks are used. Thus, try to integrate some type of hands-on activity into every lesson plan. Also, allow students to demonstrate learning using a variety of experiential activities, such as dramatizations, music, oral and visual presentations, and so forth.

Applying the latest brain research to your teaching is one way to ensure that you are creating effective lessons that will help your students achieve success. Ask the following question to find out if your lessons take advantage of the latest research:

6.20 Do your lessons accomplish the following?
  a. Allow students to repeat the learning task in variety of ways
  b. Show a direct link with previous learning
  c. Include a lot of hands-on learning

Take Into Account Your Students' Learning Styles

Learning styles describe how people process information. Dr. Anthony Gregorc has identified four basic learning styles: concrete sequential, abstract sequential, concrete random, and abstract random (see Coil, 1997, pp. 26–29 for more information about Gregorc's theory). Studies show that there is a positive relationship between accommodating students' learning styles in the classroom and student achievement and attitude. Therefore, it is important to design your lesson plans with these learning styles in mind.

The different styles are combinations of two pairs of opposites. Both concrete styles use objects and hands-on, experiential learning, while both abstract styles use theoretical thinking. With sequential learning styles, students process information in a linear, orderly fashion, whereas students with random styles process information in no particular order.

Concrete sequential students usually do well in school because most schools reward concrete sequential behavior. Students with this style of learning like to read and follow directions in the order that they are given. They like to take notes, make charts, and create outlines; enjoy hands-on activities; and do well with assignments that have concrete products. A weakness of concrete sequential processors is that they often are unimaginative and appear to lack creativity.

Students with the abstract sequential style are similar to concrete sequential processors in that they usually do very well academically and in school. Like concrete sequential processors, abstract sequential students like to read. They also like to listen to audiotapes, watch videos, see films, and work on the computer. Abstract sequential processors enjoy finding the answer to a problem and have difficulty accepting multiple answers and possibilities. They like to look at things logically, even when a logical solution might not be the best. A weakness of the abstract sequential type is that they are often socially immature because their intuitive and emotional skills tend to be weak.

Many students find it difficult to stay organized, especially when it comes to doing and handing in homework. Increase students' organization skills by giving each one a "turning in assignments" folder that remains in class. Color-code the folders for each class to help you stay organized. Hand out a weekly or biweekly outline that shows what you will be doing in class plus all of the assignments and due dates for that time period, and place a duplicate copy in the left pocket of students' "turning in assignments" folder. Each day, students remove any graded papers from the folder and replace them with any that are due that day. To further help your students stay on top of turning in their assignments, you can use the outline in the folder as a checklist for each student, making it easy for you to communicate what was or was not turned in on time.

Schools usually have a more difficult time accommodating concrete random learners. Students with the concrete random style of processing like to complete a product for a classroom assignment but might not turn it in on time. They are not afraid to take risks and will contribute many ideas to classroom discussions because they usually don't worry about being incorrect. They do things by trial and error, not by following directions, prefer to work alone rather than in groups, and like to solve problems by tinkering with concrete objects until something works out. Concrete random style processors usually do not do very well on multiple-choice, true/false, or other types of objective tests because they can see the possibility of multiple correct answers; even the incorrect answers seem justifiable to them.

Finally, abstract random processors are usually the ones always talking. They like to work in groups and like to listen to, learn from, and respond to classmates. Short reading assignments are best for abstract random processors because they find it hard to sit still for long periods. They use a lot of intuition and emotion instead of logic to come up with answers. Abstract random processors usually have a lot of things going on at once but have a hard time following through on many of these things over time.

One way to accommodate all four learning styles is to design an array of activities for each lesson, especially for the independent practice, homework, and summative assessment pieces. For example, you might want to have certain activities in your lesson plan that every student must complete, but then offer choices of four different assignments, each accommodating a different learning style. Because no one has the luxury of always working in one particular style, structure the student-choice piece so students must choose a second assignment from a different learning style. For example, ask students to complete two or three of the four student-choice assignments. This forces students to process information using styles other than their own.

6.21 How can you design lesson activities that accommodate each learning style and meet your lesson's goals and objectives?

6.22 Does every lesson in some way allow for each of the four learning styles?

Accommodate Your Students' Learning Modalities

Unlike learning styles, which deal with how people process information, learning modalities are concerned with how people acquire or perceive information. Based on the five senses, the five modalities are visual, auditory, kinesthetic, olfactory, and gustatory. The modalities most involved in communication are visual, auditory, and kinesthetic, so these are the three that teachers must be most concerned with when teaching.

Because students learn to acquire information in all three communication modalities, they are not totally visual or auditory or kinesthetic. However, each student will have a modality preference or strength. You can identify their preferred modality by watching them.

How people use their eyes will help you determine which modality they use most of the time. When speaking, if a person tends to look at the ceiling or straight at you, they probably prefer the visual modality. Those who prefer the auditory modality will move their eyes to the right or left, or down to their left. If they move their eyes mostly to their bottom right, they probably prefer the kinesthetic modality.

Make an effort to allow students to choose their preferred modality whenever possible because some students, including those who have disabilities or are gifted, might have a weakness in a particular modality that can interfere with obtaining the information.

Students who prefer a visual modality learn by seeing and watching others. They are good with details and can recall placement of words and pictures on a page. Likewise, they recognize words by sight and remember people's faces but not their names. They are affected by visual displays and color, often remember what they have written down, have vivid imaginations, and have photographic memories. Visual learners also take in many images at once but might not concentrate on any one image for a long time. They use facial expressions that are indicative of their emotions and respond to phrases such as "Do you see what I'm talking about?" and "Look at me!"

Students who are weak visual learners often turn in assignments that are not completed neatly. They read numbers, mathematical signs, or directions incorrectly; leave out letters or words when writing; and have trouble copying from the chalkboard. To help students increase their visual skills, use visuals in your lessons—charts, graphs, illustrations, videos, and so forth—and include activities that allow students to copy, illustrate, imagine, read, and observe.

Auditory learners love to talk. They learn best through verbal instructions from others or themselves. They repeat information out loud or to themselves to aid learning and memory, talk out problems, and try out solutions verbally. These students have good auditory word attack skills, learn words phonetically, and are global thinkers. Unlike visual learners who express their emotions facially, auditory learners use pitch, tone, and volume of voice to express different emotions. They respond well to phrases such as "Do you hear what I'm saying?" and "Think out loud."

Weak auditory learners find it easier to demonstrate something than to explain it. They might have a hard time finding the right words, might ask others to repeat what they have just said, and often have difficulty listening to others. To help strengthen students' auditory skills, assign oral presentations, debates, skits, songs, audiotapes, and so forth. In your lessons, include interviews, discussion, brainstorming, paraphrasing, singing, and so forth.

To increase alertness, blood flow, and energy, get students out of their seats every 10 to 12 minutes. Ask them to take a few deep breaths, and lead them in an engaging, practical activity during this short break. For example, have pairs of students explain the concepts you just discussed to each other, or have students draw, sing, rap, create a flowchart, or list the main points of what they are learning.

Kinesthetic learners are the hands-on types. They learn best with experiential activities. They remember better what they have done than what they have seen or heard. They enjoy physical activities such as athletics and the performing arts and like to touch, feel, and play with objects. They communicate their feelings using their whole bodies and show their emotions physically—hugging and applauding, for instance. They respond best to phrases such as "How does that feel?" and "Are you in touch with that?"

Students who are weak in the kinesthetic modality usually are not good athletes, preferring to be spectators rather than participants. These students appear clumsy and awkward and have trouble putting puzzles together. To help students increase their kinesthetic skills, ask them to work on puzzles, models, murals, and dioramas, and to build, assemble, experiment, and manipulate objects.

As with learning styles, you need to ensure that you are accommodating your students' different learning modalities by using a variety of strategies to communicate with your students. In addition, when speaking with students, use a variety of words that will appeal to students' different modalities. For example, after explaining directions out loud, write them on the chalkboard or overhead projector. Then demonstrate what you are asking them to do and have them practice the activity or parts of the activity with you. Before letting your students begin their assignment, ask, "Do you see what I'm asking you to do? Do you hear what I'm asking you to do? Do you understand what I'm asking you to do?" Offer students a choice of activities so they can choose activities that match their preferred modalities, and offer additional ones that stretch their comfort levels.

6.23 How can you improve your lesson plans to accommodate the different major modalities for communication—visual, auditory, and kinesthetic?

Strengthen Your Students' Multiple Intelligences

Howard Gardner, a Harvard University psychologist, developed his theory of multiple intelligences in the early 1980s (for more information on Gardner's theory, see Coil, 1997, pp. 58–66). The premise of multiple intelligences is that intelligence involves many different ways of solving problems and creating products. According to Gardner, we are stronger in some intelligences than in others, and we can develop or strengthen our intelligences that are lacking or weak. Differences in cultures and experiences are the reason some intelligences become our dominant ones and others develop more moderately or just slightly.

Unlike learning styles, which determine how people process information, or modalities, which determine how people acquire information, multiple intelligences deal directly with the content of the type of intelligence itself. According to Gardner, each individual possesses at least eight different intelligences that are used in combination with one another most of the time. As shown in Figure 6.3, these eight intelligences are divided into three main categories: language related, object related, and personal related. The intelligences in the language category relate to written and spoken languages from around the world. Object intelligences relate to the objects a person works with to solve problems or to make products. The personal category relates to people's self-image and relationships with others as well as the knowledge of cultural norms and social skills.

Figure 6.3. Howard Gardner's Multiple Intelligences

Howard Gardner's Main Categories of Multiple Intelligences		
Language Related	**Object Related**	**Personal Related**
Verbal/linguistic	Logical/mathematical	Intrapersonal
Musical/rhythmic	Visual/spatial	Interpersonal
	Bodily/kinesthetic	
	Naturalist	

The language-related category comprises two intelligences. The first, verbal/linguistic, is characterized by the ability to use language, in all forms, for different purposes, including to communicate, entertain, memorize, and learn. Students with a dominant verbal/linguistic intelligence like to read, write, and tell stories. They are good at memorizing words, places, dates, and trivia. These students learn best by speaking, hearing, and seeing words.

The other language-related intelligence is musical/rhythmic intelligence, characterized by the ability to communicate and understand emotions and ideas through music. Students dominant in musical/rhythmic intelligence like to sing, hum, listen to music, and play an instrument. They are good at remembering melodies, keeping time, picking up sounds, and noticing pitch changes and rhythms. These students learn best with music, melody, and rhythm.

The object-related category includes four intelligences. The first is the logical/mathematical intelligence. Students dominant in this intelligence can recognize and investigate relationships, patterns, and groups using objects or mathematical symbols in a logical, ordered, sequential way. Logical/mathematical students like to work with numbers, figure things out, and do experiments. They are good at math, logic, problem solving, and reasoning. These students learn best by classifying, categorizing, and working with abstract patterns and relationships.

The second intelligence in the object-related category is the visual/spatial intelligence. Those strong in this intelligence have the ability to perceive, create, and change visual objects mentally. They can create and interpret the visual arts and navigate within a specific space or environment. Students dominant in visual/spatial intelligence like to draw, build, design, and create things. They also like to watch movies and daydream and are good at imagining things, doing mazes and puzzles, and reading maps and charts. These students learn best by visualizing and working with colors and pictures.

The bodily/kinesthetic intelligence is the third object-related intelligence. Those strong in this intelligence can use both mind and body to perform physical tasks and can easily manipulate objects within their environment. Bodily/kinesthetic students like to move around, touch, talk, and use body language. They are good at physical activities, such as sports, dancing, and acting, and at creating crafts. These students learn best by touching, moving, and physically interacting with their environment.

The last of the four object-related intelligences is the naturalist intelligence. Those strong in the naturalist intelligence can identify, classify, and discern different plants and animals. They have a keen sense of observation and are skilled at putting order to information about nature. Students dominant in this intelligence like to be outdoors and feel comfortable with nature and the natural world. They are good at making distinctions and comparisons among things in the natural world. In addition, they are good at creating categories and sorting and indexing items found in nature. These students learn best by working directly with nature, conducting experiments and categorizing the data.

The third and final category of Gardner's theory of multiple intelligences is the personal category, comprising intrapersonal and interpersonal intelligences. People dominant in the intrapersonal intelligence are very reflective and have a keen sense of themselves—their own emotions, thoughts, and beliefs. They like to work alone, pursue their own interests and goals, and follow their instincts. These students learn best by working alone using self-paced instruction and individualized projects.

The second personal intelligence is the interpersonal intelligence. Interpersonal people can sense the emotions and needs of others, build relationships, and work well in teams. Interpersonal students have many friends and like to talk to others and join groups. They are good at understanding people, leading others, communicating, and mediating conflicts. These students learn best by sharing, cooperating, relating, and interviewing.

A good way to identify students' strengths is to observe their misbehavior. Students who always talk when they should not are most likely dominant in the verbal/linguistic and interpersonal intelligences. Students who constantly doodle are probably dominant in the visual/spatial intelligence. Students who always fiddle with something in their hands are probably strong in the bodily/kinesthetic intelligence.

Schools traditionally have regarded children who demonstrate both verbal/linguistic and logical/mathematical intelligence as smarter, but it is imperative that teachers do not perpetuate this stereotype. All eight types of intelligences are important and contribute to overall intelligence. Therefore, do not belittle the student whose dominant intelligence is not verbal/linguistic or logical/mathematical.

As a teacher, you must also be aware of your students' strengths and weaknesses in each intelligence. Consider and include all the intelligences when you design unit and lesson plans and student-choice assignments so you use students' strengths to help them more easily achieve your instructional goals. In addition, use their strengths to build up their weak areas. Most important, incorporate a variety of different activities in your daily lesson plans that not only cater to your students' dominant intelligences but also help develop their weaker intelligences. This must happen because our students will need all the intelligences to function effectively in the world of the 21st century.

6.24 Do your lesson plans accommodate the multiple intelligences?

6.25 Do your lesson plans strengthen all the multiple intelligences?

Use Effective Questioning Techniques

Effective questioning practices include asking questions that reflect different levels of Bloom's Taxonomy—knowledge, comprehension, application, analysis, synthesis, and evaluation. Use these different types of questions during oral discussions, on tests, and in a variety of assignments, including textbook reading assignments and research reports.

The knowledge level has to do with the learning and memorization of facts. Questions that check for knowledge include those beginning with the words *who, what, when, where,* and *how.* Comprehension-level questions begin with the words *retell, explain,* and *summarize,* and their goal is to check for understanding. The application level is used to demonstrate the use of information in a new context. Words such as *apply, show,* and *modify* usually appear in application-level questions. The analysis level examines information in detail, one part at a time. *Differentiate, classify,* and *examine* are often used with analysis-level questions. Synthesis-level questions frequently begin with *predict, invent,* and *design* and are aimed at checking for understanding of the information in relation to the whole. Finally, evaluation-level questions begin with words such as *appraise, justify,* and *judge* and are used to assess the value of information by applying standards and criteria.

To help you vary the types of questions you pose to students during a classroom discussion, post question stems on your classroom wall as prompts. Examples of question stems include, "What are the parts or features of . . . ?" (an analysis-level question), "What might happen if you combine . . . with . . . ?" (a synthesis-level question), and "What is the most important . . . ?" (an evaluation-level question). Group the question stems according to their level of Bloom's Taxonomy. This will help you make sure that you are asking questions from each of the different levels.

Always pause about ten seconds after you pose a question to your class to give your students time to think and encourage them to be more complete in their responses. If a student's answer is correct, wait about three to five seconds before giving a verbal reward, because often the student will say more. Remember to always affirm a correct response, because positive feedback for correct responses has been correlated with increased student achievement, especially for students from low socioeconomic backgrounds. Also, if a student gives an answer that is only partially correct, give credit for the correct part. If the answer is incorrect or it does not meet acceptable criteria, avoid using the words *no* and *incorrect* in your response. Instead, repeat what was correct (if anything) and prompt the student for more information. If no part of the answer was correct, probe to find out why the student responded that way. If the student's perspective is very different than what you were looking for, simply point out that some people might share a similar perspective and then go back to your original question before your class becomes sidetracked by the student's response. Help students clarify their answers by asking them to state their responses in another way or to add more information. If the student clearly doesn't know the answer, don't ask another student or answer the question yourself. Instead, rephrase the question or give additional clues to the student to help him or her arrive at the correct answer. This approach has been found to correlate positively with student achievement because it allows the student to save face and to increase his or her feelings of self-esteem.

In addition, increase the amount of student participation by directing the question to several students at once, without constantly repeating or rephrasing the question. This technique reduces teacher talk, helps improve student listening skills, and increases student talk. Use phrases such as "Do you agree?" or "I'd like to hear another answer" to help increase the amount of student participation. Also, refer to previous answers students have given, such as "A few moments ago, Sally said . . ." to help link previous learning with new learning and to boost students' self-esteem by making them feel that their contributions are important to the overall discussion.

6.26 What can you do to improve your questioning skills?

When engaging in classroom discussions, move to the opposite side of the room from the student who is speaking, leaving most of the class in between the two of you. This helps keep you and your students' attention on the whole class and encourages the speaker to speak louder and clearer.

Use a Variety of Assessments

Assessment is gathering information about student progress and achievement using various methods to determine what changes need to be made to improve performance. On the other hand, evaluation is judging the assessment results for one purpose or another. For example, reporting that a student is "working on grade level" indicates an evaluation of the student's achievement, whereas reporting that a student is able to multiply two three-digit numbers together is an assessment of his achievement. When you assess, your students can redo their work to get a better grade. When you evaluate, your students cannot change the grade they earned. To increase student motivation, assess until you know that your students have mastered the instructional goal, and then evaluate to provide the documentation you need for the grade book. This section focuses on traditional and alternative assessments.

Traditional assessments include paper-and-pencil tests that can be graded objectively. These tests often contain multiple-choice, true/false, and matching type questions. They also include standardized tests that are often mandated by school systems and states. The advantages of traditional assessments are that they can be easily administered and easily corrected.

When calculating grades, convert all numbers and letter grades to a system based on 100 percent because it is easier to figure out overall grades and others find it easier to understand.

On the other hand, alternative assessments are based on student performances, most of which are scored using rubrics. When student performance is assessed over time, the assessments are collected in a portfolio. Performance assessments can be gathered just once or periodically for the purpose of measuring progress. The sections that follow give you a closer look at these different types of alternative assessments.

Approximately six weeks into the school year, conference with each of your students about their interim grades to make sure students are aware of their progress and achievement to date. If they are not happy with their progress or achievement, there will still be enough time to improve their performance before the quarter or trimester ends.

Use Student Portfolios

You can use a portfolio assessment as either a container or a method. As a container, it is simply a folder, box, or some other type of container that holds records created by the alternative methods of assessment, including performance products (such as writing samples and projects), rubrics used to assess the performance products, checklists that document observations of task performances, and benchmark items such as culminating projects for different units. As a method, a portfolio goes beyond being just a container and becomes a way to help you analyze student progress. Therefore, when used as a method, the portfolio also contains items collected over time, such as reading logs, anecdotal records (which are teacher-recorded student accomplishments), student-teacher contracts, and student reflections of their own work. This last piece is the biggest key to using the portfolio as a method. When used to assess progress over time, the teacher and student both do the assessing. This helps transfer ownership of learning to the student, which is where it rightfully belongs.

Students lose motivation when they feel that they are not as successful as they want to be. Increase motivation by engaging your students in tracking their progress in acquiring the content, skills, and attitudes outlined in your instructional goals. Help them do this by keeping a checklist of topics studied, skills mastered, and attitudes developed. Also, show them how to create a graph or keep a portfolio of their work that shows evidence of their progress.

The first step in implementing portfolios as a method for assessment is to make two containers for each student, labeled with the student's name. One container, the day-to-day portfolio, will hold all work that the student completes, and the other, the select portfolio, holds pieces selected at different points during the school year. The containers can be simply a folded piece of construction paper or a large box. Next, find an accessible area in your classroom to store the containers because both you and your students need to be able to reach them easily during the school day.

The second step is to decide what you want to keep in the day-to-day portfolio. Performance assessment pieces, described in the next section, and their rubrics should make up the bulk of the portfolio. Also, set up a system for filing. Either allow students to file their own work or assign a portfolio filer (perhaps a parent volunteer could do this) that does the filing for everyone.

Third, choose a logical point in the unit—for example, at the end of a short unit or midway through a large unit—for students to sort their papers and choose what goes in the select portfolio. Give your students criteria for selecting the pieces to include, but allow students to choose their own representative pieces as much as possible. For example, you might tell students that their selections must include a creative writing piece, a research paper in social studies, and a chart. The selected pieces should be filed in the portfolio container, and the remaining papers should go home.

Use the select portfolios at report card time to assess the progress of your students. Select portfolios are also excellent tools for parent-teacher conferences because they can be used to show parents examples of work that support your evaluations or grades. In addition, by the end of the semester or school year, your students will have a rich collection that shows their achievement and growth, making these portfolios great student self-esteem boosters and wonderful mementos.

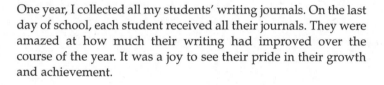

One year, I collected all my students' writing journals. On the last day of school, each student received all their journals. They were amazed at how much their writing had improved over the course of the year. It was a joy to see their pride in their growth and achievement.

Use Performance Assessments

Performances are things a student produces—written, created, built, performed, and so forth. Performances are complex because they involve a group of different learning behaviors. They are open-ended tasks, meaning that they can have more than one solution, and they are coherent because they result in a single product. Performances include projects, writing tasks, and open-ended math tasks (versus math tasks that have only one correct answer and one solution method).

Performance assessments, therefore, are assessments (rating and scoring) of the products of tasks. Rating and scoring are usually done using rubrics (designing rubrics is discussed later in this chapter). Performance assessments include observations of students actually performing tasks, such as science experiments or skits, and documenting the observations with checklists. The best way to create a checklist is to do a task analysis of the performance or project, identifying what really goes into achieving it. For instance, a checklist to assess whether a student uses the scientific method might include tasks such as identifying the problem, posing a hypothesis, creating an experiment, gathering and recording evidence, and making a generalization.

Integrate Authentic Assessments

An authentic assessment is one type of performance assessment that requires students to engage in a real-life issue or problem for an audience that needs to hear or see what the students have learned. This type of assessment helps students make meaningful connections between what they learn in school and what they experience outside school. Further, an authentic assessment allows students to demonstrate what they have learned in the course of a unit and is often used as a culminating project or activity.

Whereas performance assessments could be the result of teacher-designed assignments or prompts, authentic assessments are student generated to solve real-world problems in real time. An authentic assessment has a purpose and an audience, integrates content and skills, and involves in-depth research and inquiry. It also has explicit standards and scoring criteria in the form of rubrics. Authentic assessments allow students to demonstrate their learning in a variety of modes, including written, artistic, and oral presentations. Students use basic and higher levels of thinking and reflect both on the products and processes. Finally, authentic assessments allow students to choose the content, strategies, and time needed to complete the task.

When combined with essential questions, authentic assessments become very effective tools for helping students see the connections between learning and real life. They help students find meaning and purpose to their schooling and to their lives.

Develop and Use Rubrics

Rubrics are scoring guides that differentiate, on an identified scale, among a group of student performances in which all students respond to the same prompt (teacher or student driven). The scale identifies responses that range from excellent to inappropriate and in need of revision.

There are two types of rubrics: holistic and analytic. A holistic rubric is used to measure the overall effect of a performance product with a set of appropriate guidelines. A holistic rubric is not quantitative. On the other hand, an analytic rubric is totally quantitative and consists of elements to look for in a performance product. Because the two types of rubrics measure different things, they can be used alone or together, complementing one another. For example, a holistic rubric can be used to assess the writing process and an analytic rubric can be used to assess the basic mechanical aspects of writing.

You can use a rubric in two ways: as an assessment tool and as a teaching tool. As an assessment tool, a rubric measures or assesses achievement. When given to students ahead of time, the rubric serves as a guide, a teaching tool, to help them create a performance product that will obtain a high score. Failure is not part of a teaching rubric because students are always given the chance to try again.

Because you know what you have been teaching and what you expect from your students, you are best qualified to create rubrics for your units. You know what distinguishes excellent and average achievement from achievement that needs remediation. Ready-made rubrics usually do not accurately reflect your instructional goals or your expectations. Therefore, take the time to create your own.

To create your own rubrics, decide on a performance task that you believe would best be assessed using a rubric. Writing assignments are good candidates. Next, isolate the skills that you want students to master. Begin with a three-point rubric because it is the easiest to create. The three points are a high pass score, a pass score, and a needs-revision score. The three points parallel one another and designate different achievement levels of the same skills, the skills you want students to master. The highest score, a 3, contains all the features of a pass score, a 2, but includes a more advanced variation of the features. A score of 1 denotes the work needs revision. A score of 0 indicates no response given or no performance product turned in.

When using a rubric, if you find that you get no 3 products, check to see if the assignment required something you did not teach or if the rubric includes something that was not asked for in the prompt or assignment directions. If you find that you have all 3 products, either all your students have mastered the instructional goals or you set your expectations too low. If you receive no passing papers, check to make sure that your directions for the assignment were clear and that your students are familiar with the product format you were expecting. If you get results that appear to be inconsistent with how you feel your students are doing in class, check your rubric again or reassess your beliefs about your students' achievement. Finally, because rubrics are very useful teaching and assessment tools, take the time to learn more about how to develop quality rubrics by consulting professional resources and participating in available training on the topic.

A Final Word About Assessments

It's especially important to use alternative assessments because they offer a more complete picture of each student's progress and achievement than traditional assessments. But don't abandon the use of traditional assessments unless your school has done so. Most school systems still use traditional assessments as the basis for measuring and reporting student achievement and schoolwide achievement and for assessing teacher effectiveness. In addition, most parents understand traditional assessments better than alternative assessments.

Most school systems use report cards to report student achievement, using grades to report assessment data collected over time. Other school systems use their report cards to report evaluations of student achievement, using grades to compare students with one another. One way to find out which way your school system uses report cards is to read the back of the report card or any other information your school system provides for its teachers that explains what the grades mean. If the explanation refers to a comparison to the "average" student at that particular grade level or refers to a comparison to peers, then you know that the report card is an evaluation, not an assessment, of the student's achievement.

Obtain a copy of the report card that you are required to use and look at the categories listed on it. Make sure you collect enough data to accurately assess each student's achievement in each of those categories. Collect at least one piece of work for each category per week, and by the end of the quarter or trimester, you should have collected enough data to make an accurate overall assessment and evaluation.

Further, find out what grading scale is required on your report cards. For example, are grades reported as percentages or as letter grades such as A, B, and C? Many report cards for primary grades use letters such as S (usually denotes satisfactory), I (usually denotes showing improvement), and N (usually denotes needs improvement). Find out what letters or symbols are used on your report cards, and make sure you understand how other teachers at your school determine what is an A, S, and so forth. You probably do not want to be the only one who determines them in a certain way because parents and administrators might not understand your grading system.

With respect to report card comments, keep them succinct. Begin with a positive statement about the student's progress or achievement, and close with a statement that identifies an area that needs improvement plus what the student and family can do to help improve that area.

As mentioned in Chapter 2, it's important to impress on your students that their grades are earned, not given by you or anyone else. Teach them that they are responsible for their own learning, and prepare them for their report cards. Although your students should have been told at the beginning of the year or semester how grades would be determined, review the grading system periodically with them so that there are no surprises.

Finally, because alternative assessments give you more information about your students' progress and achievement than traditional assessments, make an effort to use this type of assessment as often as possible. Make the effort to create effective rubrics and to use portfolios to assess student progress and achievement. During parent-teacher conferences, Open House, Back to School Night, and so forth, take some time to educate parents on the value of using alternative assessments in addition to traditional assessments. You'll gain the support and encouragement you need to make alternative assessments an integral part of your teaching repertoire.

6.27 Which types of assessments and evaluations are required?

6.28 Which types of alternative assessments can you incorporate into your teaching to make your teaching more effective and your students' learning more successful?

Screen your telephone calls the day report cards go home. If you receive calls from parents or students, return the calls within 24 hours. When you do, make sure you have in front of you copies of their report cards and all your supporting assessment data.

SUMMARY

This chapter discussed how to create an instructional plan. It highlighted an 11-step process to create effective unit plans. In addition, strategies that enhance the effectiveness of lesson plans were highlighted and discussed. Strategies included accommodating individual differences with respect to how people learn and implementing alternative forms of assessment.

7

Develop a Climate Plan

INTRODUCTION AND OBJECTIVES

Climate is the atmosphere created by the emotional health of the relationships that exist among the members of your classroom and between your classroom and everyone else. A supportive classroom climate helps teachers and students succeed. Studies show that there is a clear and positive correlation between student achievement and a teacher's ability to build and maintain a healthy classroom climate using sound classroom management. A negative classroom climate—one characterized as unsupportive and critical—has been found to have adverse physiological and psychological effects on students. As the teacher, you have tremendous control over your classroom climate and thus over whether your students succeed.

Establishing a supportive classroom climate is one of teachers' most difficult jobs because it deals with the affective domain, an area in which teachers are not usually well versed or well trained. Establishing a supportive classroom climate is not for the faint of heart, nor is it for those who refuse to see the world from another's perspective. However, a supportive classroom climate pays huge dividends: Teachers can reduce classroom disruptions by 65 percent to 90 percent and thereby improve student productivity.

Every year each of us hopes for a "good class," in which all our students are self-disciplined, self-motivated, cooperative, kind, and loving. Even if the majority of your students have these positive personal qualities, if you are not a good classroom manager, your class will fall apart as the year progresses. Even the best of students need affective leadership in the classroom. And if your classroom includes students who are not self-disciplined, self-motivated, cooperative, kind, or loving—as many classrooms do—strong affective leadership can and will bring the order, safety, security, and sense of belonging that students need to blossom. It's hard work, and you might have to "go the extra mile" for those students who find it very difficult to demonstrate positive personal qualities, but they, too, will move toward these affective goals. They, too, can blossom under empathetic, nurturing, consistent, firm, compassionate, and fair leadership. If you practice strong affective leadership, will you have the "perfect class" by the end of the school year? Maybe not, but you'll probably have more students who exhibit desirable affective qualities than you did at the beginning of the school year.

The first step in becoming a strong affective leader is to believe that you can lead and that your students are capable of obtaining the positive personal qualities they do not already possess. Believe that you can lead because affective leadership skills can be developed. You can learn how to exercise both empathy and active listening skills, two modes of conduct that go hand in hand and are the foundation for strong affective leadership. Second, you must continually expand your understanding of why students behave as they do. For example, are you aware that more than 80 percent of misbehavior occurs when teachers ask students to perform developmentally inappropriate tasks (academic, social, or emotional)? Do you understand that people behave as they do because they are trying to satisfy their basic needs for enjoyment, autonomy, meaningful involvement, purpose, safety, success, and belonging? And that when students believe that they do not belong or feel that they are not significant, they often adopt defensive behavior, behavior that may be seen as misbehavior? The third step in becoming a strong affective leader is becoming well versed in a variety of classroom management skills, many of which are discussed in this chapter. And fourth, you must be committed to being consistent and fair, and to never give up on the "tough ones."

Because you are the leader of your classroom, everything you do has an impact on the climate. Most important, though, is how you manage the interpersonal relationships between you and your students and among your students. These relationships are further affected by how you manage the instructional pace, the transitions between activities, and your classroom's physical environment. In addition, how you manage the interpersonal relationships between your students and people outside your class has an impact on classroom climate.

The objectives of this chapter are to help you

- Manage the interpersonal relationships within your classroom, including the relationships between you and your students and the relationships among your students
- Manage the interpersonal relationships between you and your students' parents
- Manage the interpersonal relationships between you and those with whom you work
- Manage the physical environment of your classroom

THE FIRST FEW DAYS OF SCHOOL

Climate is predominantly established in the first few days of school. Therefore, as you read the rest of this chapter, keep in mind that you should plan for or complete most of the suggestions made here before the school year begins or before you begin a teaching assignment if you are hired midyear. If this is not possible, make an extra effort to do these things within the first few weeks of school. Remember, the more you do ahead of time, the better. It gives you greater control during the first few days of school, the most critical time of the school year for establishing a positive climate.

On the first day of school, give every student a blank seating chart, and ask students to complete their charts as you complete the master copy on an overhead projector. This helps students get to know one another more quickly and promotes a sense of belonging to your class.

ESTABLISH STRONG INTERPERSONAL RELATIONSHIPS

The most important factor affecting climate is the tone of the interpersonal relationships that exist inside and outside your classroom. If you want to become a successful teacher, you need to become an effective manager of the interpersonal relationships that exist within your classroom and of the relationships between your class and everyone else.

You can manage interpersonal relationships in two ways: in real time as they happen or ahead of time by planning different ways to ensure that any interpersonal interactions that occur are positive. Look at the interpersonal relationships that exist within your classroom and the relationships between your class and everyone else in these two ways.

Relationships Within Your Classroom

The interpersonal relationships within your classroom consume most of your day. Therefore, it is very important that this part of your plan is very thorough. The following sections describe critical ways you can successfully manage the relationships within your classroom.

Use Empathy and Active Listening Skills

To establish and maintain a positive classroom climate, teachers need to show students how to develop a deep respect and sense of caring for themselves and others while understanding and accommodating others' points of view. Empathy and active listening skills will help you accomplish this goal.

Empathy is acknowledging the feelings of others. But it goes beyond saying "I understand." It includes allowing others to vent and problem solve. One barrier to empathetic understanding is fear of being influenced by another's point of view. Also, because we tend to react to any emotionally charged statement by forming an evaluation from our own point of view, we find it difficult to see another's frame of reference when the situation is emotionally charged.

Listen with understanding. See the expressed idea and attitude from the other person's perspective. Achieve her or his frame of reference.

Active listening is the skill you use to show empathy. When a student misbehaves, gather information about the situation by listening actively to the student, give the student the opportunity first to vent and then to come to a self-inspired resolution. Active listening requires that you respond, not react, to the misbehaving student. It also requires that you do not speak up for yourself until after you have restated the ideas and feelings of the student accurately and to the student's satisfaction.

The skill of active listening actually involves several skills. First, you must paraphrase the other's feelings accurately. You accomplish this by listening to what the other person is saying—both verbally and nonverbally—and then making a statement labeling the feeling or feelings the person conveyed, such as "You are feeling angry." Second, you must accurately paraphrase and repeat the content of what you just heard in your own words, as in "Sally took your paper without your permission." Third, use door openers and acknowledgment responses to show empathy. Door openers like "Tell me more" and "Sounds interesting" illicit more information and allow the other person to vent. Acknowledgment responses show your empathy and include words such as "yes," "right," and "certainly." Other phrases you can use to express empathy include

- "Please tell me more about it."
- "Because . . . , you're feeling. . . ."
- "It's okay to feel. . . . Let's talk about it."

- "Sounds like this situation makes you feel. . . ."
- "My sense is that you are. . . ."
- "I can see that this isn't easy for you. Do you want some help?"

You can also show empathy through nonverbal communication, such as nodding your head, looking at the person in the eye, and leaning toward the person.

Activities that hamper active listening and empathy include using roadblocks. Roadblocks come in many forms, but the most common include lecturing, judging, warning (for example, "You had better. . . ."), disapproving, advising, diagnosing, arguing, criticizing, sympathizing, praising, questioning (ask why, who, and what only after the person speaking has finished), using sarcasm, and joking. These are called road-blocks because they block the person speaking and they change the direction of the flow of information.

Another activity that hampers active listening is the "happy hooker"—using one thought from the speaker to hook in your own thoughts and opinions. For example, a student says she or he is angry about a grade, and you respond by saying something like "I remember when I was your age and I received a bad grade and. . . ." In addition, "ships passing in the night" is when you talk about your own thoughts without giving any indication that you have heard what the other person has said. Finally, there is the nonverbal turnoff, such as a frown, a yawn, or turning away from the speaker.

You might be thinking that active listening stuff is all well and good, but is it an effective technique for handling a misbehavior that is emotionally charged with anger? If you have a student who is angry or involved in some type of conflict, you must defuse the anger before attempting to resolve the situation. According to Davis (1998), there are two ways to deal with emotionally charged situations, both of which require that you make a conscious effort to temporarily forget your own wants and needs and focus on the needs of the angry person.

The first method is the art of CALM: calm yourself, attend to the other person, listen to what the angry person is saying, and model active listening practices. This method requires you to remain neutral and show genuine concern for the angry person. Seek first to understand, then to be understood.

The second method is to take the HEAT: hear the person out, empathize, apologize for the problem by expressing regret that the person is experiencing the problem, and take action by summarizing the problem and assuring the person that some kind of corrective action will take place.

In real time, teachers need to use empathy and active listening skills when interacting with students. Likewise, teachers need to teach their students how to listen actively to one another and to the teacher. The easiest way to teach these skills is to use instructional strategies that employ the skills, such as many different cooperative learning strategies or structures.

One cooperative learning strategy that teaches students both active listening skills and empathy is the Split Agree-Disagree Line-Up strategy outlined by Kagan (2001). In this instructional strategy, students read and discuss a controversial topic. They then line up according to their agreement or disagreement with a statement made about the topic. For example, if the topic is using animals for drug research, the statement would be, "Animals should be used for the research and development of new medications for humans." Those who most strongly agree with the statement stand at one end of the line, while those who disagree stand at the other end. Those who have mixed feelings about the statement stand in the middle. After sharing with those near them, the students fold the line so that those who most strongly agree with the statement now face students who most strongly disagree. After exchanging points of view, each student paraphrases the other's point of view. Next, the line is unfolded and split in the center. One half of the line slides down to face the other half. Now those who strongly agree and strongly disagree exchange points of view with those in the middle of the line. The benefits of using this kind of instructional strategy is that the teacher can focus on the content that must be taught and learned, while students also learn and practice how to empathize and listen actively to one another.

To help develop students' listening skills, encourage students to pay closer attention to one another during class discussions by not repeating what students say. Enhance the effectiveness of this strategy by taking the time to teach students how to respond clearly and loudly enough for all classmates to hear.

7.1 What cooperative learning strategies and structures can you use to teach your students how to listen actively and empathize with others?

Teach Character Education

Teaching character education is another way to create a positive classroom climate. Most cultures agree on the following positive character traits: respect, responsibility, courage, fairness, trustworthiness, caring, kindness, tolerance, and citizenship. It is common to find some character education programs that teach students about the different traits using a curricular approach. For example, students participate in a lesson about courage by listening to a story whose main character exhibits courage and then writing a paragraph about the definition of courage and how the main character exhibits courage. However, the best form of character education is an instructional program in which you employ teaching strategies that require students to develop and practice these traits in real time. For example, involving students in an honest, thoughtful discussion while taking turns and showing respect for others' opinions about the moral implications of a current event is a way to teach and practice several of the character traits at one time, including respect and tolerance. In addition, many cooperative learning strategies, like the Split Agree-Disagree Line-Up strategy, allow students to develop and practice desirable character traits. Class meetings, ethics-rich academic classes, and service-learning opportunities (where students do volunteer work for the sole purpose of helping others) both inside and outside school also contribute to authentic character education.

7.2 Does your school have a character education curriculum or program? Is it a curricular- or an instructional-based program?

7.3 Whether or not your school has a character education program, what can you do to implement an instructional character education program in your classroom?

Use inviting language. For example, use *we* instead of *you* when addressing your class, as in "Today we will . . ." instead of "Today you will . . ." and "How many of us . . . ?" instead of "How many of you . . . ?" Also use phrases like "It can be difficult for people to . . ." instead of "It is difficult for you to. . . ."

Monitor Your Own Behavior and Attitudes

Because you have total control over yourself, act sincerely and eliminate behaviors that could become stressors for your students. Some of these behaviors include having inadequate classroom management skills, being ill prepared for lessons, being disorganized, having unclear goals, behaving inconsistently, using sarcasm, and showing a lack of empathy.

In addition, 75 percent to 90 percent of a message is transmitted nonverbally. Nonverbal cues include tone of voice, facial expression, and body posture. Students, including very young children, understand these cues, so it is important that the cues you use match your intended message. Videotape yourself to examine the nonverbal cues you use on a daily basis. Also, take note of how your behavior is influenced by your students' nonverbal cues. Teachers can be influenced by a student's posture, physical appearance, and tone of voice. Therefore, make a conscious effort to monitor your nonverbal behavior and your reactions to others' nonverbal behavior.

7.4 What can you do to monitor your own behavior and attitudes?

7.5 When can you videotape yourself teaching?

Stand at the door and greet students by name as they enter the classroom. If this is impossible, at least acknowledge each student by making sure you make eye contact with her or him before beginning instruction.

Build Rapport

The easiest way to build rapport is to treat your students with respect. Be fair, nurturing, firm, and consistent. Allow mistakes and help your students learn from them. Do not react to inappropriate behavior. Instead, respond in a professional, supportive manner.

By exercising a few simple behaviors such as the following, you can increase rapport in your classroom:

- Use an open body posture.
- Smile.
- Make eye contact.
- Address your students by name.
- Give students choices.
- Listen actively.

The rapport you build helps you gain their respect and cooperation, removing another common stressor for teachers.

Get to know your students by writing a letter to them and placing a copy of it on each desk on the first day of school. Attach another sheet of paper, already addressed to you, for each student to respond. In your letter, tell your students a little bit about yourself and ask questions to gather more information about them, such as "What is your favorite book?" "What do you like to do in your free time?" and "What would you like to learn about this year?" This enables you to make a connection with your students on the first day of school, and it also supplies you with a meaningful writing sample.

7.6 What can you do to build rapport with your students?

Satisfy the Basic Need for Security

Make your students feel safe and secure in their environment. The basic need for security is filled by ensuring an emotionally safe classroom, a classroom where students do not fear that they will be embarrassed in any way. There are several things you can do to establish an emotionally safe classroom.

First, be tolerant of each student's individuality, avoid sarcasm, and never put students on the spot, especially in front of their peers. Accept all your students, no matter who they are or how they behave. Your students get this message of acceptance when you use empathy, acknowledging their feelings by saying, for instance, "You're frustrated with school" as opposed to saying "When I was your age. . . ."

Another way to make students feel secure is to establish classroom routines. A daily routine helps students predict what will happen next, thus reducing their anxiety. In addition, students are less likely to misbehave when there is a routine in place because it reduces their fear of being asked to do something that they are not prepared to do. It is important to help your students understand what they are supposed to be doing at all times. Remember to post a schedule or class agenda in your room to assist your students in anticipating what comes next.

7.7 How will you satisfy the basic need for security?

7.8 To foster a sense of security, what classroom routines can you put in place?

Place each student's name on a Popsicle stick and place them in a cup. This makes it easier (and more fair) to choose "volunteers."

Create a Sense of Belonging

One of the best ways to prevent violent behavior in the classroom is to establish an atmosphere of respect, inclusion, and community. All your students must learn that they belong to a group and that they have responsibilities to that group. This is especially critical when dealing with adolescents, who are continually creating "in groups" and "outcast groups." Teachers need to break down and eliminate these groups so that all students feel included.

One way to get rid of cliques is to conduct class meetings to show students how and when their actions affect the class and the school. In addition, make every student feel he or she is an important part of the class by creating a team atmosphere. To foster a team atmosphere, explain and model citizenship and courtesy, use many role-playing exercises to help your students practice and internalize these behaviors, and expect them from your students at all times. Bullying, persecution, and harassment of other students must not be tolerated, inside or outside your classroom. These behaviors create a sense of exclusion for the student being picked on, and that student might resort to violent behavior to get revenge or simply to end the harassment. Therefore, it is imperative that you stop the bullying and teach students to tolerate and include fellow classmates.

As in teaching empathy and active listening skills to your students, many cooperative learning strategies will also help you create a sense of belonging. In addition, conduct activities to increase mutual support among your students (many team-building resources are available). When students feel that they belong and are significant, their need to misbehave usually disappears.

To help foster team spirit, a third-grade teacher adopted a catchy team name and a mascot. This teacher, "Mrs. Brown," named her class "Mrs. Brown's Bears" and chose the bear as their class mascot. The room was decorated with bears, from name tags in the shape of bears to stuffed teddy bear accessories. This team identity fostered a sense of belonging and a sense of security for the children in her class.

7.9 What can you do to create a sense of belonging and community in your classroom?

Increase Your Students' Self-Esteem

Self-esteem is the picture we have of ourselves. It is our enabler. It drives our self-motivation. None of us wants to see ourselves as a failure in life, and we have three ways to make sure that we do not.

First, we can succeed within the current system. Most of us are able to conform, "fall in line," and to a large degree, make it within the system as it is. Second, we can retreat from the real world and hide in a world that we create just for ourselves, where we accept ourselves the way we are and convince ourselves that we are good enough as we are. Finally, we can act out against the world that we believe denies us of our self-esteem and success. Unfortunately, people with low self-esteem usually choose the last option and usually manifest it as misbehavior.

Students' self-esteem is based largely on how much on-grade-level schoolwork they can do correctly. Therefore, to build students' self-esteem, do not give them more than they can handle at one time. Break complex tasks into small steps or parts to help increase students' can-do attitude. For example, if an entire math assignment frustrates some students, give them only part of it to complete at one time. Offer feedback immediately on the part they completed. Praise them for their efforts and the problems they completed correctly, and then prompt them with specific directions to correct those they did not complete correctly or ask them to continue with the next part of the assignment. Remember to give immediate feedback on the next part as well.

I once was asked to substitute teach a class that had several students who lacked self-esteem. When it came time to do their independent work, I modified the assignment for those students who did not immediately grasp the math concepts being taught. It was no surprise to me that these students also misbehaved more and had lower academic achievement than their classmates. Speaking privately with each of these students, I asked them to do only a part of the assignment while the rest of the class worked on all of it. I also asked them to raise their hands when they had completed what I had assigned for them, which enabled me to come to their desks to provide them with immediate feedback. I continued this strategy until they had completed the entire assignment. The effect of this strategy was incredible! First, incorrect thought processes were nipped in the bud. In addition, their sense of pride and accomplishment fueled their self-esteem. I distinctly remember one boy's ear-to-ear smile when I told him that he had completed that part of the assignment "perfectly." Another's reaction was to excitedly tell a classmate who sat beside him that I said his work was "outstanding." These students were happy, confident, and productive, and they behaved wonderfully the entire period.

7.10 What can you do to build your students' self-esteem?

7.11 How can you ensure that you give each of your students tasks that are academically appropriate?

Make Students Feel Significant

It's a simple fact that all of us look for the little cues from others that tell us we are good, worthy, and significant. We are happy and grateful when someone provides these cues. We feel special when someone recognizes our efforts to do good things. We like to be around these nice people and are ready and willing to return their kindnesses. In that same vein, we feel hurt and resentful when others criticize or belittle us. We often become defensive and either try to strike back or avoid the people who inflict pain on us. Therefore, it is very important that we, as teachers, make a serious effort to detect desirable behavior.

We must go out of our way to find it, especially for children who exhibit undesirable behavior more often than do their peers. We must catch these poorly behaved students being good and tell them when we do. Immediate positive reinforcement increases the probability of students continuing positive behavior. Therefore, if we are consistent about finding and responding to appropriate behavior, students will begin to move toward that form of behavior more and more of the time.

7.12 How will you make your students feel significant, worthy?

Do not show favoritism toward any one student or group of students.

Use Behavior Management Strategies That Prevent Discipline Problems

Hitting, fighting, cheating, and stealing are some behaviors that most teachers believe are never appropriate under any situation. However, other "inappropriate" behaviors, such as talking, can be appropriate within the proper setting. Remember, many times it is not what the student is doing that is inappropriate, it is the time or setting that the student chooses to engage in that behavior that is inappropriate.

Sometimes the inappropriate behaviors result from inappropriate expectations of students (social, emotional, and academic), from poor interpersonal relationships, or from poor classroom management—all signs of ineffective teaching. Sometimes no matter how much you try to prevent inappropriate behavior, it still occurs. When it does, you need to have the skills to handle it. Never react, but respond to the situation. Keep your cool and remember to acknowledge the student's feelings. Often this goes a long way in diffusing the problem.

Separate the child from the misbehavior. Do not disapprove of the child; disapprove of the misbehavior.

Discipline problems can erode classroom climate. Preventing discipline problems from occurring in the first place helps eliminate this problem. To prevent discipline problems, build classroom management skills that help foster desirable student behavior. These management skills include the following:

- *With-it-ness (being alert):* being aware of everything that is going on in the room at all times so you can reinforce appropriate behavior and can stop minor problems before they become major ones. To be with-it, you need to (1) stand where you can see everyone; (2) move around the room while making sure you can see everyone at all times; (3) watch for inappropriate behaviors, signs of confusion, signs of frustration, failure to follow directions, attending behaviors, appropriate materials on desks, and completion of work; (4) avoid becoming engrossed with one student or group by scanning the room often; and (5) prohibit students from congregating around your desk, blocking your view of the rest of the class.
- *Overlapping:* handling more than one activity or problem at the same time by paying attention to the important aspects of everything going on around you. This prevents you from becoming overwhelmed and from getting sidetracked.
- *Movement management:* pacing activities appropriately and transitioning between activities effectively (more on this later in the chapter), including giving clear beginnings (such as "Begin now") and clear endings (such as "Stop working now") to activities. It is also not starting new activities until you have all your students' attention. In addition, it includes establishing classroom routines and procedures that bring structure and smoothness to your classroom (discussed later in the chapter).

Summarize instructions on the chalkboard, and immediately after giving the instructions to the whole class, review them with slower students, either individually or in a small group.

- *Group alerting:* using whole-group strategies to keep all students involved in the task at hand and getting nonresponders to participate.
- *Specific praise:* giving students praise that is believable and tells them exactly what they did well or did correctly. An example is "You remembered to put your name on the top of your paper so I could see who did the work. Super!" Specific praise must be genuine, and the student must believe you. Specific praise should be given for correct academic responses as well as for appropriate behavior. Note that sometimes specific praise works better if it is delivered only loud enough for the student receiving the praise to hear it. If other students hear the praise, they might reject the student or make fun of him or her. This might create discipline problems, which can erode the relationships in your class.
- *Encouragement:* giving students nonjudgmental approval focused on the task, process, product, or behavior, and not on the student. An example is "This essay is excellent!" Encouragement can also be an encouraging comment, such as "Let's look at it this way . . ." and "Keep at it!" or a feed-forward comment—a direction that shows the student what to do next—such as "This sentence needs a punctuation mark" and "Use rule 3 here."
- *Assertiveness training:* teach your students how to be assertive. Model, role-play, and practice using "I statements" (discussed in Chapter 1) and other assertive behavior. Assertiveness training will give students the skills they need to effectively communicate their wants and needs without having to resort to inappropriate behavior.

I once had a female student who was being bullied by a boy from another class on the same grade level. He would tease and taunt her every chance he got—in the hallway, in the cafeteria, and on the playground. Consequently, she was afraid of him and became paranoid every time she left our classroom. Adults tried intervening, but the boy would not stop. Only after I taught my student how to stand up to the bully did he finally stop harassing her. I role-played the boy and had her practice being assertive with me, providing her with assertive phrases and postures. It took a few days, but she mustered up the courage to stand up to him the next time he teased her. Although I was not there when it happened, she recounted the event and showed me how she was forceful, confident, and assertive in her dialogue with him. She had even come up with her own assertive phrases! As a result, the teasing stopped and the boy never bothered her again.

7.13 Which prevention strategies do you need to learn more about to be able to use them effectively? Where will you obtain the training or knowledge?

Handle Discipline Problems in Real Time

Misbehavior has four main goals: gaining attention, gaining power, revenge, and compensating for feeling inadequate.

When students engage in activities, constructive or destructive, that bring undue attention to themselves, their goal is to get others to notice and involve them. These students believe that they are only important or significant when they are being noticed or getting special attention. In such cases, ignore the behaviors or redirect them by involving the students in useful tasks while avoiding special attention. Give these students unexpected attention when they do what they're supposed to be doing.

When students try to be boss, they're trying to gain power. These students believe that they belong only when they are in control and when you do what they want you to do. To effectively deal with this behavior, give the students choices—usually only two or three. Also, acknowledge that you cannot make them do something, and redirect their efforts into constructive activities.

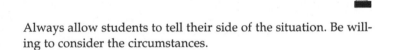

Always allow students to tell their side of the situation. Be willing to consider the circumstances.

When students are out for revenge, they believe that they cannot be liked and do not have power but that they will count if they can hurt others as they feel they have been hurt by life. With these students, use a lot of empathy and active listening. Deal with the hurt feelings and show that you care. Identify and encourage their strengths.

Students who feel inadequate usually give up and want to be left alone. They believe that they cannot do anything right, so they'll try to convince others not to expect anything from them. For these students, you need to break down tasks into small steps. Make the tasks easier until the students experience success. Show that you believe in them and will not give up on them. Encourage any positive attempt, no matter how small.

Use index cards to record "student incidents" and what you did to resolve the situations. Keep these cards to help you remember what did and did not work.

Students might exhibit more than one of these behaviors. Therefore, learn how to identify the underlying goals of student misbehavior so you can effectively manage it. In addition to the strategies presented here, the following list outlines how to manage discipline problems, often caused by the four main goals of misbehavior, as they occur:

- *Planned ignoring:* choosing not to appear to pay attention to a student involved in a minor misbehavior while maintaining your own and other students' focus to the task at hand and not on the inappropriate behavior. It also includes waiting for the student to begin engaging in an appropriate behavior and praising the appropriate behavior immediately after you observe it.
- *Physical proximity:* while continuing to teach, walking over to stand near someone who is behaving inappropriately. This involves remaining focused on the task at hand while using your physical presence to let the student know you have noticed what she or he is doing. This is often used with planned ignoring, specific praise, gestural warning/reminders, or mild desists.
- *Gestural warnings/reminders:* briefly using eye contact, a stern look, or pointing to posted classroom rules or to the task material to let a student know you are aware of her or his behavior and to remind the student of what she or he is supposed to be doing.
- *Mild desists (soft reprimands):* telling a student to stop the inappropriate behavior or telling the student what to do to start behaving appropriately. Because publicly made reprimands usually backfire, mild desists are effective when given in a calm, firm tone of voice loud enough only for the student to hear.
- *Negative reinforcement:* creating an undesirable condition that a student can avoid if behaving appropriately.

7.14 Which behavior management strategies do you need to learn about? Where will you obtain training or coaching? How will you assess how effective you are at using these skills?

Accept students' feelings. Reject inappropriate behavior. Use active listening skills to hear the emotions behind the misbehavior. Make it clear to students that they are not bad for having these emotions, but both the choice to misbehave and the misbehavior itself are wrong and unacceptable. In addition to facing the appropriate consequences for their choice of behavior, work with students to create a plan that gives them the control to prevent making this particular inappropriate choice again.

Modify Student Behavior

If the teacher behaviors described in the previous section do not work to decrease or eliminate inappropriate behaviors, try the following strategies, which are more involved practices for modifying student behavior:

- *Token economy:* creating a reward system whereby students earn points, tickets, or some other symbolic token for appropriate behavior that can be used to "purchase" a predetermined prize, such as an activity, item, or privilege, at a later time. This requires a list of exactly what students must do to earn the tokens (usually different amounts of tokens can be earned for different types of behaviors) and a list of what the tokens can purchase (usually different amounts for different prizes).
- *Contracts:* students, teachers, and sometimes parents signing written agreements that specify what particular privilege or reward students earn if they engage in a particular behavior.
- *Response cost:* taking away a privilege, activity, or item a student already has if the student behaves inappropriately (for example, taking away recess privileges for breaking a classroom rule).
- *Time-out (social isolation):* briefly removing a student from the situation and isolating her or him from other people and materials for short lengths of time to immediately stop the misbehavior. While in time-out, have the student complete the following questions to help her or him change the behavior: (1) Why do I think I was sent here? (2) What am I missing right now? What is the class doing? (3) What is my side of the story? (4) Is my behavior getting me what I want in a responsible manner? (5) What do I think should happen to me? (6) How can I change my actions? (7) Here is my plan (short,

specific, and doable). If the student is too young to write, allow her or him to record the answers onto a tape. Also, modify the language of the questions to match the developmental level of the student. The student, teacher, and parent or principal must sign the document.

- *Modeling:* using a model (such as another student, an adult, or a fictional character from a film or story) to help a student acquire a new response, inhibit a previously acquired unacceptable response, or make a response the student already exercises more important or more frequent. For modeling to work, the student must be able, physically, to perform the desired behavior and must be attentive enough to notice and recall the details of the desired behavior. The model must be important to the student. To enhance the model for the student, choose someone who the student highly values or admires, who is like the student in some way (sex, race, or age, for instance), who shares similar values with the student, or whose actions are realistic and rewarded (or punished if it is a behavior you want to inhibit).

Remember that to modify behavior, if the student is completely unskilled in the desired behavior, extrinsic motivation will probably be necessary at first. Use extrinsic motivation when the student has no intrinsic motivation to learn a particular appropriate behavior or to behave in a certain way. After successful learning of either the academic task or the appropriate behavior, the student becomes intrinsically motivated to learn and to behave appropriately.

There are four types of extrinsic motivators: (1) material reinforcers, such as toys and trinkets; (2) privileges or activities reinforcers, such as helping the teacher or playing a classroom game; (3) social reinforcers, such as attention, praise, and feedback; and (4) token reinforcers, such as tickets that can be exchanged for material, activity, or social reinforcers at a later time.

Privileges, activities, and social reinforcers are often considered natural reinforcers because they are usually less costly, easy to arrange, and already part of the classroom environment. Use them the most, especially social reinforcers because they are most readily available, cost nothing, and are very powerful motivators.

To find out which positive reinforcers motivate your students the most, watch and ask them. Use a written survey if your students are old enough, and include sentence starters such as "The best way to reward a person is to . . ." and "If I could do anything in school that I wanted, I would. . . ."

Sometimes it is necessary to use token reinforcers, such as a token economy, to condition naturally available reinforcers. They have been especially useful in special education environments and in situations where students have not responded well to social reinforcers alone. If the student receives adult approval and is praised for a job well done while receiving tokens, the tokens can usually be withdrawn gradually and the social, natural reinforcers will take over. Therefore, adult approval and doing a good job become established as conditioned reinforcers and eventually turn into the natural reinforcers or natural consequences of their behavior. Because token systems can be a lot of work for the teacher, they should be kept as simple as possible so that record keeping and the "cashing in" of tokens are not burdensome.

If you have only a few students who need material or token reinforcers to learn or to behave appropriately, it is not necessary to establish an entire classroom token economy program. Instead, impress on the students who need the program that they will get the tokens they need, and appeal to the other students' value system for help. After discussing in private the arrangements with the students who need these reinforcers, ask the rest of your class to cooperate and encourage the students' changing behavior. From time to time, reward the class as a whole for helping you and the troubled students by giving the whole class extra recess time or a 10-minute break to socialize.

Finally, you must teach students that they choose how to behave, good and bad, and that there are consequences, positive and negative, for all behaviors. Students must learn that what largely happens to them is the result of their choices. Just as good grades are largely affected by effort, positive consequences are largely affected by choosing to exercise good behavior. Without this understanding, students will blame everyone but themselves and won't develop the necessary life skills of self-control and problem solving.

7.15 Which classroom management skills do you need to develop or improve? How and when do you plan to develop or improve them?

To prevent discipline problems, set up a chart in front of your classroom that lists activities students should do when they finish their work early.

Prevent Bullying

Bullying occurs when a student or group of students repeatedly taunts or picks fights with a weaker student. Bullying implies an imbalance of strength or power, where one student is victimized by another. Most incidents occur in places with little adult supervision, such as hallways and playgrounds. Reactions to bullying can result in very serious consequences. Victims often feel vengeful, angry, and sorry for themselves after an incident. If left to fester, these feelings can evolve into depression, physical illness, suicide, and extreme violent behavior. We need only to watch television to find incident after incident where victims of bullying resorted to extreme violent behavior to get revenge and to make the harassment stop.

In classrooms that have several bullies, the classroom climate feels unsafe. Unfortunately, most bullying is tolerated and ignored. It has been found that teachers intervene in a fraction of all incidents. Therefore, teachers need to send the message that bullying is unacceptable behavior and that they will make it stop.

To prevent bullying, you must first identify the bullies and their victims. At the same time you that clarify to your class that bullying is inappropriate behavior, you must figure out why the bullies behave as they do. Bullies usually hope to gain power over others to help mask their feelings of inadequacy and powerlessness. Their choice of victims sometimes gives clues as to specifically what they might be trying to gain control over, but often their victims are just those that they believe they can easily manipulate and overpower.

In addition, it is imperative that victims' needs be met. Use empathy and active listening skills to diffuse any anger or vengeful feelings. Work on rebuilding victims' self-esteem and ensure that they feel significant and that they belong to the group.

It requires great commitment on your part to prevent and eliminate bullying, but for the health and safety of all, it is imperative that you do so.

7.16 What antibullying programs exist in your school or school system? If none exist, what steps can you take to prevent bullying in your classroom?

7.17 What steps can you take to punish bullies and to modify their behavior?

7.18 What steps can you take to protect victims and to make sure that they get the help they need after they have been victimized by bullies?

Keep Students On Task

Approximately 80 percent of all classroom management problems occur during off-task moments in the school day. Therefore, it is very important to keep students on task. To do this, first get students on task as quickly as possible when class begins. For example, have a question or quick activity written on the chalkboard or overhead projector ready for your students as soon as they come to class. In addition, save time by having assigned seats or by taking roll as students enter the classroom. Hand out materials to students as they enter the room. Have older editions of textbooks on hand for those who forget to bring them to class. Always have extra materials for lab assignments in case of spills or breaks, and always have your materials ready to begin class. Use clear phrases like "Begin working" and "Stop working" to help manage students' on-task behavior. And finally, signal to students a few minutes ahead of a transition that a transition will be occurring soon so that they can bring some type of closure to what they are working on before transitioning to another activity.

Prevent opportunities for misbehavior by getting students engaged within the first 90 seconds of class. To get students engaged as soon as possible, have something meaningful for students to do as soon as they enter the classroom, or ask questions as they enter the classroom that require every student's engagement.

During a lesson, you can keep students on task by calling on students randomly to answer questions, asking all the students to answer in unison, and using instructional strategies that allow every student to become actively involved in a lesson. Also, make sure that you have clearly stated all assignment directions and behavior expectations and that all students understand them. Plan lessons carefully so you have established appropriate developmental goals for all your students. Ensure a high success rate for every student by giving each one an appropriate level of difficulty. Keep students on task by keeping them motivated with high, yet reasonable, standards for achievement, because all of us want to feel industrious. Also, make the lessons relevant and engaging so students will want to stay focused and on task.

To help keep students on task while they work independently on an assignment, give each student a red cup, flag, sign, or some other small token that they can place on top of their desks to signal that they need additional help. This allows them to continue working (with both hands) while letting you know that you need to attend to their needs as soon as possible.

After assigning independent class work, ask your students to place a heading on their papers (the heading that you taught them to use) and to do the first two questions or problems. Then announce the answers and work the problems on the board quickly, if applicable. Ask that students who did not get the questions correct and feel they might have trouble with the assignment to place their "I need help" signs or tokens on top of their desks. Ask them to continue working doing the best they can and assure them that you will get over to help them as soon as possible.

In addition, circulate around the classroom, check students' work and progress, and give them specific feedback about their work. One way to accomplish this efficiently and effectively is to use the "praise, prompt, leave" method described by Steere (1988). As you pass a student, praise them for their hard work and effort, prompt them by stating what they should do next, and leave. An example of a prompt is telling students to check a particular part of their assignment. The "praise, prompt, leave" method should not take more than 30 seconds per student. Within a 15-minute period, you will be able to see 30 students. This method allows you to see as many students as possible and it gives your students the necessary feedback they need for successful learning. It also helps you avoid getting overly involved with one student, forsaking the others.

If you have difficulties keeping students on task, first analyze the situation to determine exactly what activity or what teaching behavior is causing the off-task behavior. Steere (1988) suggests the following questions to help you identify off-task behavior that could be damaging the climate you want to establish and maintain. A peer coach might be helpful for collecting the data needed to answer some of these questions.

How many minutes are spent each day:

- taking roll, collecting money, and attending to other homeroom activities?
- locating, distributing, and collecting materials?
- cleaning up, standing in line, going to the restroom or water?
- reviewing management rules and giving nonacademic directions?
- reprimanding students, thereby causing other students to be disturbed and pulled off task?
- by students being unengaged while waiting for the teacher?
- during which the staff members interfere with children's assigned tasks (examples: engaging in irrelevant talk, giving additional directions, having visitors, announcement of PA, being overemotional and loud in correcting behavior)?
- with one (or a few) students while others need assistance?
- during which the teacher is unavailable to assist students (examples: speaking to a visitor, handling emergencies, and being tied up with one group)?
- on activities with marginal or little value to the instructional objectives?
- on lengthy student recitations before the teacher regains "leadership"?
- exceeding the time allotted for recess and lunch?
- allowing pupils to get drinks and go to the restroom during instructional time?

- when students are out of the room, during a lesson, for the convenience of scheduling remedial instruction? (p. 95)

7.19 Which strategies do you plan to use to keep your students on task?

Motivate Your Students

The research tells us that there are several paths to motivation. To motivate students to take risks in a learning environment, they must believe that the risks are manageable. The degree of risk perceived is unique for every individual, and the fear of failure dampens motivation. Therefore, as a teacher, you need to create learning opportunities where risk taking is part of the learning process. Student learning and personal growth result from students mastering challenges that teachers present to them. Students learn best when they are fully involved and are challenged with tasks that are developmentally appropriate.

The number-one motivator for all of us is the opportunity for success. Therefore, it is very important to show students the payoff for their efforts, especially if motivation is to be maintained. Structure lessons with flexibility so each student has an opportunity for success. Make the lessons engaging and relevant for students to prevent boredom, because boredom also decreases motivation.

Encouragement is necessary for students to perceive high-risk learning activities as manageable. Encouraging statements are nonjudgmental in nature. This means that the statements focus on the task, process, product, or behavior. Encouraging statements are positive and accepting, focus on effort and improvement, are enthusiastic and optimistic, and respect students' feelings. Examples of encouragement include "Your hard work is showing improvement," "Please check your work and you'll know if you need to spend more time on this," and "You're off to a good start. Please finish so we'll know what to work on next." Encouragement is given effectively with the "praise, prompt, leave" method previously described.

Encouragement is not the same as praise. Praise, when delivered randomly and not specifically, can have a detrimental effect. However, effective praise can help motivate students. Effective praise is genuine and is delivered contingently. It also specifies the details of the accomplishment. It attributes success to effort and ability, implying that similar successes can be expected in the future if the same effort is put forth.

7.20 How can you structure lessons to make them more motivating?

7.21 What additional phrases can you use to encourage your students?

Manage Instructional Time Appropriately

Instructional time deals with managing the pace of the lesson and the flow of activities. The pace of the lesson has to be developmentally appropriate for your students. A steady, comfortable pace is best. When the pace of a lesson is appropriate, students have fewer opportunities to misbehave.

Plan for every class. Never try to wing it.

Minimize the time it takes to get lessons going by having all materials ready to go before the school day begins. Many teachers will either come to school early or stay a few minutes late the day before to gather materials and set things up for the next day. Do whichever fits best into your schedule. Also, keep materials in containers, such as plastic baskets, to make storing and moving them around easier for you and your students.

Be careful not to dwell on a certain part of a lesson, spending too much time on directions or on information that is irrelevant to the topic or goal. And try not to fragment the lesson, breaking it up into too many unnecessary steps.

Share your daily agenda with your students. All students, no matter what grade level, benefit from having an overview of what to expect during the day or class period. Revisit the agenda throughout the day or class period to help you stay on task.

You also need to pay attention to the flow of your activities. A variety of activities is usually preferred. Transitions between them need to be short and organized. A poor transition can negatively affect your climate because it provides students with the opportunity to engage in inappropriate behavior.

Transitions occur both inside and outside your classroom: during and between lessons, when you or your students arrive at and leave the classroom, and during activities in which your entire class participates outside the classroom (such as going to the restrooms or to the cafeteria). To help you with your transitions, first identify all the possible transitions you could have in a given day, both inside and outside your classroom. Second, choreograph the transitions to be short and organized. Third, practice them yourself. Finally, practice them with your students, and teach students the signal you will use to alert them when a transition is about to occur.

If you still tend to "lose" your students during transitions, get help. Ask your colleagues about how they handle their transitions. Observe other teachers. Ask veteran teachers to observe you and your class and to offer suggestions. There are also books and chapters of books that cover this topic. Again, if you need help on transitions, seek help. There is plenty available.

When I began teaching, I had horrible transitions. A few of my colleagues and administrators observed me and my class and offered suggestions, many of which focused on allowing a few children to transition at one time. One example was to allow only about five or six students to line up at the door at one time. These simple strategies became my saving grace that year.

Finally, the lengths of the lessons need to correspond to your class's attention span. Therefore, the general rule is to keep the lengths of lessons shorter for both younger children and children with learning difficulties. Knowing the ages and developmental levels of your students, answer the following questions:

7.22 What should be the pace of your lessons?

7.23 How long should the lessons or activities be? Does the time you allocate to the lessons or activities reflect your students' instructional and developmental needs?

7.24 What flow of activities would be more appropriate for them?

7.25 What kinds of games can you use to help your students transition quickly and smoothly between lessons?

To prevent discipline problems, use single-word, direct instructions, such as "sit" or "walk." These convey your expectations clearly and are easily understood.

Use Cooperative Learning Strategies

Cooperative learning strategies not only help students practice and develop empathy and active listening skills, they also help reduce tension and hostility among students by minimizing excessive competition. Cooperative learning strategies demand that all students make a combined effort to attain a common goal. Because students depend on one another, cooperative learning gives students a sense of belonging and of being significant.

Here are some tips for successful cooperative learning activities:

- Keep the group size small; two is best, and four is the maximum.
- Establish norms for behavior such as how to express opinions and how to disagree appropriately; role-play and practice these skills ahead of time.
- Select groups carefully to maintain balance.
- Define roles for each member and role-play ahead of time.
- Assess and evaluate each member's work separately (this prevents groups from having one person do all the work while the others get a free ride).
- Use an ice-breaker activity when the groups are first formed to help group members get to know one another.
- Provide feedback to the cooperative groups on their group skills, and coach the groups to function at a constructive, productive level.

7.26 What cooperative learning strategies can you use with your students? Where can you learn more about the various strategies?

7.27 What are the skills you need to teach your students before you can have effective cooperative learning groups? How and when will you teach them?

Cooperative learning teams of greater than two students usually do not function effectively until students have been taught and have practiced group process skills.

Establish Classroom Procedures

Efficient and effective classroom procedures set up ahead of time positively affect the climate of your classroom. Introduce them throughout the first week of school as needed. Teach, model, role-play (especially with younger children), and review them as often as necessary (perhaps every day for younger children) for the first few weeks of school. Remember that many children, especially younger ones, take your words literally. Therefore, if you want your students to stop doing something, say "Stop." Do not use confusing phrases such as "Cut it out." These procedures help ensure that students know what to do and when to do it, increase industriousness, and reduce the opportunities for discipline problems. Use the next set of questions to help you identify which classroom procedures you need.

7.28 What are your classroom procedures for the following daily routines?

   a. Waiting for class to officially begin

   b. Taking attendance

   c. Arriving late

   d. Obtaining transportation changes, especially for younger students, to help ensure your students get home safely

   e. Taking lunch count

   f. Recess (if applicable): How long is it? Is it the same time every day? Where does it take place (playground, classroom, or gymnasium)? Does this change for different weather conditions? What kinds of activities are allowed during indoor recess? Are they whole-group activities or are they individualized free-play activities? What are the rules for any games your students might play?

   g. Snack time (if applicable): What time does it take place? What are the rules during snack time? Who provides the snacks?

   h. Transitioning between any two activities

   i. Entering and leaving the classroom

   j. Class meetings

   k. Dismissing after class officially ends

Because students' attention decreases when they are hungry, thirsty, or need to use the restroom, provide ample opportunities for students to fulfill these basic human needs. If there are long lapses between breakfast and lunch or between lunch and the end of the school day, provide opportunities for your students to have a nutritious snack during these times, even if the only time is between classes. Also, make sure your students have access to water whenever they feel thirsty. If leaving the classroom is a problem, provide bottles of water and drinking cups. In addition to having set restroom breaks, find a way to make it safe for students to be able to use the restroom whenever they need to.

7.29 What are your procedures for the following classroom operations?

   a. Getting your students' attention when you need it

   b. Using the lavatories and water fountains found inside and outside the classroom

   c. Eating food and drinking beverages in class

   d. Sharing materials and supplies

   e. Obtaining supplies during class time (such as pencils, pens, paper, glue, scissors, books, and so forth)

    f. Touching or borrowing things from the teacher's desk and elsewhere in the classroom

    g. Using any math manipulatives or science apparatus

    h. Using any type of audiovisual equipment, including computers

    i. Borrowing classroom library books

    j. Returning school library books during a time other than the designated classroom library time or in between classes

    k. Sharpening pencils, including when and how to use the sharpener and what can and cannot be sharpened in the classroom sharpener

    l. Cleaning up after themselves

    m. Keeping their desks or workspaces and classroom neat and clean

    n. Working classroom jobs

    o. Handling classroom lost and found items

    p. Handling disagreements or problems that arise in class (for example, if a student refuses to do work or refuses to remove him- or herself from the group)

    q. Using a time-out area in the classroom

    r. Giving feedback about the classroom (for example, using a classroom suggestion box)

If you have ever taught young children, you know never to take anything for granted! I'll never forget the day my classroom's pencil sharpener jammed. I opened it and found crayon shavings and evidence of other things that should not have been placed in the sharpener. And I discovered my students did not know how to use other basic office supplies, such as scissors, staplers, glue, paper clips, rubber bands, staple removers, and three-ring binders. I learned my lesson—to teach young children (and older ones sometimes) how to properly use common office supplies and tools (and to keep a spare electric pencil sharpener in the closet). Do not leave it to chance if you want to prevent stress!

7.30 What are your classroom procedures for the following instructional events?

    a. Asking a question and joining class discussions

b. Telling you that they cannot see or hear you

c. Handing out and collecting papers, textbooks, and other items and supplies

d. Evaluating each other's work (such as when students switch papers to check one another's work)

e. Working in groups, such as reading groups, lab groups, project groups, and other cooperative learning groups

f. Coming to a small group: What do they bring? What do they do while waiting for the group to start?

7.31 What are your classroom procedures for working independently, such as the following?

a. Asking for help

b. Talking during seatwork

c. Finishing an in-class assignment before their classmates

d. Obtaining extra time to finish an in-class assignment

e. Leaving their seats: When is it allowed?

f. Sitting on the floor or in other places around the classroom: Where, when, how can they sit?

g. Interrupting you when you are working with another student or a small group of students

7.32 What are your classroom procedures for the following infrequent classroom events?

a. Interruptions by the intercom or visits from an unexpected guest or messenger

b. Buying lunch when a student forgets her or his lunch or lunch money

c. Borrowing P.E. equipment from the gymnasium for recess

7.33 What are your procedures for written assignments with respect to the following?

a. Headings on papers

b. Kinds of paper to be used

c. Kinds of writing tools, such as pen or pencil, to be used

7.34 What are your procedures for the following types of paperwork?

a. Homework: How often is it assigned? Is it to be done in pen or pencil?

b. Weekly folders that go home

c. Finding out and making up missed class work, including tests, after returning from an absence

d. Tests: Are parents expected to sign them? Are students allowed to keep tests at home or do they return them to you? Are students asked to keep track of their own grades to help them keep tabs on what their final grade will be?

Some teachers write the names of absentees on extra handouts from class and use a three-ring binder or folder to hold them. They also keep an assignment sheet or index card for each day showing what work was assigned (in-class independent work and homework) and due dates. A student helper is usually assigned the task of recording the assignments to free up the teacher. Students are taught that they are to check the binder or folder on arriving after an absence for any work that they missed. They are taught to take their copies of the handouts and copy the assignment from the assignment sheet or index card. In addition, procedures are set in place to extend the due dates for absentees. One procedure I have seen gives the student one extra day for each day of absence. For example, if the student was absent two days, the due date is extended by two days.

7.35 What are your classroom procedures for handing in the following?
   a. Homework
   b. Notes from home, including signed permission slips, tests, and report cards
   c. Completed in-class assignments

7.36 What is your procedure for storing class work that is not completed in the allotted time?

7.37 Do any of these procedures need to be written down and posted in the classroom?

7.38 Do all the procedures support all that is expected of you and your class?

Because asking why questions tends to put people on the defensive, use other prompts, such as what, where, or how questions.

Establish Classroom Rules

Effective teachers have expectations for behavior that are understood by all their students, whether or not the rules are written and posted on the wall. Rules stated positively help to define how you and your students should behave and encourage positive interpersonal relationships more than negative statements do. For example, it is better to say "Keep hands and feet to ourselves" than to say "No hitting," which fails to tell students that kicking or pinching others is also inappropriate. The rules should be clear about which behaviors are allowed some of the time, such as talking, and which are never allowed, such as hitting. The number of rules should be kept to a minimum so the larger goals stay in focus and don't get muddled with the little stuff. Two to seven rules should be enough. They should be reasonable, necessary, observable, and enforceable. Words that are difficult to understand for children, such as *respect* and *responsible*, should be clearly explained. Logical, reasonable consequences—positive and negative—should be part of each rule. The consequences should be related to the offense and should be respectful to the perpetrator. Remember, choosing the right behaviors to emphasize can help you prevent discipline problems, so choose your rules carefully.

Your classroom rules communicate your discipline plan, which should be consistent with your school's overall discipline philosophy, appropriate for the age of your students, and flexible for adapting to individual differences. The plan needs to provide students with feelings of safety, belonging, and security. It also needs to be easy to administer and easy to communicate to students, parents, and administrators.

Some teachers create their classroom rules with their students. If you would like to do this, begin the process by using questions like "Why do we have rules?" and "What rules do you think we need in our classroom?" These questions help begin the conversation. Some teachers create contracts or classroom constitutions with their students. You can determine which strategy is right for you and your students. However, regardless of which strategy you use, you should identify ahead of time the rules you believe will benefit your entire class. This ensures that these important rules are included in your final list and not accidentally overlooked.

After establishing the rules, you need to teach them to your students and review them as often as possible. Many teachers discuss their classroom rules daily. They also role-play situations where the rules are demonstrated until they become a part of the classroom culture. You know when this has happened when students are following the rules without having to be reminded of them.

You also need to share your classroom rules with parents so they understand the expectations for classroom behavior. You can include the rules in your classroom handbook (discussed in Chapter 2), or you can send a note home with a tear-off response slip that parents and students must sign to acknowledge that they are aware of your classroom rules and will support them.

Throughout the day, you might have to prompt your students to follow the rules. You can do this by sharing your expectations of how they should behave during a particular activity. You can also praise students who are following the rules by identifying the specific behavior you want others to follow. For example, thank a student for turning to page 10 so that you are also repeating the directions for another student who needs the prompt for the expected behavior. Finally, if none of these prompts work, you can issue a warning. If the student still chooses to break the rules, follow it with a consequence. Remember, the consequence must be appropriate for the offense.

I taught as a substitute teacher for one full year. During that time, I learned that it was imperative to state and explain my classroom rules within moments of arriving to my assigned class. Today, I still have the same two classroom rules: "Respect others" and "Do what you are supposed to be doing." I explain to my students that respect means never, in any way, to hurt another person. This includes making fun of another person, even if the person is not present. To explain the second rule, I first give examples. One example I use is to tell them that if they are supposed to be working with another student on an assignment, they should be working together and talking (I often see a slight surprise on their faces when I use this example). I go on to tell them that there's nothing wrong with not knowing what you're supposed to be doing—it happens to everyone, even me—but behaving badly to try to hide the fact that you don't know what is going on is never acceptable. With deep sincerity, I add that not knowing is not a problem, and I encourage them to simply raise their hands and ask me for the information again. Consequently, I usually do not have any major discipline problems. In fact, I had so few problems as a substitute teacher that I was consistently called to substitute the more "difficult" classes. I will never forget the day I was a few minutes late to one such class and they told me that the students were upset that I had not yet arrived! For me, this was a testament to the power of simple, clear, reasonable rules and empathetic leadership.

7.39 How can you establish effective classroom rules?
   a. Keeping in mind the school rules, which behaviors are acceptable and which are unacceptable?
   b. What rules, if any, are needed to maintain appropriate behaviors?
   c. What are positive consequences (rewards) and negative consequences for following or breaking the rules, respectively?

d. How and when do you plan to share these rules with your students?

e. How and when do you plan to share these rules with your students' parents? Do they support the expectations of you and of your class?

f. Should you post any of these rules to avoid confusion or forgetfulness?

Successfully Integrate New Students

Much of your classroom climate is established during the first few days and weeks of school. What happens if a new student arrives in mid-December? At any time during the school year, new students may join your class and need to be acclimated into your classroom. You want this to occur as smoothly and as quickly as possible to avoid detracting from the healthy classroom climate you have created. One way to ease the process is to buddy the new student with one of your more trustworthy students. Another way might be to create a "new student kit," which includes a classroom handbook and other things the child (and his or her parents) need to be successful in your class. Determine how you can effectively integrate new students so that when a child arrives at your class midyear, you can just refer to your notes and not have to worry about how to handle the situation.

I had a half dozen new students one year. I had not anticipated it, nor did I have much warning. In fact, I remember one student showing up at my door with the school secretary around 10 o'clock in the morning. There was absolutely no warning and no prep time. So I had to think on my feet and quickly figure out a way to welcome the child and to successfully integrate her into our class. If I had come up with a plan in advance, it would have prevented a lot of stress.

7.40 How can you integrate new students during the school year to maintain the climate of your classroom?

a. How can you successfully acclimate a new student to your classes, both socially and academically?

b. How can you successfully acclimate a new student to your classroom's rules and procedures?

c. What items, such as books and supplies, do you need to make sure a new student receives?

d. What kinds of information do you need to assess a new student's achievement to date?

Put together a survival kit for new students that includes a map of the school, a map of the community, locations of favorite student hangouts or entertainment facilities, your classroom handbook, and a list of what has already been covered in each subject.

Your Relationship With Your Students' Parents

Your classroom climate is also affected by your relationships with those outside your class, such as your students' parents. Your relationships with your students' parents can make or break your career without you ever realizing it. Although this is not what you usually focus on, these relationships must be established and nurtured, just like the relationships with your students. Some of these relationships can be the most difficult challenges you face as a teacher.

To be successful, establish rapport with your students' parents using several positive interactions early in the school year. Then maintain the rapport with favorable opinions and images of your classroom. Basically, this boils down to a proactive public relations program.

It has been found that schools are more highly rated by those who know them best, and that students and newspapers are the top sources of information for parents about what is going on in school. Therefore, review with your students the learning goals and achievements each day, providing them with accurate words to describe to their parents what goes on in school. Also, invite the media to your school often to see and report the good things that go on in your school instead of waiting until something bad happens and they invite themselves.

The Beginning of the School Year

There are things that you can do ahead of time to help ensure that you and your students' parents get off on the right foot. You need to think of yourself as a public relations manager whose task it is to make parents feel confident about you and about what is going on in your classroom. This is not an easy task. Here are some suggestions:

- Before the school year begins, send a letter to your students and their parents introducing yourself and welcoming them back to school.
- Before the school year begins, host your own open house if your school does not have a meet-the-teacher day, inviting both your students and their parents to meet you and to become familiar with the school and your classroom.
- Provide parents with weekly newsletters highlighting students' accomplishments.
- After the first two weeks of school—an opportune time of the school year—do some type of public relations activity, such as a telephone call or a postcard to each student and his or her parents relating the good things the student has done. Continue this activity period- ically throughout the school year to ensure that you are contacting parents when there is something good to share, not only when there is a problem.
- Plan a parent tea or student presentation for parents within the first six weeks of school to show off your students' accomplishments.

Notice that many of these suggestions should be done at the beginning of the school year. This is important because parent involvement and en- thusiasm run higher at the beginning of the school year than at any other time. Take advantage of the excitement and energy by planning as many of the suggested activities at the beginning of the school year as possible.

For ongoing communication with parents, use take-home journals. One way to use a take-home journal is to ask your students to write a letter home to a family member every Friday. Ask them to summarize what they learned in school that week and to high- light their personal accomplishments for the week. The students take their journals home for the weekend, and the family mem- bers receiving the letters write responses on the backs of the letters. Students return their journals to school on Monday so they can use them in class during the week. This is a great way to help keep parents in touch with what is happening in school, and it provides parents and children a meaningful way to com- municate about school.

7.41 What can you do to promote a positive image of you and your students, especially at the beginning of the school year?

Open House or Back to School Night

These events are usually organized at the school level and are great opportunities to put your public relations plan in high gear. The following are some suggestions for making these events a success:

- If possible, send home a questionnaire before the event asking parents what they are interested in hearing and seeing.
- Display your students' best work proudly and neatly both inside and outside your classroom.
- Provide refreshments if the school does not.
- Provide name tags with space for the names of both parent and child.
- Make the classroom neat, clean, and inviting.
- Dress neatly, cleanly, and professionally.
- Provide sign-up sheets for parent volunteers (if applicable).
- Make it clear that you will not discuss individual student's problems but that parents can sign up to schedule a conference with you at a later time.
- Take the time to reiterate your expectations for their children's behavior and for homework.
- Explain the goals and objectives of the class and the major units of work you will cover during the year.
- Consider involving students in a sample lesson or hands-on activity at the event. For parents, a demonstration of your teaching strategies speaks volumes.
- Explain how grades are determined.
- Allow time for parents to ask questions.
- Explain your procedure for parents to voice concerns and how you plan to handle the concerns.

7.42 What can you do to make Open House or Back to School Night a success?

Involving Parents

Getting parents involved in the classroom is another way to promote the good things that are happening in your classroom. Invite them to participate in organized, effective educational activities with their children. Parents are invaluable resources for you and your students. Use a parent survey, such as Resource 3.1 in the Resources for Successful Teaching section, the first few days of school to find out the interests, hobbies, and skills parents want to share with you and your students. Parents can also be tutors, assistant teachers, and clerical assistants for you and your class.

Resource 3.1

With many options available, you must first decide how you want to integrate parents into your classroom. Think your strategy through very carefully. If you are not organized, you could be setting yourself up for some bad publicity. Remember, parents talk to one another. If a parent is in your classroom and an activity goes terribly wrong, many more people will hear about it. On the other hand, if the activity goes smoothly and your students are successful, the parent will probably gain more confidence in you and your class. This situation can be a wonderful source of positive publicity. Therefore, careful planning is imperative.

7.43 In what ways do you want parents involved in your classroom?

After you figure out how you want parents involved, you need to figure out how to recruit them. One way is just to ask for parents' help and involvement on an as-needed basis. Another way is to set up a group of parent volunteers ahead of time, such as a classroom parents committee.

If you plan to organize your classroom parents, you must decide how you will do it and how often you want them in the classroom during the instructional day. Determine these things before the first day of school. One idea is to limit parent volunteers to one time each during the first month of school, increasing time as needed during the year. By starting out this way, you can see how each parent works with the children, what each parent's attitudes and intentions are, and how the children react to the parent. If it is not in your or the students' best interest to have a certain parent working in the classroom, this setup makes it easier to reduce that parent's time in the classroom. Regardless of how you choose to involve parent volunteers, be prepared to explain your policy. Have your ideas outlined before the first day of school because you might have some parents asking you about this even before school opens!

One year before school even began, students and parents dropped by my classroom to meet me. Many of these parents expressed their interest in helping out during the school day. Although I did tell them briefly how I planned to involve parents in my class, I did not have a sign-up sheet for specific activities. This was a missed opportunity to get more help for my students. I learned my lesson and now plan well in advance of the first day of school how I will involve parents and am prepared with specifics when parents express their interest.

Your classroom parents committee needs just as much structure as your classroom. Establish procedures for the committee. Decide which parent will chair it and define the different roles of committee members. Identify tasks or events in which they will be involved and how they will be involved. Keep an open mind and get input from parents, but do not leave the final decision to them—if you do, you might lose control over this precious resource, and your stress level will rise. Organizing your classroom parents ahead of time as carefully as you organize your classroom will pay huge dividends later.

7.44 How do you want to organize your classroom parents into a classroom parents committee?
 a. How do you want to ask for classroom parent volunteers? For example, do want to post a request in your weekly newsletter, send a note/memo to parents, use telephone calls, and/or put out a sign-up sheet during Back to School Night or other time?
 b. Do you state that "no experience is required" or that they need particular skills?
 c. How will you decide who, if anyone, chairs the committee?
 d. What is each individual's role on the committee?
 e. What tasks or events will each parent work on?
 f. How often will you meet with the committee?
 g. How often do you want parents to be involved in your classroom during the instructional day?
 h. What procedures do you need to establish to help keep the committee running smoothly?

7.45 How do you involve parents who will not volunteer to be classroom parents?
 a. How can you let them know you would like them involved in a particular activity or event?
 b. How can you use the classroom parents committee to help get other parents involved?

Working With Parents

When working with parents, remember always to treat them as very important partners in your students' education. You are the teacher, not a buddy or enemy. You are on the same team and are working with parents for their children. Practice good communication skills and use active listening. Treat them with respect and act professionally. Use tact, empathy, kindness, and consideration. When speaking, avoid educational jargon and use a tone that makes parents feel comfortable with you and confident in you and your skills.

When working with parents, also remember that they have different personalities and that you might need to interact differently with each one. For example, the timid parent usually has a high regard for teachers and does not say much to you, positive or negative. To elicit more responses from the timid parent, offer sincere compliments and be as friendly as possible without overdoing it. Also, ask questions that cannot be answered with a simple yes or no.

Another type is the egotistical parent. These parents are very confident, probably very intelligent, and often brag about themselves and their families. When working with these parents, acknowledge their knowledge and abilities and use them as resources for their children and possibly the entire class. Be careful not to deflate their balloon or you will create a difficult working relationship with them.

Worried parents are usually concerned about more than just their children. They tend to believe that any request for a parent-teacher conference is a bad sign. For parents who are worriers, acknowledge and respect their concerns. If their children are doing well in school, assure the parents of this, and if their children aren't doing well, assure the parents that there are very few learning or behavior problems that cannot be solved. Action plans on how to help their children often give parents some relief.

Finally, critical parents are those who come in with "expert" opinions on how to teach children. They are usually very demanding and skeptical of what most teachers do. Do not argue with such parents; empathize instead. Discuss only those areas in which you are knowledgeable, and admit that educators do not have all the answers. Who does?

Because no parent wants to feel ambushed at the end of the school year, keep parents informed of student progress and achievement throughout the year. If you have any concerns about promoting a particular student to the next grade level, tell parents about your concerns as soon as possible. It is best to begin talking about the possibility of retention long before the first semester or first trimester is over because this will give parents enough time to get their children more help, such as tutors, to try to catch up before the year is over. Keeping parents informed not only improves your working relationship with them but also is in the best interest of your students.

Conducting Effective Parent-Teacher Conferences

Conducting an effective parent-teacher conference plays a big part in a successful school year. For required parent-teacher conferences, you might want to send home a positive letter inviting the parents and asking them to check off the top three times they are available to meet with you. Whether or not the conference is required, include a questionnaire when you write back to confirm the appointment. The questionnaire should include questions about what parents feel are their children's strengths and weaknesses, how they can help their children at home, and any questions they might have for you. If a parent has requested the meeting, it is imperative that you find out in advance exactly what the parent wants to discuss. If it is a complaint, perhaps taping the meeting or inviting witnesses, such as your principal or other staff members, might be necessary.

The following questions can help you examine possible teacher behaviors that can establish and nurture your relationships with parents when meeting with them. Resource 2.4 has parent-teacher conference tips you might want to consider.

7.46 What can you do to improve the chances of a successful parent-teacher conference?

a. What does your conference invitation say?
b. What questions can you include in your questionnaire?
c. How can you schedule your conferences to avoid having too many in a row?
d. Are students allowed to attend the conference? Are their siblings allowed?

I once had a scheduled 20-minute parent-teacher conference last longer than 60 minutes. The parents had a very long list of questions for me, and I wasn't prepared to discuss most of them. The conference was a disaster. And parents who had scheduled their conferences right after this one ended up waiting a very long time, so I had to deal with their complaints. I learned the hard way that it is imperative to find out what parents want to discuss, whether it is a routine parent-teacher conference or not, and to agree on the focus of the conference ahead of time so that concerns with the highest priority get addressed. I also learned that if a conference is running more than a couple of minutes over the allotted time, to be fair to the other parents who are patiently waiting their turn, I need to ask the parent that we schedule a follow-up meeting to continue our discussion.

Communicating Parents' Role in Homework

Parents need to understand their role in their children's homework. They need to know how much assistance they should be giving their children. Remember to take into consideration all the expectations about homework discussed in Chapter 2. Make your expectations clear to them in your classroom handbook, in a letter, or in a newsletter to parents on the first day of school.

Homework is a way to teach students about responsibility. It should also be used to practice skills that you have already taught and students have practiced under your supervision and understood. Homework assignments should ensure a high level of success, minimizing frustration for both students and parents. Before students go home, they should understand exactly what is expected in the assignment. Careful planning helps create a positive climate during homework time and helps build a favorable impression of you, the teacher.

7.47 What is the goal of homework?

7.48 What do you expect to be parents' role in homework?

7.49 How can you communicate this expectation?

7.50 What things can you do to ensure a high success rate on home-work?

Showing Parents That Their Children Are Special to You

Another way to improve your relationship with parents is to make sure that you show them that their children are special to you. Some parents are especially concerned about their children being recognized. A student recognition plan is one way to address this concern. Even if one is not required, establish a student recognition plan in your classroom. Teachers often use Student of the Week, Show and Tell, and other programs to highlight students and their accomplishments. Find out what your colleagues are using. To get the most out of the activity, choose one that you feel is worthwhile, is developmentally appropriate, and helps students achieve some of your instructional goals.

7.51 Do you have a student recognition program in your class?
    a. Is it worthwhile and developmentally appropriate, and does it help students achieve some of the instructional goals?
    b. How is it structured?

Another way to show parents that you believe their children are special is to celebrate students' birthdays. This makes your students feel special and allows parents to get involved in the celebration. Some teachers try to schedule the day or week when a student is recognized as Student of the Week with the child's birthday. This is very efficient and does not let a student's birthday dampen anyone else's special week. To simplify matters, some teachers schedule one birthday party per month. Whatever you decide, make sure that it follows school policy.

7.52 What do you want to do to celebrate a student's birthday (if their family's religious beliefs permit celebrating birthdays)?
    a. When and how do you want to celebrate birthdays that fall over weekends and vacations?
    b. How do you want to involve parents in the celebration?

Plan how you will thank your parent and community volunteers. Find out what is customarily done at your school, and plan accordingly.

Your Relationships With Your Coworkers

Colleagues, administrators, and other staff members are part of your support network, so nurture these relationships as you would any other. Act professionally and assertively. Be considerate of others' feelings, and respect their experience and opinions. Brainstorm ways in which you can strengthen these relationships.

7.53 What can you do to build and support relationships with the people you work with?
a. Colleagues
b. Administrators
c. Other school staff
d. Central office personnel

MAKE YOUR PHYSICAL ENVIRONMENT INVITING

As your primary environment, the classroom itself plays a major role in your classroom climate. Stress decreases when your classroom environment is organized, interesting, and clean. To become a successful teacher, you must learn to manage your classroom's physical environment effectively and efficiently. This is very important because this is an area in which most teachers have a considerable amount of control. The classroom environment consists of the floor plan (including furniture and storage areas) and decor (including walls, bulletin boards, and accessories).

Your Classroom's Floor Plan

A classroom floor plan that works to help you avoid potential stressors must address two critical issues: students' need to function with the maximum degree of independence, which also increases their self-esteem, and your need to optimize the use of classroom space while providing for the free movement of people within the room.

To meet both these needs, take into account the traffic pattern in your classroom. Take note of high-traffic areas such as the doors, cubbies (lockers or places where students keep their personal belongings, such as coats, books, and lunches), and other storage areas as well as the classroom sink, bathroom, and water fountain. To promote safety and prevent your students from getting in each other's way, these areas need to remain free of any physical obstacles.

If you plan to work with your students in small groups or in stationary learning centers, you need to create a floor plan that accommodates these separate areas. These areas should not be totally hidden from the rest of the room. You need to be able to see everyone in your room from all vantage points at all times. You also need to make room to allow assistants and volunteers to work with your students during class time. If you teach younger children, you might also want a large floor area where your students can gather when you read a story to them. Regardless of your students' age, you might also want to set aside some desks in quieter spots in the classroom so students can work alone when they feel they need to. Remember to take note of the location of the intercom button or telephone, light switches, heating and cooling controls, and computer and telephone jacks before deciding on your floor plan.

You can place your students' desks or tables in a variety of ways. Note that the most common instance of visual distraction occurs when students are seated around tables looking at one another while the teacher is talking. Placing students with attention problems around tables only makes their attention problems worse. Therefore, the seating arrangement should both maximize students' ability to stay focused and on task and minimize the transition time between activities.

Four effective seating arrangements are paired desks, the horseshoe configuration with the teacher facing the students, the horseshoe with rows and center aisle, and the chevron design composed of tables of four desks each. Figure 7.1 shows these seating arrangements.

Figure 7.1.   Effective Classroom Seating Arrangements

X = Teacher
⌂ = Student desks

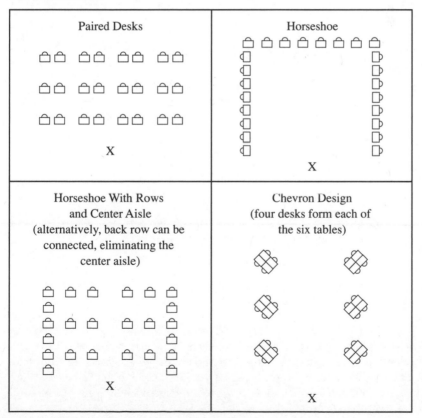

For elementary school students, any of these arrangements works well. At the middle and high school level, it might be more appropriate to place students in the horseshoe most of the time. This configuration fosters discussion, unity, and belonging. It also helps establish a sense of equality among classroom members, helping to break down adolescent cliques that often have a negative impact on classroom climate.

Some arrangements will be better than others for helping you achieve your goals. Experiment. Most schools do not bolt their desks down anymore, so if one arrangement doesn't work, don't be afraid to change it. Visit your colleagues' classrooms to get ideas.

Whichever way you decide to arrange the desks or tables, sit at every seat. While imagining all the seats filled, make sure that each student will be able to see you clearly no matter where you are teaching. And make sure that you can see everyone from any vantage point in the room. If you plan to rearrange your students' desks for different activities, remember to teach your students how to move furniture safely and practice this transition until your class can do it safely and smoothly.

Finally, no matter which seating arrangement you decide to use, teach your students to face you when you are speaking. For example, teach them that they should not only be looking at your face, but they should have their knees and shoulders facing you—knees to knees, shoulders to shoulders. Encourage them to turn their chairs or change positions in their chairs so they face you.

Use the following questions for assessing your floor plan:

7.54 Can every student see the chalkboard?

7.55 Can every student see you from anywhere you stand?

7.56 Can every student see the pull-down screen (used for an overhead projector and a film projector), television, and any other visual aid you plan to use?

7.57 Can you see everyone from anywhere in the classroom?

7.58 Are high-traffic areas clear?

7.59 If you have learning centers, are quiet ones away from noisy ones?

7.60 Does the floor plan support your educational objectives, your teaching style, and your students' learning styles?

7.61 Are seats and cubbies assigned?

7.62 Have you made name tags for each student's desk and cubby so they know what space belongs to them?

Where you place your desk and your assistant's desk (if you have an assistant) is another variable. You need to decide how much time you spend at your desk during the school day and where you want it in relation to the classroom door. Again, if you are unsure about where to place it, ask your colleagues where they place theirs and why. You might find it interesting to hear their reasons.

When I taught first grade, I had many parents bring their children to class each morning. At the beginning of the year, I had my desk in the far corner of the room away from the door. As a result, parents would come in and end up staying a long time—looking at all my bulletin boards and talking with their child's classmates. This became a huge distraction for most of my students. Other teachers had similar problems and solved it by placing their desks closer to the door. I placed my desk near the door, resembling a receptionist's desk. I also tried to spend more time at my desk during arrival time. It worked beautifully, and as a bonus, it made it easier to greet my students as they entered the door, which helped establish a positive classroom climate for the day!

Storage Areas for You and Your Students

Other things you must consider are where you plan to store materials that your students need access to during the school day, such as personal belongings, books, glue, scissors, and math manipulatives. Keep them easily accessible so that your students can be self-sufficient.

7.63 Is there a place in the room for your students' personal belongings, such as coats, book bags, and books?

7.64 Where can you store materials that your students need? that you need?

Storage areas can get messy. Motivate your students to keep their desks, cubbies, and other personal work spaces neat and clean by giving them time to straighten up the areas and sponges to wipe them down, if necessary.

Your Classroom Decor

Your classroom decor complements your floor plan. It includes your window and wall treatments, plants, odors, and accessories. To foster a stress-free, positive climate, the room needs to be soothing, comfortable, and inviting. Colors used to decorate the room, including bulletin boards, should be in soothing colors, such as blues, greens, pale pink, peach, and other pastels. Avoid bright red and orange. Window curtains, even very inexpensive ones, plants, and fresh cut flowers add an inviting touch to any room. They help to soften the hard lines and surfaces of chalkboards, windows, bookshelves, and tables. If permitted, air fresheners (remember to use them only if no one has any allergies to the chemicals in them) and opening the windows to change the air in the classroom help the room smell fresh and pleasant.

Bulletin Boards

Bulletin boards can be entertaining, act as display areas, or be interactive, inviting students to do an activity. Decide how you want to use each of your bulletin boards. They can send powerful messages to anyone who visits your room about what kind of teacher you are and how your classroom is run.

To save time, use fabric or paper that doesn't fade to make longer-lasting backgrounds for bulletin boards. To save money, use string, yarn, or strips of construction paper as bulletin board borders. Also, for easier reading, remember to use larger lettering on the top one-third of wall space and smaller lettering on the lower two-thirds.

Some teachers like to fill the walls with bulletin boards, posters, and other things to make the room stimulating. Others like to keep it simple yet attractive, believing the environment should not distract students. Because there are good arguments for both sides, you must decide for yourself. How? Again, experiment. Try each way for a few weeks and see how your students respond. If stimulating walls help you and your students achieve your goals, keep them. If they make it more difficult to keep your students on task, then go with the simple look. Every class is different. Every teacher is different. The decor that helps your students work well helps you become a more effective teacher.

7.65 How do you plan to decorate your classroom to make it conducive to learning?

7.66 How do you plan to use your bulletin boards to support and enhance your goals?

7.67 Does your decor (especially curtains and bulletin board background paper) violate any fire codes?

If you must share other teachers' classrooms throughout the day, identify how much input you have in those classroom environments and influence them as much as you can. An option might be to rearrange the desks while you conduct class and to put them back when you are through. Be creative!

SUMMARY

In this chapter, different elements that can either assist or detract from a positive classroom climate were discussed. These elements include the physical environment of the classroom and the interpersonal relationships among all the members of the class, including the relationships with students' parents and colleagues. Teachers have a significant amount of control over these elements, and it is very important that they exercise this control because a positive classroom climate is necessary for strong student achievement.

8

Revisit Your Schedule

INTRODUCTION AND OBJECTIVES

In Chapter 5, you allocated time for personal and professional development activities and outlined your teaching schedule. In Chapters 6 and 7, you developed your instructional and climate plans. Now it's time to revisit the schedule you outlined in Chapter 5 to make sure that you have enough time to carry out your instructional and climate plans.

The objectives of this chapter are to help you

- Review your entire schedule to ensure that you will have enough time to achieve all your instructional and climate goals
- Closely examine your planning time to ensure that you have enough time to work on your highest-priority items

TAKE ANOTHER LOOK AT YOUR INSTRUCTIONAL SCHEDULE

Use your Pacing Chart (see Resource 6.1) to take another high-level look at your instructional schedule. Ask yourself the following questions:

8.1 Knowing the units you have chosen and the number and types of goals in each unit, does it appear you have enough time to cover all the goals? Do some units have to be further combined or integrated?

Resource 6.1

During the school year, periodically check to see if you are on track to cover all the units you have planned for the school year. If you are not, make adjustments as soon as possible. These periodic checks help you maintain a steady instructional pace for the remainder of the school year, avoiding the need to cram too much material into the last marking period.

In addition, develop the first couple of units before the first day of school because you will need to use lesson plans from your first unit during the first days and weeks. So set aside time before the school year begins to work on these units.

8.2 When will you work on creating your first and second units so you will have your lesson plans ready for the first days and weeks of school?

GET A HEAD START ON IMPLEMENTING YOUR CLIMATE PLAN

Because the first few days and weeks of school are critical to establishing your classroom climate and your desired tone with parents and colleagues, it is very important that you begin working on your climate plan before the first day of school. The parts of your climate plan that you can and should complete before school begins include setting up classroom procedures, writing your classroom handbook, sending a "welcome back to school" letter to students and parents, creating a floor plan, and setting up bulletin boards, just to name a few. Because completing these tasks before the first day of school is very important for achieving a successful school year, you will have to set aside time during your summer break to complete these items.

8.3 When will you begin the tasks outlined in your climate plan so that you will have everything in place for the critical first days and weeks of school?

In addition, you will have to schedule the time during the first few days and weeks of school to share your climate expectations, including rules and procedures, with your students. This sharing must occur as an integral part of your unit lesson plans or as part of separate activities or lessons. Either way, make sure your schedule allows the time for sharing your climate expectations.

8.4 How and when will you share your climate expectations with your students?

REEXAMINE YOUR PLANNING TIME

Examine all the time you designated as planning time. Remember, you need to use this planning time to accomplish many tasks. The following are only some of the many tasks you need to accomplish during your planning time:

- Developing unit plans and associated lesson plans
- Designing, developing, and implementing the things that establish, maintain, or improve your classroom climate—including classroom decor, lists of procedures, newsletters, and telephone calls—before and after the first day of school
- Grading papers and recording grades
- Completing paperwork required by your employer and school (including report cards)

With so many things to do, how can you allocate your planning time so that you can get everything done that you need to get done? The answer is to first prioritize your tasks. The following questions will help:

8.5 What must you get done right away?

8.6 Can you delegate any of these tasks or parts of these tasks?

Mark a reasonable amount of time on your weekly plan book pages for each high-priority task. As each day passes, keep reevaluating your priorities, and make sure that you are scheduling enough time to complete them.

Once school is in session, you'll have completed many one-time tasks, including setting up your classroom, establishing procedures and rules, and completing your classroom handbook. However, you still need to use your planning time to complete the day-to-day tasks. To help you stay on track for achieving a successful school year, take control now by organizing your planning time to do routine tasks.

8.7 When can you schedule the time to do the following tasks?
    a. Develop your resource units
    b. Correct papers
    c. Work on weekly newsletters to parents
    d. Open and respond to parents' notes and other mail
    e. Complete other required paperwork

To prevent stress at the end of a marking period, do not have major projects and projects involving large amounts of writing due the week before you have to fill out report cards.

Get the most out of your planning time by doing your most difficult tasks during the time you identified in Chapter 5 as your "best time." Also, do not overschedule every moment of your day, because things come up. Leave some breathing room for flexibility in your daily planning time.

SUMMARY

In this chapter, you revisited your schedule to make sure that you have enough time for achieving all your instructional and climate goals. You also took another look at your available planning time and organized it in a way that will help you maintain a comfortable, steady pace for achieving a successful school year.

Section III

Your Momentum

9

Implement and Assess Your Plans

INTRODUCTION AND OBJECTIVES

As you implement the plans you've now put in place, you need to assess if they meet the goals you identified in Chapter 4 as well as the overall goal of this book—to have a successful school year and a thriving teaching career.

The objectives of this chapter are to help you

- Identify whether you are achieving your personal, instructional, and climate goals
- Determine if your action plans are helping you prevent stress so you can become an effective, successful teacher

ARE YOU ACHIEVING YOUR GOALS?

As a teacher, you know that you must continually assess your students, whether you are engaged in a testing situation or not. It's the same with your action plans. You need to be aware of your progress at all times.

To see if you're meeting your personal and professional goals, determine whether you've actually taken the time to do the things you planned. Were you able to accomplish everything you set out to do in the allotted time?

To assess progress toward your instructional goals, first check your students' progress toward and achievement of the instructional goals using formative and summative assessments and evaluations, during and at the end of a unit, respectively. Also, during a lesson, watch your students' facial expressions and listen to your students' questions. Check homework and independent practice assignments. These will give you clues as to whether they understand the material.

In addition, it is important to assess your daily lesson plans to ensure that they are appropriate for your instructional goals and behavioral objectives. The following questions will help you:

9.1 Are your lesson plans developmentally appropriate?

9.2 Are your instructional goals and behavioral objectives clearly stated?

9.3 Are the content and procedures of your lessons written clearly enough so a substitute teacher could follow them?

9.4 Are the materials and instructional resources needed clearly identified and their locations clearly described?

9.5 Do your lessons contain motivators, including a focus activity to get students on task quickly?

9.6 Is it clear how you will check for understanding during the lessons?

9.7 Are multiple opportunities for practice included?

9.8 Is there a proper closure indicated in every lesson plan?

9.9 Do the procedures outlined clearly lead to the attainment of the instructional goals and behavioral objectives?

Finally, assess your lesson presentations. Record and videotape yourself teaching your lessons, and use these tapes to build your own assessment portfolio. When listening and viewing the tapes, look for the following:

- An enthusiastic, positive attitude
- A pleasant, clear, audible voice that conveys leadership
- An organized presentation
- A seamless presentation, where one activity appears to flow into the next activity
- A command over the content and procedure of the lesson
- A demonstration of effective instructional and affective leadership

Try to review the audio- and videotapes with a trusted peer because peer review will help you see your performance through another, possibly more objective, pair of eyes.

There are a number of ways to check whether you are meeting your climate goals. To help you identify student behaviors that are detracting from your climate, keep a log of class behaviors for a week. Examine your log for patterns. Identify behaviors that are keeping you and your class from achieving your classroom climate goals. Also use the log to find clues to the causes of any inappropriate behavior. If you are still not sure what is affecting your climate, ask a trusted colleague to observe you and your class in action. He or she might be able to point out possible causes.

If your classroom climate is still not meeting your goals, take the following steps to identify and correct potential problems:

- *Your expectations:* Are your expectations developmentally appropriate? Have you clearly communicated your expectations? Do all your students understand them?
- *Your classroom arrangement:* Does it allow for smooth traffic flow? Are all students able to see you and the chalkboard? Can you see everyone from any point in the room?
- *Classroom management skills:* Is the room organized or is it chaotic? Are you able to get your students' attention when you need it? Do you have a special signal to do this? Are your students aware of the signal and have you practiced it with them?
- *Classroom rules:* Are they effective? Do all your students understand them? Do they need to be discussed, reviewed, or role-played some more?
- *Classroom procedures:* Do you need to review the procedures? Do you have procedures for all the things that could potentially cause you and your students problems?
- *Inappropriate behavior:* Are you able to nip inappropriate behavior in the bud?
- *Schedules:* Have you communicated the schedules to your students? Are the schedules too tight? Is there too much downtime?
- *Transitions:* Are transitions smooth and orderly?
- *Lesson plans:* Are your lessons developmentally appropriate for your students? Have you individualized instruction to accommodate different learning styles, learning modalities, and other learning needs in order to reduce opportunities for inappropriate behavior?

To determine whether you are achieving your climate goals dealing with the relationships between your class and everyone else, examine the feedback you are getting from parents, colleagues, and administrators. If their overall tone is negative, figure out why they don't think highly of you and your class, and then adjust your climate plan accordingly. If their overall tone is positive, you are probably meeting your goals. Continue the bulk of what you are doing, adjust any of the activities you think might still need tweaking, and eliminate those that do not affect your climate at all.

9.10 Are you achieving the personal and professional, instructional, and climate goals you identified in Chapter 4?

9.11 If you are not achieving your goals, why not? What aspects of your plans need adjusting?

ARE YOU PREVENTING STRESS?

Are your plans helping you prevent stress? The way to determine this is to redo the Stress Inventory you completed in the introduction (see Figure A.1) after you have been executing your plans for several weeks. Again, copy the inventory into your notebook and give yourself as many lines as you need. Remember that answering the questions below the inventory will help you complete it. Redoing this inventory may help you identify whether or not you are still affected by the same stressors. It can also help you identify any new stressors in your life.

Analyze the results of your latest Stress Inventory. Are you able to group your stressors in any way? Compare the results of this inventory with the results you obtained the first time you completed it.

9.12 Are the stressors in your life different now?

9.13 Have you been able to reduce the number of stressors related to your job?

If your plans have not reduced the number of stressors in your life, you need to make some adjustments, but what kind? First, identify which stressors or groups of stressors are causing most of your stress. Then examine your goals and your plans with respect to your current stressors.

9.14 Which stressors or groups of stressors are causing most of your stress?

9.15 Do your goals or plans include ways to address your current stressors?

If you answered no to the last question, you need to act now to address your stressors. By asking yourself empowering questions, like those found throughout this book, you can identify what you might need. If you answered yes to the last question but still experience stress, you must figure out why your plans aren't working. To help you determine where breakdowns occur, answer the following questions:

9.16 Are the goals you chose in Chapter 4 appropriate for addressing your stressors? Do your plans achieve those goals without adding new stressors?

9.17 Do your plans contain activities that help you achieve your goals?
a. Are you following your plans?
b. Is your schedule comfortable, too tight, or too slow?

9.18 Do your plans take advantage of all the resources that are available to you?

If breakdowns occur because your goals are inappropriate or ineffective or your plans are inefficient, make necessary adjustments. Check to make sure your goals and your plans are in sync, and try again. If you determine that your plans are not working because you are not implementing or following them properly, get motivated! If you do, you have so much to gain and only pain to lose. Work your plans. It might not be easy, but the rewards can be great!

SUMMARY

After you know where you want to go and have plans to get you there, you must figure out if you're on the right path. If your plans aren't working, try to figure out why, and then try something else. Make some adjustments to your plans and keep going. Never stop watching for progress. Analyze and evaluate your plans on a daily basis. Make this step a part of your everyday routine. Work it in like your breathing; do it unconsciously yet always be aware of its importance.

10

Become a Reflective Practitioner

INTRODUCTION AND OBJECTIVES

Reflective practice is critical for your continued growth and a thriving teaching career. Reflective practice involves examining your actions by asking questions about them and about the beliefs behind them. This process needs to be a part of your life because it helps you evaluate your growth as a teacher and as a person.

Although this topic is related to Chapter 9, it takes a different approach. Whereas Chapter 9 focused on your plans, this chapter broadens its view, asking you to reflect on your entire planning journey—to look at where you are today compared with where you started.

The objectives of this chapter are to help you

- Begin and maintain the reflective process
- Assess how much you've grown after using this planning guide
- Identify any changes you might want to make in your goals or plans for the future

ENGAGING IN THE REFLECTIVE PROCESS

Reflection is not an automatic process. It is a skill that needs to be nurtured. One way to begin the reflection process is to keep a journal. As often as possible (preferably on a daily basis), record focused accounts of your ideas and feelings before, during, and after your teaching experiences, and continue recording throughout the school year. The purpose of journaling is to provide you with an increasingly complex account of your thoughts and emotions.

Although you should not censor your writing, focus on the issues of teaching. Your journal entries should not simply be descriptions of your activities, nor should they compose a running commentary of your daily life. If you find it difficult to get started, begin your entries by answering the following questions:

- What did you learn from your teaching experiences today?
- After documenting and reviewing the experiences, what questions do you have?
- Were there any notable student actions and reactions during these teaching experiences? Describe and analyze them.
- What concerns you most at this moment?
- How would you rate your performance during each of today's teaching experiences—weak, neutral, or strong?

A rule of thumb is for each entry to be between one and four pages long. Also, avoid becoming too critical of your initial entries. The more entries you make, the more efficiently and precisely you will write.

Every week or so, reread your entries and see if you are becoming more analytical and reflective. As you read several days' worth of entries, ask yourself the following reflective questions:

10.1 Over time, are your feelings changing? How?

10.2 With each new lesson plan, are you changing your teaching strategies to better meet your students' needs?

10.3 With each day that passes, are you finding it easier to establish and maintain a positive classroom climate?

10.4 In your view, do you see evidence that shows that you are moving toward more effective teaching?

Finally, let your journal become your springboard for making the changes you need to help you become the most effective, successful teacher you can become.

HOW MUCH HAVE YOU GROWN?

Reflect on your overall growth as a teacher. To identify areas in which you have (or have not) grown, assess and evaluate your current teaching skills by looking at others' assessments and evaluations of your skills and by conducting a self-assessment and a self-evaluation.

Others' Assessments and Evaluations

One way to judge your skill as a teacher is to ask your principal or other supervisors to assess and evaluate your teaching. In many schools, these are requirements, not options. Regardless, they can be helpful. Another way is to ask a trusted colleague to observe you and give you feedback.

Your students can be another source of evaluations, especially if your students are older. If you do ask your students to evaluate your teaching, make sure that it is done in writing. You can use a classroom suggestion box during the year, or you can ask your students to respond to the following questions about your class:

- What do you like or hate about this class?
- If there is one thing that you could change, what would it be?
- What are the most important classroom procedures? rules?
- What have you learned so far this year?

Your students' answers can be invaluable because they have a different perspective of your class than you do.

Your Self-Assessment and Self-Evaluation

You also need to do a self-assessment and a self-evaluation. Take an honest look at your teaching skills. Using Figure 10.1, rate your teaching skills as they were at the beginning of your current teaching assignment (for many, this equals the beginning of the year) and as they are now. Use a scale of 1 to 10, with 1 being totally unskilled and 10 being highly skilled. Calculate an average for each column.

Figure 10.1.   How Much Have You Grown?

	Beginning of Year	Today
Making enough time to take care of your health		
Managing your emotional state		
Having enough time to fulfill your personal responsibilities		
Staying on top of your employment details		
Getting actively involved in professional development activities		
Sharing your time and expertise with your colleagues		
Identifying and effectively communicating your expectations to students, parents, administrators, and colleagues		
Identifying and understanding federal and state expectations		
Identifying and understanding your school system's policies and procedures		
Identifying and understanding your school system's curriculum for your grade level or subject area		

	Beginning of Year	Today
Identifying and understanding programs and procedures for exceptional students		
Identifying and understanding your responsibilities with respect to paperwork		
Identifying and understanding parents' expectations		
Handling extra duties		
Using your planning time wisely and effectively		
Identifying and understanding how others can help you		
Identifying and gathering the teaching tools and materials you need to be effective		
Determining your personal goals		
Determining your instructional goals		
Determining your climate goals		
Efficiently developing quality unit plans		
Increasing your knowledge of the subject matter you are teaching		
Efficiently developing effective lesson plans		
Varying teaching strategies		
Making your lessons interesting and motivating		
Reaching all students		
Accommodating individual differences and needs, including the needs of exceptional students		
Designing and using effective assessment strategies		
Getting your paperwork done on time		
Maintaining adequate records		
Establishing a positive classroom climate		
Maintaining a positive classroom climate		
Managing student behavior		
Managing your own response to student misbehavior		
Using empathy, active listening skills, and assertiveness when communicating with others		
Identifying and developing effective classroom rules and procedures		
Getting along with administrators and colleagues		
Working with parents successfully		
Conducting effective parent-teacher conferences		
Total		
Final Average		

10.5 Is today's average higher or lower than your average at the beginning of the year (or when you first started this teaching assignment)?

10.6 Are you pleased with your progress? Why or why not?

10.7 Can you identify areas of strength?

10.8 Can you identify areas of weakness?
   a. What goals can you put in place to improve these areas?
   b. What plans do you need to accomplish these goals?

You must also evaluate your growth as an individual. Use today and the day you started reading this book as points of reference. The following questions will help you start evaluating your personal growth:

10.9 How "stressed out" do you feel today compared to the day you began reading this book?

10.10 Are you feeling stronger and more in control?

10.11 Is your self-esteem higher?

10.12 Do you have hope for a better tomorrow?

10.13 Do you feel you have grown as a person?

10.14 Do you feel you have grown as a professional?

CHANGES FOR NEXT TIME

Examine the effective and not-so-effective elements of your journey toward a successful school year and a thriving teaching career. Are there things that you wish you had done differently? Identify what they are. Use the following questions to help you explore the things you can, and want, to do differently next time—for tomorrow or for the next school year:

10.15 Has the journey toward a successful school year and thriving teaching career been satisfying? difficult?

10.16 Was the pace of your journey steady? realistic? comfortable?

10.17 Do you want to keep the same goals, or do you want to change some of them?

10.18 Has your plan been simple to implement?

10.19 What mistakes do you want to avoid in the future?

10.20 What could you do differently? What do you want to do differently?

YOUR FUTURE

Now look to the future. "Where do you go from here?" Perhaps a better question might be, "Where do you *want* to go from here?" Ask yourself the following questions:

10.21 What kind of teacher and person do you want to be five years from now?

10.22 What do you need to do to become that teacher and person?

10.23 How far away are you from your vision of the ideal teacher for your present teaching assignment? What do you need to do to become that ideal teacher?

10.24 Can you apply what you have learned in this book to other areas of your life? How?

Remember, you can be as good a teacher, parent, friend, or person as you want to be. You are in control of your life.

Continually reflect on your actions and beliefs so that you can grow and reach your full potential. Never become complacent, for it will kill your motivation and your desire to become all that you can.

Believe that no matter what the stressor is, you have some control over it and you determine your response to it. Control over stressors is the key to preventing stress and becoming a successful teacher.

Finally, look forward to a better tomorrow and to a better you. Take heart. There is a light at the end of the tunnel.

SUMMARY

This book has been a journey to achieve a successful school year and a thriving teaching career. At the beginning, you looked at where you were and where you wanted to go. You created plans and implemented those plans. Finally, you reflected on the success of your plans and on your growth as a teacher and as a person. For the future, continue to reflect on the effective teaching process you experienced with this planning guide and make any adjustments to your goals and plans to help you continue your journey toward success.

Epilogue

Enabling Successful Teaching: What Educational Leaders at All Levels Must Know

INTRODUCTION AND OBJECTIVES

In today's educational environment, becoming an effective, successful teacher can be difficult, and it can take many years to perfect the necessary skills. However, changes in the way teachers are currently trained and in the amount and kind of support teachers receive at the school level can dramatically decrease both the difficulty and the time it takes to become an effective, successful teacher.

The objectives of this chapter are to

- Outline changes that must be made to teacher training to enable successful teaching
- Highlight several changes at the school level that will enable successful teaching

CHANGES IN TEACHER TRAINING

Teaching is a profession. But the training teachers receive is not typical of that required for the majority of professions. Most professionals receive a lot of on-the-job postgraduate training. For example, a newly hired engineer usually works very closely with more experienced engineers for several months or years. During that time, the novice receives a tremendous amount of training, support, and feedback while gaining invaluable experience. Gradually, the novice engineer becomes competent enough to work alone, but colleagues are always available to answer questions or offer assistance at virtually any time.

On the other hand, most teachers are given very little, if any, on-the-job training. Most teachers are expected to go from novice to expert in one giant leap. They are not eased into their positions as are most other professionals. They are often expected to know everything and to do everything well from day one. For most teachers, this is an impossible task, and failure is inevitable. Consequently, changes must be made to the teacher induction process.

Like other professionals, teachers need a time to be "in training." For at least the first two years of practice, every new teacher should be assigned a mentor. The mentor should work with the new teacher in the classroom on a full-time basis for at least one full semester. A mentor should be assigned to only one new teacher so the two can work together the entire school day. Retired teachers who were very effective and successful teachers make great mentors. With increasing numbers of retired teachers, they are a tremendous resource to those who are still struggling to succeed.

Mentors in turn need training to be effective. The state licensure office should either organize the training or be heavily involved in the training, because mentors should also understand the new initial licensure and portfolio requirements that many states now have in place for teachers. One of the mentors' responsibilities should be to help teachers complete these requirements. Mentors' other responsibilities should include demonstrating effective instructional practices and coaching of all the requirements for successful teaching outlined in this book.

A concern that might be raised at this point is who should pay for all these mentors. Because mentoring is on-the-job training, the employer will probably be the one to pay the mentor's salary. This is similar to when a corporation hires and pays someone to train its employees. However, where will the money come from? It is a matter of priorities. There is grant money, from both private and government sources. And just as in any budget, if an item is a priority, there will usually be enough money set aside for it.

In addition, peer coaching must become an integral method of professional development for all teachers. Peer coaching is a confidential process where two or more teachers work together to reflect on current teaching practices, to explore and implement new teaching strategies, and to solve problems they face in the workplace. Studies show that peer coaching is one of the most effective methods for implementing new learning of successful teaching strategies.

For peer coaching to work, teachers must be trained how to be peer coaches. Also, the administration and school leaders at all levels must take active roles in establishing and supporting peer coaching teams by providing time for the teams to meet. Effective peer coaching demands a culture that rewards collegial planning, experimentation, and reflection.

In addition, please let us stop believing that a crash course in teaching is enough time to prepare someone from industry for the intricacies of teaching! A better place to spend the money is to help retain the teachers that are already employed. The rate of attrition is high for college- and university-trained teachers, but it is even higher for teachers trained with a crash course in teaching. This is not to say that we should not recruit or encourage career changers or retired people! We need them. We want them—their expertise, their life experiences, and their fresh perspectives. In fact, I was recruited from industry and strongly believe that career changers have a lot to offer schools. But please, give career changers the training and support they need to succeed.

Teaching is not an easy job, and just because career changers were once students themselves does not mean they are experts on teaching. Just because they might have successfully raised their own children does not mean career changers automatically have the skill to deal with others' children—many of whom come from homes very different from those of the prospective teachers, with different beliefs, traditions, expectations, and so forth. Just because they might have successfully tutored their own children or others' children does not necessarily mean career changers will be successful when teaching a group of 25 to 30 (or more) students at one time, all with different ability and achievement levels—even if the students are "tracked," as in most middle and high schools.

Finally, we cannot underestimate all the other things teachers have to manage—everything mentioned in this book. It is a disservice to those who want to teach, who want to be part of a noble, wonderful profession, to give them only a few weeks of training to do such a complicated job in an effective way. We need to improve teacher training and allow that path to be taken by all preservice teachers, whether they are coming to the profession from undergraduate settings or from industry.

Student teaching must be increased to an entire year. In no way does an 8- or even 15-week student teaching experience fully prepare anyone for teaching. Unfortunately, student teaching usually occurs during the final college semester—in the spring for most students. As a result, a student teacher enters a classroom that has already been under way for several months. Procedures, expectations, and rules all have been identified and internalized. Usually, the student teacher finds him- or herself in an environment that is already running like a well-oiled machine. But how did it get like that? How was the routine established? How were the rules and procedures learned? These are the things, among so many others, discussed in this book. These are the things established during the first days and weeks of school, so most student teachers do not get the benefit of having them modeled. They do not experience first hand how to establish all the things that teachers must establish during the first days and weeks of school to achieve a successful school year.

In addition, all prospective teachers should substitute teach at least during their junior year in college. This would have multiple benefits. For the many districts struggling to fill positions, having an army of substitute teachers would alleviate a lot of problems. For the student teachers, having this wealth of experience would set them on course for a successful career. Student teachers should substitute in all different grade levels, from kindergarten through Grade 12, including special education, art, music, physical education, and so forth. They should be exposed to all different experiences because (1) it would help them decide if teaching is the right career for them; (2) it would help them decide which grade level or special area they would like to teach; (3) they would gain insight into how different teachers do the myriad of things required of them (this is a great way to learn about how teachers manage classroom rules and procedures); (4) they would get a feel for different schools' cultures, which would give them insight into the environment they would like to work in after graduation; (5) they would get a foot in the door for future employment opportunities; and (6) they would earn money while gaining invaluable experience and exposure in the profession they are pursuing.

For this type of student teaching to occur, colleges and universities need to develop the junior-year academic schedules with classes in the afternoons and evenings, so students have the time during the day to substitute teach. Ideally, students would have all weekdays available for substitute teaching so they could experience the difference between teaching on a Monday versus a Friday and teaching at the beginning of a school year versus the end.

CHANGES AT THE SCHOOL LEVEL

In addition to changes in how teachers are trained and inducted into the profession, things must change at the school level. Many of the changes recommended here would support the topics discussed in this book. For some schools, the following discussion is not pertinent. But in too many schools, these changes need to occur to enable successful teaching. School leaders, including principals and school system leaders, are in positions to make the changes discussed here.

First, help teachers take care of their personal needs. One of the easiest ways to do this is to provide teachers with enough planning time during the school day so they don't have to bring work home with them. This would leave them with plenty of time to be with loved ones, rest, exercise, and take care of their personal responsibilities. In addition, take care of teachers' needs by providing them with clear information about their job responsibilities, teacher evaluations, salary, benefits, and legal rights and responsibilities. Also, make sure that teachers understand the role of their local education association or union.

Second, review with teachers different school procedures, rules, and policies. Distribute this information to teachers in the form of a handbook and review it together. The handbook should be very thorough and should include at least the items outlined in Chapter 2. Examples include fire drill procedures, how to respond to student illness or injury, securing parental permission for field trips and other special activities, school policies on student discipline, homework, attendance, and so forth.

Third, make sure that all teachers have the tools and other resources to do their jobs effectively, including copies of the latest curriculum guides and state and federal laws that pertain to their positions. In addition, provide every teacher with a computer, preferably a laptop. Also, provide every teacher with voice mail, accessible via the school's main telephone number, and access to a private office with an outside telephone line to enable them to have confidential conversations with parents. To ensure that teachers have the necessary tools and resources, principals and other school leaders should do the legwork to provide teachers with these things before the school year begins instead of expecting teachers to scramble to gather the resources they need.

Fourth, make instructional changes at the school level. For example, institute block scheduling and reduce class size. If reducing class size is not possible, establish teams of collaborating teachers to team teach larger classes. Also, make sure that teacher workloads are equitable and that new teachers are not given the most difficult assignments.

Fifth, establish a climate that expects, values, and rewards collaboration. In addition to establishing and supporting peer coaching, use faculty meetings to provide ongoing training instead of using the meeting to disseminate information that is easily shared with teachers using a newsletter or e-mail.

Sixth, establish a climate that expects, values, and rewards a high level of professionalism and encourages teachers to take risks. Provide substantial support and feedback to teachers to help them assess and improve their instructional skills. Establish high expectations for teaching effectiveness, and provide incentives and time for improving teaching skills.

Seventh, become strong affective leaders and establish a positive school climate for teachers, students, and parents. Build a sense of community. Use empathy and build rapport with teachers, students, and parents. Establish schoolwide behavioral expectations for everyone and communicate them clearly.

Finally, make sure that every teacher has enough planning time built into every school day to plan, collaborate, assess, and reflect. Time is the greatest resource you can provide for your teachers. It is absolutely necessary for personal and professional growth and the catalyst for effective, successful teaching.

SUMMARY

Become teacher advocates. This book outlines what teachers need to become effective, successful teachers, most of which can be supported by educational leaders at every level. Take advantage of the wealth of information in this book to determine what teachers need from their administrators and other school leaders. Provide them with proper training, adequate resources, and sufficient time to do their jobs effectively, and the rewards to your school system will be great.

Resources for Successful Teaching

Resource 1.1

Professional Development Plan

The following is a list of items usually found on a professional development plan:

- Your name, position, school, grade levels and subject areas, areas of certification, and the dates of the plan's cycle (for example, the 2002–2003 school year)
- No more than three professional or educational development goals written as concise statements of what you want to accomplish
- Two or three strategies (steps you will take to accomplish the goal) for each goal
- The number of certification renewal, workshop, or college credits received for completing each strategy, if any
- The estimated completion date for each strategy
- The resources, such as people, funds, material, and time, needed to complete each strategy
- A place to write in the date when each strategy is accomplished
- The types of assessments that will be used to assess the extent to which the goal has been accomplished
- Your and your principal's signatures indicating that the plan was initially reviewed
- A checkmark by each goal you accomplished and for any goal you did not accomplish, an explanation of why you did not
- Additional signatures indicating that the plan was reviewed during and at the end of the plan's cycle

Resource 2.1

Planning Celebrations

To prevent potentially stressful celebrations, use these questions when planning a classroom celebration or party:

1. When and where will the celebration take place?

2. Will there be food and beverages?
   a. What kinds?
   b. Who is in charge of bringing or buying it?
   c. How much does it cost and how is it paid for?
   d. How are the food and beverages served? By whom?
   e. What serving utensils and containers are needed? Who supplies them?
   f. Who supplies the plates, cups, napkins, and eating utensils?

3. Will there be decorations?
   a. Who buys or makes them?
   b. Who does the decorating?

4. Who cleans up afterward? What cleaning supplies are needed?

5. Will there be music?
   a. What kind?
   b. Who can bring the stereo, radio, or other necessary equipment?
   c. Who can bring audiocassettes or CDs?
   d. Will the noise disturb other people?
   e. Who is in charge of choosing and changing the music?
   f. Who regulates the volume?

6. Will there be games?
   a. Who can bring the games?
   b. Who is in charge of selecting and organizing participants?
   c. Are there prizes? Where do they come from?
   d. Who decides the winners?

7. Has the necessary permission been given?

Resource 2.2

Taking Class Trips

There are four major stages for taking class trips. The first stage includes planning an educational purpose for the trip and selecting where you and your class will go. Second is organizing the trip. Third is taking the class trip. The last stage is evaluating the trip.

The first stage is done when you create your unit plans (see Chapter 6). Your destination should have some relevance to your curriculum. Also, ask the following:

1. How many trips are you allowed?

2. Where are you allowed to go?

3. How do the places chosen support your curriculum?

The second stage is where all of the "leg work" takes place. You need to familiarize yourself with the site, including any overnight accommodations, and any school procedures for taking a class trip. Answering the following questions will help you with this stage:

4. What is the procedure to get the following?
   a. Permission (from school and from parents)

If your school does not have a standard form for permission slips and you have to create your own, make sure you include the following information: the date of the trip, the departure time, the return time, and information about your destination, the cost, and the mode of travel. In addition, on the slip, ask each parent for the following: family physician's name and telephone number, any prescription drug information, other medical information, emergency phone numbers, emergency medical aid permission, and parent signature and date.

---

   b. Transportation: Which types of transportation are allowed?
   c. Insurance clearance
   d. Chaperones
   e. Funding for students', teachers', and chaperones' admission and transportation costs (including any tips for the driver, if applicable)

5. Is a check or cash used to pay for admission? transportation?

6. How far in advance of the actual trip are you required to have it planned and paid for?

7. Do you need reservations? Are large groups only admitted on certain days or during certain hours?

8. What and where are the site's facilities for the following?
   a. Restrooms
   b. Eating
   c. Disabled students

     d. Overnight accommodations (if applicable): Is round-the-clock security provided, or must you provide your own? Is an effort made to keep your rooms together?

     e. Souvenirs

9. What are the rules regarding the use of cameras?

10. What are the rules regarding sleeping arrangements if overnight accommodations are necessary?

11. How do you arrange for chaperones?

     a. What is the maximum chaperone-to-student ratio that is allowed?

     b. Besides parents, can other teachers who work with your students be asked to chaperone?

     c. Are chaperones allowed to take the same transportation as the students?

     d. If parents must drive themselves, are they allowed to drive their own children to and from the destination? Are they allowed to drive other students?

     e. Are chaperones allowed to bring other children who are not a part of your class?

     f. Are chaperones allowed to take students directly home from the site, or must students return to school first to sign out?

12. If the trip extends through the time for breakfast, lunch, or dinner, do students need to bring their own food and drink, or are they provided?

     a. If food and drink are provided, is there an additional cost?

     b. If you bring your own food and drink, do you need to provide coolers to prevent spoilage?

13. If you take a bus, what are the bus driver's rules and procedures with respect to seating arrangements, noise levels, eating food and beverages on the bus, and so forth?

After the trip is planned, both students and chaperones need to be made aware of several things. Use the following questions to help you identify them:

14. Do your students and chaperones know the following?

     a. The educational purpose of this trip

     b. What kind of things they should be looking for on the trip

     c. What kind of follow-up work they will need to do when you return from the trip

15. Do your students and chaperones understand the following?

     a. What they should and should not wear and bring

     b. When money and permission slips are due

    c. Appropriate behavior at the site

    d. Appropriate behavior on the bus (or other transportation vehicle)

    e. Where they must sit on the bus or at the site (if applicable)

    f. What they should do in case they get lost or hurt

    g. When and where they need to meet the group

Before the day of the field trip, ensure that you have taken care of things that are necessary for a successful class trip. Answering the following questions can help:

16. Do you have the following items before your scheduled class trip?
    a. A confirmation letter from the host of your class trip
    b. A confirmation from the transportation company hired
    c. A confirmation of insurance clearance
    d. Administrative approval and clearance on arrangements
    e. All the required permission slips

17. Have you notified the cafeteria of your trip so that they know fewer students will be eating at school that day?

18. Have you informed other teachers of your trip, especially those whose schedules will be impacted?

19. Have you arranged for the following?
    a. Meals
    b. Restrooms
    c. Transportation, including the route approved if walking

20. Have you created and sent a cover letter to parents that describes the purpose, itinerary, meal provisions, and special clothes required for your trip?

On the day of the trip, use the following questions to help you with last-minute concerns:

21. Have your students and chaperones been given necessary name tags, maps, instructions, and directions?

22. Have you packed extra Band-Aids and a first-aid kit, Handi-Wipes, paper towels, tissues, and trash bags?

23. Do you have emergency telephone numbers for all your students?

After returning from the trip, you and your students should evaluate it. Look at different aspects of the trip to make changes and improvements for next time. Use the following questions to help you pinpoint the things you need to review:

24. Did your students gain the knowledge you hoped they would?

25. Did your students see how the trip related to their curriculum?

26. Were your students behaved during every stage of the trip?

27. Was the site appropriate for your goals? for the interest and developmental level of your students?

28. Were the size and accommodations of the site adequate?

29. Did the transportation arrangements provide adequate space and safety? Were they affordable?

30. Was the length of the ride too long?

31. Were the chaperones on the trip adequately prepared for their assignments?

32. Were there any problems or complications that you had not anticipated?

Resource 2.3

Substitute Teacher Kit

The following is a list of the information and plans to include in your substitute teacher kit:

1. Lists
   a. Class rosters
   b. Names of students who are helpful and trustworthy
   c. Names of students who have behavior or academic difficulties
   d. Names of students who have behavior or academic contracts and an explanation of how the contracts work
   e. Names of students who need to take medication, when, and who is allowed to administer the medication
   f. Names of students that have existing health problems and emergency procedures to handle the problems
   g. Members of different reading, lab, or other groups you have in your class
   h. Assistant teachers and volunteers, including the time they are available and their responsibilities
   i. Names and titles of all staff and faculty members, including names of teachers next door, who can answer any questions during the day
   j. Transportation information for each student

2. Maps
   a. School
   b. Classroom seating charts
   c. Cafeteria seating chart
   d. Emergency escape routes and locations for your class during severe weather emergencies

3. Schedules
   a. Daily class-related activities, including but not limited to
      i. Arrival and dismissal times
      ii. Class periods
      iii. Schedule of lessons and other classroom activities
      iv. Lunch
      v. Recess
      vi. Special classes, such as art, music, etc. (also note day, time, and place)
   b. Students' volunteer activities, such as main office helpers, custodial helpers, and safety patrol helpers
   c. Your extra duties (such as bus, lunch, etc.) and a description of associated responsibilities
   d. Students' pull-out (when your students leave your classroom to work with another teacher) or push-in (when another teacher comes into your classroom to work with your students) activities, including resource, band, and others

4. Important school and classroom rules to ensure a smooth day, including but not limited to
   a. Classroom management and discipline system
   b. When it is appropriate to send a student to the office and the procedure to follow when doing so

5. Important school and classroom procedures to ensure a smooth day, including but not limited to
   a. Emergencies (fire, severe weather, first aid, etc.)
   b. Arrival and dismissal routines
   c. Sign-in and sign-out procedures for students and teachers
   d. Attendance procedures (including collecting absentee notes)
   e. Hallway, restroom, and water fountain use
   f. Students' free time
   g. Sending a student to the health office

6. Plans
   a. Lesson plans with all needed materials or the location of the plans and materials denoted in the plans
   b. Grade book, if necessary
   c. Extra activities in case students finish their work early or in case lesson plans do not go as planned

7. A substitute feedback form that includes areas to write
   a. The substitute teacher's name and home telephone number
   b. A way to indicate which plans were completed
   c. A list of names of absent students
   d. A list of names of students who were helpful
   e. A list of names of students who needed extra assistance
   f. Any extra work that was done
   g. Any behavior problems
   h. General notes and comments

Resource 2.4

Tips for a Successful Parent-Teacher Conference

- Schedule breathing room before and after the conference.
- Make an outline of the points you want to cover.
- Review the student's record from previous years, and check for indications of changes in behavior or academic achievement.
- Send home an upbeat letter before the conference.
- Select one or two goals for the conference, and communicate to parents in advance the main purpose of the conference, such as giving information, receiving information, or solving problems.
- Find out if your school system requires that the student attend the parent-teacher conference.
- Find out what you are expected to do if parents bring younger children along. Can the main office watch the children? Are they allowed to play outside unsupervised while you conference with the parents?
- Be ready to discuss the student's social, emotional, and academic progress and achievement with accuracy, and have specific supporting information available to share with parents.
- Estimate the degree to which the purpose of the conference will be achieved in one meeting. If there is too much to cover in one meeting, limit the goals for the conference and plan for a follow-up conference.
- If other teachers will also attend the conference, hold a briefing before the conference to make sure everyone has the same information and is aware of the goals of the conference.
- Anticipate parents' responses that indicate whether successful communication has occurred.
- Be ready to discuss the student's academic level.
- Be able to explain what standardized tests measure, how to interpret the test scores, how accurate the score is, and what effect, if any, the test will have on the student's schooling or placement.
- Avoid using educational jargon and presenting irrelevant material.
- Have all of the student's work that you want to share and any notes you need ready. Share the work with the student prior to the conference, if possible.
- Use a table and adult-size chairs.
- Dress professionally.
- Be on time.
- Be positive and enthusiastic.
- Have a place to put coats and umbrellas.
- Have paper and pencils available for parents to use.
- Sit where you can see a clock.
- Avoid physical barriers such as desks and uncomfortable chairs. Sit beside parents, not across from them.

- Keep a chair outside your door for parents who arrive early and must wait their turn.
- Smile, use a firm handshake, make eye contact, use parents' names as you greet them, and make sure you use the correct name—do not assume that the parents' last names are the same as the child's.
- Make parents feel welcome.
- Review the purpose of the conference, how long it will take, and give an agenda (verbal or written).
- Begin on a positive note by pointing out the student's strengths.
- Do not use labels or generalizations.
- Present proof of student's growth; there should not be any surprises.
- Give parents a chance to talk early in the conference.
- Watch parents' body language and tone.
- Listen attentively and actively. Listen to both verbal and nonverbal messages.
- Be empathetic.
- Strive to set a tone of partnership, cooperation, and understanding because the overall tone or mood of the conference will probably be remembered long after the content of the conference is forgotten.
- Gather information about the child from the parents, including what works for them when helping their child at home.
- Do not overwhelm parents; present one or two problem areas only.
- If you suspect that a problem at home is affecting the student's learning or behavior, report the problem and ask parents if they have any ideas about the cause; do not pry.
- Let parents talk and ask questions; if they disagree with what you are saying, hear them out and respond with, "I hear what you are saying. Let's work things out together."
- Avoid becoming defensive when parents question your judgment. Keep an open mind to parents' ideas.
- Try to see the student from the parents' point of view.
- Serve as a resource person to the parents.
- Present a fair, impartial, complete, and meaningful evaluation of the child.
- Use anecdotal data consisting of objective facts to provide examples of behavior instead of labeling a child as lazy, disobedient, and so forth.
- Keep the conversation focused on the student.
- Do not compare the student with others.
- Do not interrogate the parents; they will be more open to you if you do not put them on the defensive.
- Do not criticize or argue.
- Have resources handy to send home with the parents, such as telephone numbers of counseling services and tutors (if allowed), book lists, lists of activities to do at home, and homework tips.
- Be prepared to explain services offered by the school system for children with different kinds of special needs.

- If parents ask for help with a problem, respectfully suggest ways they might solve it, but be careful not to function as a therapist or to give too much advice. Stick to your role as a teacher and consider referring the parents to another resource, if needed.
- Identify ways you can work together to help the student.
- Determine a follow-up schedule to inform parents about their child's progress.
- Do not make any promises that you might not be able to keep.
- Let them know how to set up another conference with you in the future.
- Keep the conference to about 20 minutes.
- Keep the conference focused.
- Whenever possible, reassure parents with information on what is normal developmentally.
- Give a warning about the ending of the conference when there is approximately 5 or 10 minutes left, and summarize what was discussed.
- Ask parents to summarize what they heard you say so you can make sure you communicated clearly.
- Offer parents the opportunity to bring up final questions or comments.
- End on a positive note; it sets the tone for future interactions.
- End the meeting on time.
- See the parents to the door and thank them for coming.
- Keep the conversation confidential.
- Make a record of the conference, using your school's procedure and forms, if available.
- Reflect on what happened during the conference and document ideas to help improve future parent-teacher conferences.
- Send a follow-up note summarizing key points of the conference.
- Follow up with parents and the student to make sure follow-up plans were carried out.

Resource 2.5

Sample Table of Contents for a Classroom Handbook

The following are possible sections of a classroom handbook that you can create to help others learn about your expectations. Some of these items may already be listed in your school's student handbook and, therefore, might not need to be repeated in your classroom handbook. Also, consider creating your entire handbook in an easy-to-read FAQ (frequently asked questions) format. The possible sections include the following:

- Your teaching and instructional philosophies
- Overview of the curriculum for the school year
- Critical tasks that children are expected to accomplish at this grade level

- How students will be grouped for instruction
- What teaching strategies will be used in the major subject areas
- How grades are determined
- When report cards are distributed
- Dates set aside for fall and spring semester parent-teacher conferences, including interim conferences
- Homework policy
- Homework folders or weekly folders procedures
- Classroom rules and consequences (positive and negative)
- School policy on the use and care of instructional materials, such as textbooks, supplementary teaching materials (for example, maps, globes, and science kits), audio-visual equipment (for example, films, videos, CDs, and filmstrips), computer hardware, and computer software
- Arrival and dismissal times
- How absences are handled, including how and when a student must make up the work missed
- Schedules of special classes such as art, music, media, and physical education
- List of necessary school supplies, including what not to bring to school
- What kinds of snacks to bring for snack time
- Special classroom activities such as Student of the Week, birthday celebration procedures and rules, and others
- Special programs that are available at the school, such as speech, psychological services, reading resource, bilingual services, programs for the gifted and talented, and after-school instructional assistance
- List of extracurricular activities available at the school, including sports and clubs
- Key calendar dates for the school year
- Classroom parents committee information
- Parent volunteer guidelines
- How you will communicate with parents (for example, newsletter, telephone calls, and notes)
- How a parent can contact you
- How a parent can request a conference with you
- Dress code (if school has one)
- Map of the school with the location of your classroom(s) highlighted
- Safety, fire, and severe-weather procedures
- How to apply for free or reduced lunch benefits
- Description of school nurse/health office services available

Resource 3.1

Sample Parent Survey

This is a sample parent survey that you can use to gather information about your students' parents. The information collected can be used to help you effectively integrate parents into your classroom.

Name:
Address:
Daytime telephone:
Please circle the activities you are interested in doing for your child's class:

Informal talks
Demonstrations
Sharing items from your home

If you are interested in doing an informal talk, please circle the general subject you would like to present and specify what the particular topic would be:

Job:
Hobby:
Travels:
Country of origin or of family's ancestors:
Other:

If you are interested in sharing any special talents by doing a demonstration, please circle the general topic and specify what the demonstration would be:

Child care:
Crafts:
Cooking:
Dance:
Drawing/painting:
Exercise:
Financial investing:
Gardening:
Hobbies:
Music (voice or musical instrument):
Pets:
Other:

If you are interested in sharing any collections or items from your home, please specify:

Videos, films, CDs (music), and so forth:
Souvenirs, figurine collections, costumes, and so forth:
Computer software or hardware:
Other:

Resource 3.2

Professional Organizations

American Alliance for Health,
  Physical Education, Recreation
  and Dance
1900 Association Drive
Reston, VA 20191-1598
(800) 213-7193

American Association of Physics
  Teachers
One Physics Ellipse
College Park, MD 20740-3845
(301) 209-3311

American Council on the Teaching
  of Foreign Languages
6 Executive Plaza
Yonkers, NY 10701
(914) 963-8830

American Federation of Teachers
555 New Jersey Avenue, NW
Washington, DC 20001
(202) 879-4400

American Library Association
50 E. Huron Street
Chicago, IL 60611
(800) 545-2433

American School Counselor
  Association
801 North Fairfax Street, Suite 310
Alexandria, VA 22314
(703) 683-2722 or (800) 306-4722

American Speech-Language-
  Hearing Association
10801 Rockville Pike
Rockville, MD 20852
(800) 638-8255

Association for Career and
  Technical Education
1410 King Street
Alexandria, VA 22314
(800) 826-9972

Association for Childhood
  Education International
17904 Georgia Avenue, Suite 215
Olney, MD 20832
(301) 570-2111 or (800) 423-3563

Association for Educational
  Communications and
  Technology
1800 N. Stonelake Drive, Suite 2
Bloomington, IN 47408
(877) 677-AECT or (812) 335-7675

Association for Experiential
  Education
2305 Canyon Boulevard, Suite 100
Boulder, CO 80302-5651
(303) 440-8844

Association for Supervision and
  Curriculum Development
1703 North Beauregard Street
Alexandria, VA 22311-1714
(800) 933-2723 or (703) 578-9600

Council for Exceptional Children
1110 North Glebe Road, Suite 300
Arlington, VA 22201-3660
(888) 232-7733

Council for Learning Disabilities
P.O. Box 40303
Overland Park, KS 66204
(913) 492-8755

International Reading Association
800 Barksdale Road
P.O. Box 8139
Newark, DE 19714-8139
(302) 731-1600

Kappa Delta Pi
3707 Woodview Trace
Indianapolis, IN 46268-1158
(317) 871-4900 or (800) 284-3167

Learning Disabilities Association
of America
4156 Library Road
Pittsburgh, PA 15234-1349
(412) 341-1515

Lutheran Education Association
7400 Augusta Street
River Forest, IL 60305
(708) 209-3343

Modern Language Association of
America
26 Broadway, 3rd Floor
New York, NY 10004-1789
(646) 576-5000

Music Teachers National
Association
441 Vine Street, Suite 505
Cincinnati, OH 45202-2811
(513) 421-1420 or (888) 512-5278

National Alliance of Black School
Educators
2816 Georgia Avenue, NW
Washington, DC 20001
(202) 483-1549

National Art Education Association
1916 Association Drive
Reston, VA 20191-1590
(703) 860-8000

National Association for Bilingual
Education
1030 15th St. NW, Suite 470
Washington, DC 20005
(202) 898-1829

National Association of Biology
Teachers
12030 Sunrise Valley Drive,
Suite 110
Reston, VA 20191
(703) 264-9696 or (800) 406-0775

National Association for the
Education of Young Children
1509 16th Street, NW
Washington, DC 20036
(202) 232-8777

National Association of Elementary
School Principals
1615 Duke Street
Alexandria, VA 22314
(703) 684-3345 or (800) 386-2377

National Association for Gifted
Children
1707 L Street, NW, No. 550
Washington, DC 20036
(202) 785-4268

National Association for Industry-
Education Cooperation
235 Hendricks Boulevard
Buffalo, NY 14226-3304
(716) 834-7047

National Association of School
Psychologists
4340 East West Highway, Suite 402
Bethesda, MD 20814-4468
(301) 657-0270

National Association of Secondary
School Principals
1904 Association Drive
Reston, VA 20191-1537
(703) 860-0200

National Business Education
  Association
1914 Association Drive
Reston, VA 20191-1596
(703) 860-8300

National Catholic Educational
  Association
1077 30th Street, NW, Suite 100
Washington, DC 20007
(202) 337-6232

National Council for the Social
  Studies
8555 Sixteenth Street, Suite 500
Silver Spring, MD 20910
(301) 588-1800

National Council of Teachers of
  English
1111 Kenyon Road
Urbana, IL 61801-1096
(800) 369-6283

National Council of Teachers of
  Mathematics
1906 Association Drive
Reston, VA 20191-1502
(703) 620-9840

National Education Association
1201 16th Street, NW
Washington, DC 20036
(202) 833-4000

National Middle School
  Association
4151 Executive Parkway, Suite 300
Westerville, OH 43081
(800) 528-6672

National Rural Education
  Association
c/o Bob Mooneyham
University of Oklahoma
820 Van Vleet Oval, Room 227
Norman, OK 73019
(405) 325-7959 www.nrea.net

National Science Teachers
  Association
1840 Wilson Boulevard
Arlington, VA 22201-3000
(703) 243-7100

Phi Delta Kappa
408 N. Union Street
P.O. Box 789
Bloomington, IN 47402-0789
(800) 766-1156 or (812) 339-1156

Teachers of English to Speakers of
  Other Languages
700 South Washington Street,
  Suite 200
Alexandria, VA 22314
(703) 836-0774

Resource 3.3

Possible School Supplies

This is a general list of school supplies (consumable and nonconsumable) that you might need. Create additional lists of supplies you require to teach the specific curriculum for your grade level or subject.

1. Furniture
   a. Desks (students', teacher's, assistants')
   b. Chairs (students', adults')
   c. Tables
   d. Bookshelves

2. Classroom accessories
   a. Globe
   b. Maps
   c. Flannel board
   d. Pocket chart
   e. Chart paper easel, big book stand
   f. Dictionary
   g. Thesaurus
   h. Timers, bell
   i. Recess equipment (such as balls, jump ropes, and cones)

3. A/V equipment
   a. Projectors (overhead, slide, film)
   b. Television and VCR (with necessary cables)
   c. Filmstrip viewers
   d. Screen
   e. Extension cords
   f. Slides, films, videos, filmstrips
   g. Computers, printers, software
   h. Tape recorder

4. School equipment
   a. Keys to classroom, storage rooms
   b. Laminating machine
   c. Book binding machine
   d. Electric or heavy-duty three-hole punch
   e. Large paper cutter
   f. Photocopier and your assigned confidential key or code
   g. Die-cut machine for making bulletin board letters and shapes

5. "Office" supplies
   a. Lesson plan book
   b. Grade book (or software)
   c. Paper (plain copier, colored copier, lined notebook paper, newsprint, lined newsprint, construction, tissue, spiral and marble notebooks, printer, legal pads, notepads, chart, butcher, colored bulletin board)
   d. Regular and colored pencils, pens (black, blue, and colored), magic markers (washable and permanent), overhead transparency pens, dry-erase markers, crayons
   e. Pencil sharpener
   f. Erasers (pencil top, rectangular)
   g. Glue (white glue, rubber cement)
   h. Thumbtacks
   i. Stapler, staples, staple remover
   j. Paper clips (all kinds and sizes)
   k. Scissors ("righty" and "lefty," adult and student sizes)
   l. Rulers, yardsticks, meter sticks
   m. Rubber bands

n. Tape (transparent, masking)
o. Hole puncher (handheld, three-hole punch)
p. Chalk, whiteboard markers
q. Overhead transparencies (for photocopier, for transparency maker, for just writing on)
r. Chalkboard or whiteboard eraser
s. Clipboard
t. Envelopes
u. School stationary
v. Manila file folders
w. Hanging file folders
x. Pocket folders
y. Three-ring binders
z. Divider inserts for three-ring binders
aa. Safety pins
bb. Stamp pads, stamps, ink
cc. Craft supplies (such as pipe cleaners, felt, yarn, paint, and cloth)
dd. Stickers and labels (for folders and for student rewards)
ee. Sticky note pads
ff. Blank audiocassettes, videotapes, computer diskettes
gg. Printer cartridges
hh. Toner for photocopying machines

6. Cleaning supplies
    a. Soap, cleansers, detergents
    b. Broom, mop, dustpan
    c. Buckets
    d. Paper towels
    e. Tissues
    f. Sponges
    g. Scrub brushes
    h. Rags

Resource 5.1

Your Personal Schedule

Time	Sunday	Monday	Tuesday	Wednesday
6:00 a.m.				
6:30				
7:00				
8:00				
8:30				
9:00				
9:30				
10:00				
10:30				
11:00				
11:30				
12:00 p.m.				
12:30				
1:00				
1:30				
2:00				
2:30				
3:00				
3:30				
4:00				
4:30				
5:00				
5:30				
6:00				
6:30				
7:00				
7:30				
8:00				
8:30				
9:00				

Time	Thursday	Friday	Saturday	Notes
6:00 a.m.				
6:30				
7:00				
8:00				
8:30				
9:00				
9:30				
10:00				
10:30				
11:00				
11:30				
12:00 p.m.				
12:30				
1:00				
1:30				
2:00				
2:30				
3:00				
3:30				
4:00				
4:30				
5:00				
5:30				
6:00				
6:30				
7:00				
7:30				
8:00				
8:30				
9:00				

Resource 5.2

Schedule of School Events

Date	July	August	September	October	November	December
1						
2						
3						
4						
5						
6						
7						
8						
9						
10						
11						
12						
13						
14						
15						
16						
17						
18						
19						
20						
21						
22						
23						
24						
25						
26						
27						
28						
29						
30						
31						

January	February	March	April	May	June	Date
						1
						2
						3
						4
						5
						6
						7
						8
						9
						10
						11
						12
						13
						14
						15
						16
						17
						18
						19
						20
						21
						22
						23
						24
						25
						26
						27
						28
						29
						30
						31

Resource 5.3

Sample Lesson Plan Book Pages

Week _____   Beginning: ____/____/____
Units: _____

	Time/ Subject	Time/ Subject	Time/ Subject
M O N			
T U E			
W E D			
T H U			
F R I			

Reminders: _____
_____
_____
_____

Time/ Subject	Time/ Subject	Time/ Subject

Resource 6.1

Pacing Chart

July	August

November	December

March	April

September	October

January	February

May	June

Bibliography

Allen, R. (2001, Fall). Technology and learning: How can schools map routes to technology's promised land? *Curriculum Update*, p. 1.

Bozzone, M. A. (1995, January/February). A teacher's stress survival guide. *Instructor*, pp. 55–57.

Brophy, J. (1981). Teacher praise: A functional analysis. *Review of Educational Research, 51*, 5–32.

Canady, R. L., & Seyfarth, J. T. (1979). *How parent-teacher conferences build partnerships* (Fastback 132). Bloomington, IN: Phi Delta Kappa Educational Foundation.

Cockburn, A. D. (1996). *Teaching under pressure*. London: Falmer Press.

Coil, C. (1997). *Teaching tools for the 21st century*. Dayton, OH: Pieces of Learning.

Cummings, C. (2000). *Winning strategies for classroom management*. Alexandria, VA: Association for Supervision and Curriculum Development.

Davis, A. H. (1998). *Becoming a better communicator: How to improve employee productivity, resolve conflict and build collaborative relationships*. Holly Springs, NC: Performance Plus Consulting.

Davis, M., Eshelman, E. R., & McKay, M. (1995). *The relaxation and stress reduction workbook*. New York: MJF Books.

Eckman, A. (2001, September). Beyond bullying: Knowing when to step in—and when not to. *Education Update*, p. 1.

Farber, B. A. (1991). *Crisis in education: Stress and burnout in the American teacher*. San Francisco: Jossey-Bass.

Gold, Y., & Roth, R. A. (1993). *Teachers managing stress and preventing burnout: The professional health solution*. London: Falmer Press.

Gordon, S. P. (1991). *How to help beginning teachers succeed*. Alexandria, VA: Association for Supervision and Curriculum Development.

Gordon, T. (1974). *Teaching effectiveness training* (3rd ed.). New York: Longman.

Grusko, R., & Kramer, J. (1993). *Becoming a teacher: A practical and political school survival guide*. Bloomington, IN: EDINFO Press.

Gupta, N. (1981). *Some sources and remedies of work stress among teachers*. Austin, TX: Southwest Educational Development Laboratory. (ERIC Document Reproduction Service No. ED 211 496).

Hall, R. V. (1975). *Managing behavior, part II: The principles of operant and respondent conditioning*. Lawrence, KS: H & H Enterprises.

Halpin, G., Harris, K., & Halpin, G. (1985). Teacher stress as related to locus of control, sex, and age. *Journal of Experimental Education, 53*(3), 136–140.

Hardiman, M. M. (2001). Connecting brain research with dimensions of learning. *Educational Leadership, 59*(3), 52–55.

Hlidek, R. (1980). Creating positive classroom environments. In M. Reynolds (Ed.), *Social environment of the schools* (pp. 61–77). Reston, VA: ERIC Clearinghouse.

Hoppenstedt, E. M., & Thomas, C. C. (1991). *A teacher's guide to classroom management*. Springfield, IL: Charles C. Thomas.

Indiana University, Safe and Responsive Schools Project at the Indiana Education Policy Center. (2001). Understanding school violence. Retrieved June 22, 2001, from http://www.indiana.edu/~safeschl/guide.html

Inlander, C. B., & Moran, Cynthia K. (1996). *Stress: 63 ways to relieve tension and stay healthy*. New York: Walker and Company.

Jasmine, J. (1993). *Portfolios and other assessments*. Huntington Beach, CA: Teacher Created Materials.

Johnson, S. M., Birkeland, S., Kardos, S. M., Kauffman, D., Liu, E., & Peske, H. G. (2001, July/August). Retaining the next generation of teachers: The importance of school-based support. *Harvard Education Letter's Research Online*. Retrieved July 17, 2001, from http://www.edletter.org/past/issues/2001-ja/support.shtml

Kabat-Zinn, J. (1990). *Full catastrophe living: Using the wisdom of your body and mind to face stress, pain, and illness*. New York: Delta.

Kagan, S. (2001). Teaching for character and community. *Educational Leadership, 59*(2), 50–55.

Kelly, D. (1999, December/2000, January). Creating web units. *Classroom Connect*, p. 4.

Kronowitz, E. L. (1992). *Beyond student teaching*. White Plains, NY: Longman.

Kyriacou, C. (1987). Teacher stress and burnout: An international review. *Educational Research, 29*(2), 146–152.

Laborde, G. Z. (1987). *Influencing with integrity*. Palo Alto, CA: Syntony Publishing.

Lombardi, J. D. (1995, January/February). Do you have teacher burnout? *Instructor*, pp. 64–65.

Martin-Kniep, G. O. (2000). *Becoming a better teacher: Eight innovations that work*. Alexandria, VA: Association for Supervision and Curriculum Development.

Mathews, J. (2001, September 4). Taking more time for teacher training. *The Washington Post Online*. Retrieved September 4, 2001, from http://www.washingtonpost.com/wp-dyn/education/A37308-2001Sep3.html

Megay-Nespoli, K. (1993). *The first year for elementary school teachers: A practical plan for dealing with the short- and long-term management of teaching duties and responsibilities*. Springfield, IL: Charles C Thomas.

McGrath, M. Z. (1995). *Teachers today: A guide to surviving creatively*. Thousand Oaks, CA: Corwin Press.

McGreal, T. L. (1983). *Successful teacher evaluation*. Alexandria, VA: ASCD.

McQueen, C. (2001). Teaching to win. *Kappa Delta Pi Record, 38*(1), 12–15.

Miller, A. (1988, April 25). Stress on the job. *Newsweek*, pp. 40–45.

Minner, S. (2001, May 30). Our own worst enemy. *Education Week on the Web*. Retrieved May 31, 2001, from http://www.edweek.com/ew/ewstory.cfm?slug=38minner.h20

Moran, C., Stobbe, J., Baron, W., Miller, J., & Moir, E. (1992). *Keys to the classroom: A teacher's guide to the first month of school*. Newbury Park, CA: Corwin Press.

National Center for Education Statistics. (2000). Indicators of school crime and safety, 2000. (2001). Retrieved September 4, 2001, from http://nces.ed.gov/pubs2001/crime2000/nfteacher.asp?nav=3

Nelson, J., Lott, L., & Glenn, H. S. (1997). *Positive discipline in the classroom*. Roseville, CA: Prima Publishing.

Pappano, L. (2001, June 10). First-year teachers discover what it's really like. *The Boston Globe*. Retrieved June 11, 2001, from http://www.boston.com/dailyglobe2/161/m . . . s_discover_what_it_s_really_like+.shtml

Partin, R. L. (1995). *Classroom teacher's survival guide*. West Nyack, NY: The Center for Applied Research in Education.

Powell, J. R. (1994). *The working woman's guide to managing stress*. Englewood Cliffs, NJ: Prentice Hall.

Purkey, W. W., & Novak, J. M. (1988). *Education: By invitation only* (Fastback 268). Bloomington, IN: Phi Delta Kappa Educational Foundation.

Renwick, L. (2001, September). Weaving in technology: Integrating technology into your lessons will grow more valuable with each step. *Scholastic Instructor,* pp. 83–87.

Rogers, S. (1999). *Teaching tips: 105 ways to increase motivation and learning.* Evergreen, CO: Peak Learning Systems.

Scaros, B. C. (1981). *Sight on sites: An approach to coping with teacher stress—Preventing burn-out.* New York: New York City Teacher Centers Consortium. (ERIC Document Reproduction Service No. ED 236 131).

Schaps, E., Schaeffer, E. F., & McDonnell, S. N. (2001, September 12). What's right and wrong in character education today. *Education Week on the Web.* Retrieved September 12, 2001, from http://www.edweek.com/ew/newstory.cfm?slug =02schaps.h21

Schwartz, W. (2001). A guide to community programs to prevent youth violence. ERIC Clearinghouse on Urban Education. Retrieved June 22, 2001, from http://eric-web.tc.columbia.edu/guides/pg9.html

Selye, H. (1974). *Stress without distress.* New York: The New American Library.

Shalaway, L. (1989). *Learning to teach: Not just for beginners.* New York: Scholastic.

Showers, B. (1985). Teachers coaching teachers. *Educational Leadership, 42*(7), 43–48.

Singh, G. R. (2001). How character education helps students grow. *Educational Leadership, 59*(2), 46–49.

Sprinthall, N. A., & Sprinthall, R. C. (1990). *Educational psychology: A developmental approach* (5th ed.). New York: McGraw-Hill.

Stedman, C. (2000). *Identifying good teaching: What research tells us.* Indianapolis, IN: Kappa Delta Pi.

Steere, B. F. (1988). *Becoming an effective classroom manager: A resource for teachers.* Albany: State University of New York Press.

Survival guide for new teachers. (1996). Raleigh, NC: North Carolina Association of Educators.

Swick, K. J. (1989). *Stress and teaching.* Washington, DC: National Education Association.

Swick, K. J. (1987). *Student stress: A classroom management system.* Washington, DC: National Education Association.

Warner, J., & Bryan, C. (1995). *The unauthorized teacher's survival guide.* Indianapolis, IN: Park Avenue Publications.

Wichert, S. (1991, March). Solving problems together! *Scholastic Pre-K Today,* pp. 46–53.

Wilkins-Canter, E. A., Edwards, A. T., Young, A. L., Ramanathan, H., & McDougle, K. O. (2000). Preparing novice teachers to handle stress. *Kappa Delta Pi Record, 36*(3), 128–130.

Williams, C. C., Farthing, A., Spragely, K., Emerson, B., & Drinkard, L. (1999). *Tools for success: A handbook for first year teachers' professional growth.* Raleigh: North Carolina Association of Educators.

Williamson, B. (1993). *A first-year teacher's guidebook for success* (Rev. ed.). Sacramento, CA: Dynamic Teaching Co.

Wilson-Brown, G. (1994). *The assertive teacher.* Hants, England: Arena.

Index